Derrel R. Watkins, PhD
Editor

Practical Theology for Aging

Practical Theology for Aging has been co-published simultaneously as *Journal of Religious Gerontology*, Volume 15, Numbers 1/2 2003.

Pre-publication REVIEWS, COMMENTARIES, EVALUATIONS . . .

"THOUGHT-PROVOKING, ENLIGHTENING, INSIGHTFUL, AND PRACTICAL. As I read through the book, I repeatedly found myself thinking, 'what AN EXCELLENT SUPPLEMENTAL TEXT for the Introduction to Gerontology course.' AN EXCELLENT TRAINING RESOURCE for health care providers working with older adults, as well as religious leaders of all denominations as they seek to enhance their pastoral care programs with older adults.

Patricia Gleason-Wynn, PhD
Lecturer
School of Social Work
Baylor University

" **A** MUST-HAVE for any religious organization's library as well as that of anyone interested in exploring this topic. . . . EMINENTLY READABLE AND FILLED WITH MATTER-OF-FACT INFORMATION regarding an array of topics, including sexuality and the older individual, pain and suffering, and preaching to an older population."

Connie E. Beran, BAS
Assistant Director
Center for Aging and Community
University of Indianapolis

" **I** n a time of longer life spans and increasing numbers of senior adults, the publication of this valuable resource is a welcome event. This book addresses a full range of issues, from biblical and theological foundations to the practice of ministry. THE AUTHORS ARE THEOLOGICALLY DIVERSE AND HAVE A WEALTH OF EXPERIENCE. This is a book for all in the church who seek to understand aging and its implications for ministry."

Henry H. Knight III, PhD
E. Stanley Jones
Professor of Evangelism
Saint Paul School of Theology

" **E** XCELLENT, HIGHLY PRACTICAL. . . . Readers will be pleasantly surprised. This is NOT another book extolling the need to give deference and platitude to the white haired among us. Readers are given a wealth of practical suggestions for addressing difficult issues of late life such as creativity, worship, spiritual growth, dementia, preaching to older members, social myths, physical suffering, death and dying, and productivity in later life. I HIGHLY RECOMMEND THIS BOOK."

Charlie D. Pruett, PhD
Director
Pruett Gerontology Center
Advisor for Graduate Gerontology
Abilene Christian University

"**P**ROFOUND YET PRACT-ICAL! No serious pastoral care worker will want to be without this very useful resource. This comprehensive collection demonstrates how theological reflection can enlarge our understanding of the process of aging and enhance our work with senior adults. The chapter entitled 'The Caleb Affect' is A MUST-READ FOR PASTORS AND PASTORAL EDUCATORS. This fascinating chapter highlights the new challenges and opportunities of a rapidly aging society. With its numerous examples and models, ministers, educators, and students will read this book again and again."

Lindell E. Anderson, DMin
ACPE Supervisor
VITAS Healthcare Corporation
of Texas, LP

"**A** MUST-READ FOR EVERY PASTOR and especially for ever Senior Adult Minister. The book provides a solid theoretical rationale for senior adult issues, but the practical applications for the minister are what I found invaluable. THE LIST OF CONTRIBUTING AUTHORS READS LIKE A WHO'S WHO OF SENIOR ADULT MINISTERS. This is one book that should be on the shelf in every pastor's library, but it won't stay there. The minister will be taking it down to read it again and again."

Bob Harper, DMin
Pastor
First Baptist Church
White Hall
Arkansas

The Haworth Pastoral Press®
An Imprint of The Haworth Press, Inc.

New York • London • Victoria (AU)
www.HaworthPress.com

Practical Theology
for Aging

Practical Theology for Aging has been co-published simultaneously as *Journal of Religious Gerontology,* Volume 15, Numbers 1/2 2003.

The *Journal of Religious Gerontology*[TM] Monographic "Separates" (formerly *Journal of Religion & Aging*)*

Below is a list of "separates," which in serials librarianship means a special issue simultaneously published as a special journal issue or double-issue *and* as a "separate" hardbound monograph. (This is a format which we also call a "DocuSerial.")

"Separates" are published because specialized libraries or professionals may wish to purchase a specific thematic issue by itself in a format which can be separately cataloged and shelved, as opposed to purchasing the journal on an on-going basis. Faculty members may also more easily consider a "separate" for classroom adoption.

"Separates" are carefully classified separately with the major book jobbers so that the journal tie-in can be noted on new book order slips to avoid duplicate purchasing.

You may wish to visit Haworth's website at . . .

http://www.HaworthPress.com

. . . to search our online catalog for complete tables of contents of these separates and related publications.

You may also call 1-800-HAWORTH (outside US/Canada: 607-722-5857), or Fax 1-800-895-0582 (outside US/Canada: 607-771-0012), or e-mail at:

docdelivery@haworthpress.com

Practical Theology for Aging, edited by Rev. Derrel R. Watkins, PhD (Vol. 15, No. 1/2, 2003). *THOUGHT-PROVOKING, ENLIGHTENING, INSIGHTFUL, AND PRACTICAL. As I read through the book, I repeatedly found myself thinking, 'what AN EXCELLENT SUPPLEMENTAL TEXT for the Introduction to Gerontology course.' AN EXCELLENT TRAINING RESOURCE for health care providers working with older adults, as well as religious leaders of all denominations as they seek to enhance their pastoral care programs with older adults."* (Patricia Gleason-Wynn, PhD, Lecturer, School of Social Work, Baylor University).

New Directions in the Study of Late Life Religiousness and Spirituality, edited by Susan H. McFadden, PhD, Mark Brennan, PhD, and Julie Hicks Patrick, PhD (Vol. 14, No. 1, 2/3, 2003). *Refreshing. . . . encouraging. . . . This book has given us a gift of evolving thoughts and perspectives on religion and spirituality in the later years of life. . . . Of interest not only to university students, researchers, and scholars, but also to those who provide services to the aged." (James Birren, PhD, Associate Director, UCLA Center on Aging).*

Aging Spirituality and Pastoral Care: A Multi-National Perspective, edited by Rev. Elizabeth MacKinlay, RN, PhD, Rev. James W. Ellor, PhD, DMin, DCSW, and Rev. Stephen Pickard, PhD (Vol. 12, No. 3/4, 2001). *"Comprehensive . . . The authors are not just thinkers and scholars. They speak from decades of practical expertise with the aged, demented, and dying." (Bishop Tom Frame, PhD, Lecturer in Public Theology, St. Mark's National Theological Centre, Canberra, Australia)*

Religion and Aging: An Anthology of the Poppele Papers, edited by Derrel R. Watkins, PhD, MSW, MRE (Vol. 12, No. 2, 2001). *"Within these pages, the new ministry leader is supplied with the core prerequisites for effective older adult ministry and the more experienced leader is provided with an opportunity to reconnect with timeless foundational principles. Insights into the interior of the aging experience, field-tested and proven techniques and ministry principles, theological rationale for adult care giving, Biblical perspectives on aging, and philosophic and spiritual insights into the aging process." (Dennis R. Myers, LMSW-ACP, Director, Baccalaureate Studies in Social Work, Baylor University, Waco, Texas)*

Aging in Chinese Society: A Holistic Approach to the Experience of Aging in Taiwan and Singapore, edited by Homer Jernigan and Margaret Jernigan (Vol. 8, No. 3, 1992). *"A vivid introduction to aging in these societies. . . . Case studies illustrate the interaction of religion, personality, immigration, modernization, and aging." (Clinical Gerontologist)*

Spiritual Maturity in the Later Years, edited by James J. Seeber (Vol. 7, No. 1/2, 1991). *"An excellent introduction to the burgeoning field of gerontology and religion." (Southwestern Journal of Theology)*

Gerontology in Theological Education: Local Program Development, edited by Barbara Payne and Earl D. C. Brewer* (Vol. 6, No. 3/4, 1989). *"Directly relevant to gerontological education in other contexts and to applications in the educational programs and other work of church* congregations and community agencies for the aging." (*The Newsletter of the Christian Sociological Society*)

Gerontology in Theological Education, edited by Barbara Payne and Earl D. C. Brewer* (Vol. 6, No. 1/2, 1989). *"An excellent resource for seminaries and anyone interested in the role of the church in the lives of older persons . . . must for all libraries."* (David Maldonado, DSW, Associate Professor of Church & Society, Southern Methodist University, Perkins School of Theology)

Religion, Aging and Health: A Global Perspective, compiled by the World Health Organization, edited by William M. Clements* (Vol. 4, No. 3/4, 1989). *"Fills a long-standing gap in gerontological literature. This book presents an overview of the interrelationship of religion, aging, and health from the perspective of the world's major faith traditions that is not available elsewhere . . . "* (Stephen Sapp, PhD, Associate Professor of Religious Studies, University of Miami, Coral Gables, Florida)

New Directions in Religion and Aging, edited by David B. Oliver* (Vol. 3, No. 1/2, 1987). *"This book is a telescope enabling us to see the future. The data of the present provides a solid foundation for seeing the future."* (Dr. Nathan Kollar, Professor of Religious Studies and Founding Chair, Department of Gerontology, St. John Fisher College; Adjunct Professor of Ministerial Theology, St. Bernard's Institute)

The Role of the Church in Aging, Volume 3: Programs and Services for Seniors, edited by Michael C. Hendrickson* (Vol. 2, No. 4, 1987). *Experts explore an array of successful programs for the elderly that have been implemented throughout the United States in order to meet the social, emotional, religious, and health needs of the elderly.*

The Role of the Church in Aging, Volume 2: Implications for Practice and Service, edited by Michael C. Hendrickson* (Vol. 2, No. 3, 1986). *Filled with important insight and state-of-the-art concepts that reflect the cutting edge of thinking among religion and aging professionals. (Rev. James W. Ellor, DMin, AM, CSW, ACSW, Associate Professor, Department Chair, Human Service Department, National College of Education, Lombard, Illinois)*

The Role of the Church in Aging, Volume 1: Implications for Policy and Action, edited by Michael C. Hendrickson* (Vol. 2, No. 1/2, 1986). *Reviews the current status of the religious sector's involvement in the field of aging and identifies a series of strategic responses for future policy and action.*

Published by

The Haworth Pastoral Press, 10 Alice Street, Binghamton, NY 13904-1580 USA

The Haworth Pastoral Press is an imprint of The Haworth Press, Inc., 10 Alice Street, Binghamton, NY 13904-1580 USA.

Practical Theology for Aging has been co-published simultaneously as *Journal of Religious Gerontology*, Volume 15, Numbers 1/2 2003.

Cover design by Lora Wiggins

Library of Congress Cataloging-in-Publication Data

Practical theology for aging / Derrel R. Watkins, editor.
    p. cm.
    Includes bibliographical references and index.
    ISBN 0-7890-2226-5 (hard cover : alk. paper)–ISBN 0-7890-2227-3 (soft cover : alk. paper)
    1. Christian aged–Religious life. 2. Aging–Religious aspects–Christianity. 3. Church work with the aged. I. Watkins, Derrel R., 1935–
BV4580.P73 2003
259'.3–dc22
                                       2003017503

Practical Theology for Aging

Derrel R. Watkins, PhD
Editor

Practical Theology for Aging has been co-published simultaneously as *Journal of Religious Gerontology*, Volume 15, Numbers 1/2 2003.

The Haworth Pastoral Press®
An Imprint of The Haworth Press, Inc.

New York • London • Victoria (AU)
www.HaworthPress.com

Indexing, Abstracting & Website/Internet Coverage

This section provides you with a list of major indexing & abstracting services. That is to say, each service began covering this periodical during the year noted in the right column. Most Websites which are listed below have indicated that they will either post, disseminate, compile, archive, cite or alert their own Website users with research-based content from this work. (This list is as current as the copyright date of this publication.)

Abstracting, Website/Indexing Coverage . . . . Year When Coverage Began

- *Abstracts in Social Gerontology: Current Literature on Aging* **1991**
- *AgeInfo CD-Rom* **1994**
- *AgeLine Database* **1994**
- *Applied Social Sciences Index & Abstracts (ASSIA) (Online: ASSI via Data-Star) (CD-Rom: ASSIA Plus) <http://www.csa.com>* **1994**
- *ATLA Religion Database, published by the American Theological Library Association <http://www.atla.com>* **1991**
- *CNPIEC Reference Guide: Chinese National Directory of Foreign Periodicals* **1995**
- *Educational Administration Abstracts (EAA)* **1995**
- *Family & Society Studies Worldwide (online and CD/ROM) <http://www.nisc.com>* **1996**
- *Guide to Social Science & Religion in Periodical Literature* **2000**
- *Human Resources Abstracts (HRA)* **1991**
- *IBZ International Bibliography of Periodical Literature <http://www.saur.de>* **1996**
- *Index Guide to College Journals (core list compiled by integrating 48 indexes frequently used to support undergraduate programs in small to medium sized libraries)* **1999**

(continued)

     * **Exact start date to come.**

Special Bibliographic Notes related to special journal issues (separates) and indexing/abstracting:

- indexing/abstracting services in this list will also cover material in any "separate" that is co-published simultaneously with Haworth's special thematic journal issue or DocuSerial. Indexing/abstracting usually covers material at the article/chapter level.
- monographic co-editions are intended for either non-subscribers or libraries which intend to purchase a second copy for their circulating collections.
- monographic co-editions are reported to all jobbers/wholesalers/approval plans. The source journal is listed as the "series" to assist the prevention of duplicate purchasing in the same manner utilized for books-in-series.
- to facilitate user/access services all indexing/abstracting services are encouraged to utilize the co-indexing entry note indicated at the bottom of the first page of each article/chapter/contribution.
- this is intended to assist a library user of any reference tool (whether print, electronic, online, or CD-ROM) to locate the monographic version if the library has purchased this version but not a subscription to the source journal.
- individual articles/chapters in any Haworth publication are also available through the Haworth Document Delivery Service (HDDS).

Practical Theology for Aging

CONTENTS

ABOUT THE EDITOR

Derrel R. Watkins, PhD, served as Professor of Social Work Emeritus at Southwestern Baptist Theological Seminary. He holds the Oubri A. Poppele Chair in gerontology and health and welfare ministries at Saint Paul School of Theology. After retiring in 2000, he continued to teach courses in gerontology at the Institute for Gerontological Studies at Baylor University in Waco, Texas and the University of Indianapolis.

Dr. Watkins has written a number of articles for the *Southwestern Journal of Theology*, the *Journal of The Academy of Evangelism in Theological Education*, the *Journal of Family Ministry*, and other publications. He contributed articles to several books including *Aging and Spirituality* (Haworth) and has a monograph published entitled *Christian Social Ministry*, and is the editor of *Religion and Aging: An Anthology of the Poppele Papers* (Haworth).

Dr. Watkins is an ordained Baptist minister and has served as pastor or associate pastor in 12 congregations in Arkansas, Michigan, and Texas. He is currently a member of the National Association of Social Workers (NASW), the Academy of Certified Social Workers (ACSW), the North American Association of Christian in Social Work (NACSW), and the Association for Gerontology in Higher Education (AGHE). He has been a licensed marriage and family therapist, a licensed social psychotherapist, and a member of the American Association of Marriage and Family Therapists, the Council on Social Work Education, the Gerontological Society of America, the National Council on Aging, the American Society on Aging, and the Mid-America Congress on Aging.

Introduction
to Practical Theology for Aging

The authors of the articles contained in this volume are essentially educators or practitioners in what I call practical theology. While I firmly believe that all theology that addresses the everyday-lived-lives of people is by definition, practical, there is a specialization in many theologically based institutions that operates under the practical theology rubric. Some of the specific disciplines are pastoral care, pastoral psychology and counseling, church administration, preaching, evangelism, missions, Christian education, church and community studies, rural church ministries, urban ministries, youth ministries, children's ministries, communication ministries, recreational ministries, social ministries, family ministries and ministries with adults, including senior adults. The lines between those ministries can be blurred and there is often a great deal of overlap in the theoretical foundations that support them.

Often these "practical" disciplines depend more on information gleaned from non-theological sources than from theology. Some have said that there simply isn't enough theologically based literature available for these practices in churches and synagogues. One of our goals in producing this volume is to make a contribution to the available resources for the training and practice of these faith based practical disciplines. Each of the writers possess a rich background in theological studies and in professional practice.

The first two papers were chosen in honor of Barbara Pittard Payne Stancil. She was a pioneer in the development of the field of gerontology. She made significant contributions to the field of religion and aging, as well. I would have to say that she was a primary example of a practical theologian. Her death has left a large vacant spot in the hearts of all of us who knew her. Stephen Sapp delivered the address at the lectureship that honors her memory at Georgia State University. That address is printed here as Chapter 1: "To Learn, To Teach, To Care: Gerontology As It Should Be Practiced." Barbara broke the

[Haworth co-indexing entry note]: "Introduction to Practical Theology for Aging." Watkins, Derrel R. Co-published simultaneously in *Journal of Religious Gerontology* (The Haworth Pastoral Press, an imprint of The Haworth Press, Inc.) Vol. 15, No. 1/2, 2003, pp. 1-3; and: *Practical Theology for Aging* (ed: Derrel R. Watkins) The Haworth Pastoral Press, an imprint of The Haworth Press, Inc., 2003, pp. 1-3. Single or multiple copies of this article are available for a fee from The Haworth Document Delivery Service [1-800-HAWORTH, 9:00 a.m. - 5:00 p.m. (EST). E-mail address: docdelivery@haworthpress.com].

http://www.haworthpress.com/store/product.asp?sku=J078
Digital Object Identifier: 10.1300/J078v15n01_01

mold of religious persons who were embarrassed to talk about sex. She wanted church leaders and the public at large to understand that older persons are also sexual beings. Thus, we include one of her articles here, Chapter 2: "Sex and the Elderly: No Laughing Matter in Religion." It was originally published by the Poppele Center, in the *Quarterly Papers on Religion and Aging*, Vol. V, No. 4, Summer 1989.

Chapter 3 is a more theoretical article entitled "A Practical Theology for Aging." I attempt to provide a brief overview of some of the basic theological concepts out of which a practical theology might be more thoroughly developed. In Chapter 4, Brian McCaffery, from Luther Seminary, contributes a theological reflection based upon Process Theology entitled "Needing to Make Room for Change: A Theology of Aging and Life." Kellie A. Shantz, a Roman Catholic and a Psychiatric Nurse with a master's degree from a school of theology, contributes important insights regarding suffering in Chapter 5: "The Kyrios Christos as Ultimate Hope: A Response To Pain and Suffering."

DeeAnn Klapp, a United Methodist minister, contributes two articles to this volume, Chapters 6 and 11. Chapter 6: "Biblical Foundations for a Practical Theology of Aging" is foundational to any ministry with frail older persons. Chapter 11: "A Practical Theological Model for Worship with Alzheimer's Patients: Using the Validation Technique" develops a conceptual framework for including persons not generally considered in need of spiritual services, in the ministry of the church.

In Chapter 8, Pamela S. Harris, MD, a specialist in rehabilitation medicine, Karen Lampe, a rehabilitation therapist, and Brian Chaffin, a pastor, team up to contribute a theological reflection regarding wholeness in later life. The title of their article is " 'Always Green and Full of Sap': Facilitating Wholeness in Aging."

Martha S. Bergen, a professor of Christian Education, contributes Chapter 9: "A Christian Education for the Spiritual Growth of Senior Adults." It is an insightful article highlighting a wide range of topics the church educator must consider when planning and implementing spiritually enriching programs for older persons. Professor Al Fasol, a distinguished professor of preaching, reflects on some basic considerations for "Preaching to Senior Citizens," in Chapter 10.

Julie A. Gorman, a specialist in spiritual formation, contributes two articles to this volume. Chapter 7: "The Dilemma of Aging" explores the process of aging and the formation of attitudes about aging. In Chapter 12: "New Significance and Identity: A Practical Theological Perspective," Gorman discusses the essential elements that are available to older persons whereby they may find new significance and a new sense of purpose in later life. Lucien Coleman and I wrote Chapter 13: "Live A Little Before You Die A Lot" with the idea that older persons can learn to be creative and as a result find greater joy and fulfillment in their retirement years.

Chapter 14: "The Caleb Affect: The Oldest-Old in Church and Society" addresses the fact that the 80+ generation is essentially overlooked by church and community planners. In this article, Ben Dickerson and I stress the fact that the oldest-old cohort is the fastest growing segment of the senior adult population. They constitute an "age crescendo" because the 80+ population is rapidly growing in volume and intensity.

Perhaps a majority of books and magazines articles on aging published by religious publishing houses are, by nature, practical theology. We do not claim to add radically new materials to the field. Nor do we believe that we have exhausted the subject. It is our hope that what we share with the readers of this volume will at least be thought provoking and even helpful to some.

Derrel R. Watkins, PhD
Editor

Chapter 1

To Learn, To Teach, To Care: Gerontology As It Should Be Practiced– A Tribute to Barbara Pittard Payne Stancil

Stephen Sapp, PhD

SUMMARY. This article highlights the life and contributions of Barbara Pittard Payne Stancil to the field of gerontology in general and to the issue of spirituality and aging specifically. Her identification with a practical theology that underscores the lived lives of older persons is highlighted. *[Article copies available for a fee from The Haworth Document Delivery Service: 1-800-HAWORTH. E-mail address: <docdelivery@haworthpress.com> Website: <http://www.HaworthPress.com> © 2003 by The Haworth Press, Inc. All rights reserved.]*

KEYWORDS. Pioneer, giant, groundbreaker, pillar, gadfly, social sciences peak, learn, caring, religious gerontology, sexuality, intergenerational, clergy

---

Stephen Sapp is Professor of Religious Studies, University of Miami, Coral Gables, Florida. Dr. Sapp is a popular speaker on the subject of spirituality and aging and has written a number of articles and books on religion and aging. He served as editor of the *Journal of Religious Gerontology.*

[Haworth co-indexing entry note]: "To Learn, To Teach, To Care: Gerontology As It Should Be Practiced–A Tribute to Barbara Pittard Payne Stancil." Sapp, Stephen. Co-published simultaneously in *Journal of Religious Gerontology* (The Haworth Pastoral Press, an imprint of The Haworth Press, Inc.) Vol. 15, No. 1/2, 2003, pp. 5-16; and: *Practical Theology for Aging* (ed: Derrel R. Watkins) The Haworth Pastoral Press, an imprint of The Haworth Press, Inc., 2003, pp. 5-16. Single or multiple copies of this article are available for a fee from The Haworth Document Delivery Service [1-800-HAWORTH, 9:00 a.m. - 5:00 p.m. (EST). E-mail address: docdelivery@haworthpress.com].

Digital Object Identifier: 10.1300/J078v15n01_02

"Pioneer" . . . "Giant" . . . "Pillar in the Field" . . . "Groundbreaker" . . . All of these terms are often applied to people judged to have made exceptional contributions in some area of human endeavor. Often they are even deserved! In the case of the person we are gathered here this evening to honor and, sadly, for the first time to *remember*–Barbara Pittard Payne Stancil–they and many others we could all think of are unquestionably appropriate.

As I struggled to get a handle on what Barbara meant to the field of gerontology, the three-fold structure reflected in the title of this lecture came to my mind as truly reflective of her approach, a way of doing gerontology that we would all do well to emulate if we seek a real "best-practices model" for our work in the field. I'm going to use this structure to share with you my impressions of this remarkable woman, often through her own words, either as they appear in some of her many publications or from an interview that Mel Kimble and Jim Ellor of the Center on Aging, Religion, and Spirituality at Luther Seminary conducted with Barbara in 1994.[1] Along the way I'll also offer a few of my own thoughts on some of the issues Barbara addressed so passionately and so well.

In preparing this lecture, I reread many of Barbara's publications and read others for the first time, and I talked with a number of people who had known her much longer and better than I. As I did so, one of the first things that came to my mind was a quotation from scripture that I think she might have appreciated in this context (and, given her lifelong devotion to the Methodist Church, it's certainly appropriate in a lecture bearing her name); it comes from the gospel of John, where John the Baptist is quoting the prophet Isaiah: "I am the voice of one crying in the wilderness" (1:23). Indeed, that is what Barbara must have felt like at various times during her career in gerontology (of course, I've also heard her described by the distinctly nonbiblical term *gadfly*, but then that term also could apply to biblical prophets like Jeremiah and Amos). As the child of Methodist ministers' children, Barbara's whole life had revolved around the church, and thus she knew something in the very core of her being that other gerontologists seemed bent on ignoring (and many still do). As she expressed it back in the mid-1980s in classic "social-sciencespeak," "The treatment of religion by gerontologists is not consonant with the importance that older people place on religion in their lives."[2] So she set out to correct this incongruity, often–it must have seemed at times–single-handedly, that lone "voice crying in the wilderness."

To do this, of course, she first had to *learn* a great deal, to credential herself so that she might have some chance of being listened to, though she had several strikes against her: First, she was a woman; next, she came out of a Christian education background (primarily because that was about all that was really available to women at that time); and finally, she was simply ahead of her times, carrying the banner for the importance of religion at a time when the topic of religion was basically forbidden as a legitimate subject in scientific disciplines. Nonetheless, she persevered in her quest for knowledge against formidable odds; and as I have read much of her writing recently, I have been struck constantly by her familiarity with the literature of gerontology in particular, sociology and psychology more broadly, and theology, a familiarity that was both exceptionally broad and impressively deep.

Clearly her love of learning never waned, a love that led her to take more courses and earn more degrees (four!) than I have time to describe to you. I do have to share one anecdote, though, because it is a great illustration of how she navigated the various programs she pursued at a time when women were not encouraged to do what she was doing: When Barbara decided to get a PhD at Emory, she was asked, "What does a woman of your age want to do with a PhD? Aren't you wasting our time and yours?" Her reply? "Sir, I've got things to do. I don't know exactly what, but I want this education and I want to teach somewhere." She happily recalled that years later, when she was here at Georgia State, Emory invited her back "for a convocation–when women became important–because I was the first woman to receive a PhD with a major in religion. So, I led off the convocation, this nontraditional idiot who wanted to *learn.*"

The fact that Barbara never stopped learning is well illustrated for me by an incident that occurred in–of all places–Acapulco at a meeting of the International Federation of Gerontology in the early 1990s.[3] One of Gari Lesnoff-Caravaglia's doctoral students presented the results of his doctoral dissertation, which he had based on the Pittard Religiosity Scale. After he finished, Barbara stood up and asked, "Why'd you use that old thing? It was out of date years ago" (can any of you hear her saying that?). The poor student, who had no idea who this outspoken woman was, gave the expected dissertation-defense reply: "It's the standard in the field, long-tested, proved reliable, etc., etc." Barbara concluded the exchange with the comment, "Well, I hope you'll consider using something newer and more sophisticated next time." Afterward when she was introduced to the student, she was typically gracious and supportive of his work, but the incident is illustrative for me of her determination to be on the cutting edge, to continue to seek new and better ways of exploring the rich role of the transcendent in human aging, even if it meant moving beyond and leaving behind her *own* recognized and accepted work. I wonder how many of us could so easily let go of fruits of our labors that had helped "make our name" in our profession?

So the foundation of gerontology as it should be practiced was from the outset and remained for Barbara a solid base of learning. To return now to my recounting of her early years in the field, having learned academically what she needed to know to complement the practical education that life had already brought her way, she began to *teach*, both formally here at Georgia State but also informally through her activities in various professional societies (as founder and first president of the Southern Gerontological Society, for example, and president of the Association for Gerontology in Higher Education, to mention only two of many). And of course she always taught by example as well, especially as she herself grew older! And through all of these efforts, she never failed to *care* deeply about what she was doing and for those for whom she was ultimately doing it.

Lest we fail to recognize Barbara Payne Stancil's real contributions in this arena, I want to offer a brief personal anecdote about my entry into the field we now call religious gerontology (no, I'm not about to say that *my* getting into aging studies was one of her contributions, though she was one of the first names I came to know in the field and one of the first authors I read): I began my journey into things gerontological (academically speaking, at least–Nature was taking care of the *personal* aspects quite adequately at the time!) with an internal University of Miami research grant for the summer of 1984. Starting from scratch in the field, I set out to read in those three-plus months everything I could find in any field I could find that pertained to the interface of religion and aging. A great deal of it of course bore Barbara's name or referred to her and her work. But the point I want to make here is that by the end of that summer, I found myself reading "straight" gerontology because I had exhausted the literature in religion and aging in that relatively brief span! Today–in no small part thanks to the efforts of Barbara Payne Stancil–it is impossible even to *keep up* with what comes out in this subspecialty in a steady and ever-increasing stream!

Barbara must have been especially frustrated by the stubbornness of many members of her own discipline, the sociologists, whom, as her collaborator Susan McFadden has put it, "she repeatedly urged to pay attention to religion" and "to wake up" to its importance for practicing gerontology as it should be done.[4] Bob Atchley, who delivered this lecture two years ago, agrees that "she was very concerned about gerontology's neglect of the religious aspects of aging," concluding in his typically understated fashion, "and she freely shared that view with anyone who would listen."[5] By the way (but not totally incidentally) Bob Atchley clearly did listen to her because he has devoted an entire chapter to religion and aging in last year's 9th edition of his standard text *Social Forces and Aging*. In fact, he listened so well that in 1998 he left his position as Distinguished Professor of Gerontology and Director of the Scripps Gerontology Center at "the other Miami" in Ohio to become chair of the gerontology department at the Naropa Institute in Boulder, Colorado, which is, according to its literature, "characterized by its unique Buddhist educational heritage." That seems to be a pretty clear indication that this major figure in the field now not only recognizes the importance of religion for gerontology but promotes it! I imagine Bob's move must have at least secretly pleased Barbara quite a bit.

Her impact on the field is further illustrated by an incident that occurred at a GSA meeting in San Francisco at which Andy Achenbaum was giving a talk on aging and the Bible and one of the respondents was Rick Moody. Barbara was sitting on the front row, and after the session Rick bounded around the table, grabbed her hand, and said, "I just want to thank you, Barbara." When she asked him what for, he replied, "You made me pay attention, all of us pay attention, to religion and aging." Friends, these are household names in gerontology who are giving this woman credit for introducing the discipline to the importance of religion and making it all right if not mandatory to take it seriously, whatever one's particular area of specialization.

So Barbara learned and learned well, and she taught not only individuals but her whole discipline to value the religious dimension of life as we age. I want to turn now to the third aspect of what I have suggested to be Barbara's approach to gerontology as it should be practiced–caring. I'll begin by talking about my first real interaction with Barbara, which occurred in the context of a preconference special program that the American Society on Aging's Forum on Religion, Spirituality, and Aging sponsored before the annual meeting in 1993. As chair of the special program committee, I had the pleasure of inviting Barbara to deliver the keynote, handling all her arrangements, and serving as her host for the day. Her presentation, "The Challenge of Caring: Individuals, Congregations, and Community," pulled together many of the themes and thoughts that she had advocated for decades. It was also a masterful display of sharing her learning in the clear, straightforward way that I had come to expect of her from reading her publications. It certainly taught those of us who were there a great deal, especially about that third aspect of gerontology as it should be practiced–caring–that was her primary theme that morning.

Several things Barbara said in her keynote illustrate especially well how she practiced gerontology, and they bear hearing again.[6] First and foremost, she made a point at once obvious and yet too often overlooked, I fear: *The necessary beginning of making a good gerontologist is simply love for older people.* She elaborated on this fundamental truth by reminding us that even great skill in delivery of care does not make up for lack of clarity about one's *motivation* for caring in the first place. That of course is where religion comes in because most religions teach in one way or another that it is normal, expected, and even appropriate for humans to bear burdens and that caring for others often "costs" something, however alien to our dominant cultural values that sounds. In this light, then, becoming a family caregiver is transformed from being an unacceptable intrusion upon a burdenless life that is seen as one's right; instead, caregiving and the burdens it necessarily brings are a legitimate and expected part of a certain type of life one has *chosen* to live, if one's motivation for caregiving is *religious*. That's worth thinking about, I think, at least if you're among those who have chosen that type of life.

On the other hand–or perhaps better, from the other direction–the *receiver* of care has certain obligations as well, primarily that of being willing to work with the caregiver even if it means bringing others in to mediate disputes. The American obsession with independence of course makes it very difficult for most people to be care recipients, but once again religion can be helpful here because virtually every major religious tradition teaches in one way or another that we are *not* self-sufficient atoms who can always function totally on our own. The dominant tradition in the United States, Christianity, goes so far as to say that one can come to a proper relationship with God– and thus with self and others–*only* through recognition of one's total and utter dependence on God (granted, that's my Reformed bias showing through, but it really *is* the heart of the gospel). Again, it appears to me that Barbara did a pretty good job of demonstrating in her own life both sides of what she called this "dyadic model for caring."

One important implication of much of Barbara's work that jumped out at me in reading her publications is the necessity to keep ever before us the question "Who *are* the elders of the 21st century?" and to answer that question honestly. And friends, my answer is, to paraphrase Pogo's immortal words, "We have met the age wave, and it is *us!*" If we want to have any hope of overcoming the classifying, labeling, and separating that have led even to threatened "intergenerational warfare," we need to come to understand–in our hearts as well as our heads–that we are *all aging together,* regardless of our age at any particular moment.

Now be honest: When you hear the word "aging," what image comes immediately to your mind? Think of any conference or meeting you've attended that contains the word "aging" in its title: *Who* do you just automatically assume is the focus of such a meeting? But "aging" is not something that applies only to "old" people–it applies to *all* of us because we're all aging, every day of our lives from the day we're born.

If we can genuinely comprehend that truth, no longer is it a matter of "older" and "younger"–whom we treat almost as if they are two different species–no longer a matter of *us* and *them* (depending on where you place yourself in the life span) but rather *all of us* together, engaged in a common enterprise, sharing a universal human experience, making the same lifelong journey even if we are at different points along the way. In short, we need a shift on the most fundamental level of our thinking from our current practice of classifying people by age and dealing with them on that basis–especially the "old"–to one in which we all see ourselves as *aging together.*

You see, I don't consider myself "old" (or even "old*er*"–despite my 55+ years!), and thus it is very easy for me to deny that I have any common interests with those whom I consider to fall into that "alien" category. But, if I am honest, I cannot deny that I am very definitely "aging," as is everyone else on the face of the earth, and thus we all do have something very significant in common. In fact, of all the characteristics we human beings use to categorize and therefore separate ourselves, aging may well be the only one we all really *do* share! There *are* two sexes, different races, different nationalities, different ethnicities, different religious beliefs, different socio-economic statuses, and so on. But when it comes to *aging*, we really are all in it together! In short, whatever our age at the moment, we need to learn to say to one another, "Where you are, I once was," and "Where you are, I some day will be." This seems to me to be the real thrust of Barbara's frequent use of the word "intergenerational," especially with regard to the Church.

In fact, now that I've mentioned "church" again, let me get something off my chest: I am really tired of the attitude of our churches that "older adults" are somebody "over there" to whom "*we*" must minister and for whom "*we*" must figure out programs. The elderly are *not* a needy subgroup within the Church–they *are* the Church and will only become increasingly more so, as many of you know from first-hand experience. Using my denomination–the Presbyterian Church (USA)–as an example, 67 percent of our members are over the age of 45, 57 percent over 50, and 35 percent 65 or older. The median age is 54, whereas the median age for the US population as a whole is about 36. And this is a trend that is seen across the mainline Protestant denominations, with most reporting at least 20 to 25 percent of their members 65 and older. In the Evangelical Lutheran Church of America, for example, two out of five members are over 55. And Mel Kimble of Luther Seminary in St. Paul, along with Barbara, one of the real pioneers in the field of religious gerontology, estimates that the average clergyperson spends about one-half of his or her time working with older parishioners and their families.

So we simply have to stop thinking about "older adult ministry" or "ministry with the aging" as *missionary* work to those "old folks over there." As Barbara so practically put it, "Don't feed me and pray with me on Thursday unless you're going to include me all the other days." Continuing to talk about ministering to "those old folks over there" in light of the demographic realities we all know so well just doesn't make sense when "those people over there" are who *we* are!

Indeed, the role of the Church is likely to become only more important in the 21st century because of one of the major and still too little discussed impacts of the aging of society, namely, some previously unknown changes in the family. Today some 80 percent of eldercare is still provided by families, but already the industrialized nations have a fertility rate that barely replaces people who die (and it's actually below replacement in several). So demographers are beginning to warn of the logical and unavoidable outcome of (1) the sheer numbers of aging Baby Boomers, combined with (2) their much smaller number of offspring I just mentioned, compounded by (3) increased longevity, leading to an unprecedented *great-grandparent boom*.

The result? Very few *younger* family members will be around to provide care for their elders. Today's Boomers can usually share at least some aspects of caring for Mom and Dad among several siblings; but when we grow old, we are much more likely to have at most two or maybe only one (or possibly no) adult children to care for us (in 1995, e.g., 20 percent of US women 35-39 were childless, twice the percentage of their mothers at the same age). For the first time in history, people will know more of their *ancestors* than of their *descendants*, i.e., relatives who are older than those who are younger.

In short, in the 21st century fewer and fewer adult children will have more and more elderly parents around, and those parents will tend to live much longer than in the past and thus to reach the age to be increasingly frail and in need of care (Carl Eisdorfer, one of the founders of the Alzheimer's Association and my colleague as chair of the Psychiatry Department at the University of Miami, points out that the need for care doubles for every five years a person survives beyond 65, and as we all know, the fastest-growing segment of the US population comprises those 85 and older). Already we see more and more "old old" being cared for by "young old," and that situation is only going to increase as all the factors I've just talked about come fully into play.

We've all heard of the "sandwich generation," those adult children who are "sandwiched" between the care of children still at home and older parents? Well, now the experts are telling us to prepare for the arrival of the "*club* sandwich generation" as we face multiple generations living long enough that several will need care at the same time. And I won't even mention the further problems caused by the widespread divorce and multiple remarriage that are likely only to increase as we live longer and longer, a practice that leads to jumbled intergenerational relationships and thus great confusion over which descendant is even the "responsible" or appropriate caregiver. So the question looms: Who will take care of us?

This discussion leads naturally into another area of deep concern for Barbara, one in which she made a major contribution through her involvement with the Gerontology in Theological Education project in the mid-1980s. I've already cited some numbers clearly showing that American congregations are aging even faster than the general population. Now add to that the studies that show that clergy are often the first people many of their congregants turn to, not only for "spiritual" needs but for many others as well, including various mental health concerns. In light of these two factors in the context of the question I raised a moment ago, it's obvious that clergy need to have not only passing acquaintance with gerontology but in fact serious specialized training in various aspects of working with older people.

But I'm compelled to ask–as Barbara did regularly beginning 30 or more years ago, "What are the religious institutions of this country going to offer to meet this pressing need of the 21st century?" Despite the compelling evidence, the nation's seminaries are just not recognizing the need and making gerontological education part of their curricula (just yesterday morning I gave the closing plenary address at a national interfaith symposium on aging in Florida and made some similar remarks; the first comment, from a well-known lecturer who travels widely across the country, was that that has been her observation and experience as well, and her remark prompted widespread agreement among those who were there).

The need, however, goes beyond even something as important as training clergy in gerontology to more fundamental changes in the religious institutions themselves. Already many faith communities have become surrogate families for a number of older people with the breakdown of the traditional nuclear family and the ever-increasing mobility and transiency of our lifestyle. But perhaps such religious bodies need to show a greater willingness to "decentralize"–to get out of the rigid identification with a building as "*the* Church"–and figure out ways to get to people where *they* are–aging in place–while still seeing themselves (and being seen) as "the Church."

And perhaps–though this may be more difficult from a theological perspective–religious institutions also need to be a little more open to redefining "the family" because it just isn't what we still think of it as or what many of us probably wish it still were. If the religious organizations that have played such an important role in this nation's history in providing all sorts of assistance to the elderly and others are to avoid failing to do needed ministry because the world no longer fits their preconceived–and largely outdated notions–of how it should be, then they are going to have to reconceptualize some fundamental aspects of their belief and practice to accord with the way things are now.

Yet another of Barbara's many areas of interest was sex–i.e., the sexuality of the elderly. This one especially caught my attention and represents another link between Barbara and me because when I began my career in the academic study of religion at Duke, my field of specialization was the ethics of human sexuality. In fact, the first book I published was titled *Sexuality, the Bible, and Science*. By the early 1980s, however, I began to feel the need to shift my research focus, and I decided to begin looking into ethical issues raised by aging.

As many of you know, it's important to keep the chairperson of your department informed of your academic pursuits, and when I told him about my new research agenda, he responded that he was not at all surprised. He said he had already discovered that as one approaches 40, one's thoughts (and interest) naturally shift from sex to aging!

I don't subscribe to that assessment of my motivation, by the way, because it is undeniable that even as one ages, sexuality remains an important component of a truly fulfilled life. And, as she did in so many other areas, here also Barbara Payne Stancil made a significant contribution to our knowledge and awareness by reminding us of this fact. Way back in 1975 she was co-author of *Love in the Later Years: The Emotional, Physical, Sexual, and Social Potential of the Elderly*, and if anything, this is an even more important area today because of increasing longevity and better health longer into that extended lifespan. If we are to care genuinely about and for those whom we serve as gerontologists, we need to follow Barbara's example, continuing to learn about the role of sexuality as we age and working to eliminate the disparaging stereotypes of the "dirty old man" and the predatory elderly widow.

Related to this topic, I want to cite another example of Barbara's caring that once again can serve as a terrific lesson for all of us, *whatever* our age. And this lesson is that it is simply never too late to be open to new experiences in life, to *learn* new things about ourselves and others that we can then *teach* to those around us, even things that our culture tells us we should not care about when we are "old."

I think it best here simply to let her speak for herself from the 1994 interview: To set the context, I need to tell you she has just described a situation at church where she did a couple of sessions for a young adult class on parenting and aging; two weeks later the baby of one of the couples died unexpectedly, and the class asked Barbara to come back to talk with them about the baby's death. She thought it was because they felt she would understand, and she concludes, "That understanding doesn't come overnight. I couldn't have done that forty years ago." Then she asks and answers a question that illustrates precisely how she practiced gerontology: "Who's going to help these baby boomers and younger folks understand faith and faith development? Only people who have had some history and experience in it."

She then uses that incident to begin talking about her own "growth and development" in her later years– "personal stuff," as she calls it. Next comes the part I want to share with you now:

> A lot of my personal growth is with Frank. This is the new love relationship I didn't expect. It's a gift. We have a home like I've never had before. . . . This is a home that has joy, that starts that way every day. Frank

is a "happy waking-up man." Our home is full of love and tenderness and open to people. It is so peaceful it is unbelievable. And we can share that gift as the way marriage can be, with any age group–encourage them, and open our home to others. This is a new, happy experience, and it's a maturing one.

There it is, folks, all in one short, sweet statement: gerontology as it should be practiced (and lived!)–always learning, open to new experiences; ever teaching, willing to share what you continue to learn as you "mature"; and especially caring deeply! So if you're *older*, don't ever let anybody tell you you're too old to experience profound and abiding love–even passion (Susan McFadden vividly remembers the night Barbara "called me, completely giddy, to tell me she was marrying Frank Stancil")–or that you're too old to share that love with others. And if you're *younger*–at least if you *care* about the elders with whom you interact, whether clients, patients, relatives, friends, or strangers–don't ever disparage or deny the capacity of those "old folks" for growth, development, and personal fulfillment.

I want to leave you with one last bit of wisdom from this exceptional woman whom all of us who knew her feel blessed to have had her be part of our lives. It's a bit of wisdom not original with her but in fact ancient. And perhaps in many ways that's the best kind, especially when given new life by one so wise herself.

Barbara woke up one morning shortly before she met Frank to "a very deep experience for me," as she termed it, what she said was "like a booming voice in the room" affirming, "This is the day the Lord has made. Rejoice and be glad in it!" From that day on she says she began every day with that thought, and she and Frank included it in their wedding ceremony as the anthem the choir sang.

From that experience she recaptured a sense of "the precious present" and a new outlook on the future as something no one can know but that needs to be lived one day at a time because that's all any of us is ever given. Barbara maintained that "you don't get wiser merely because you get old"; instead, because of the experiences that accumulate through a lifetime of living, you learn things to share that weren't available to you when you were younger. I tell my students that the best way I can think of to define "life" is as *experiencing* (that's why in my death and dying class I tell them–most of whom in an exercise we do to describe their "ideal death" say they want to die in their sleep–that that's the last way I want to die because death is the *last* thing in this life I will ever experience, and I don't want to miss it!)–so if we think of life as experiencing, then if we don't take advantage of every moment of every day to experience as fully as possible whatever life brings our way, then we're not really living. I think Barbara would have understood my point.

In a 1991 article on "Spiritual Maturity and Meaning-Filled Relationships," Barbara says something that is certainly appropriate for us to hear in this first Barbara Payne Lecture after her death: "I am reminded that all beginnings are endings and all endings are beginnings."[7] Through her learning, her teaching, and perhaps most of all her caring, Barbara became the personification of the wisdom that can accompany the maturity of years–the discovery of that great biblical goal of a "good old age"–and certainly she serves as an example we can all strive to follow. As Susan McFadden describes her, "She truly lived fully. . . . She was a wonderful model of living into old age with zest!" I would add that she became the consummate gerontologist as well, always focused on the real needs of those she felt called to serve (and yes, I don't think there's any doubt that for Barbara it was indeed a sacred calling, a true vocation in the classic meaning of that term).

By basing her thinking and acting on solid research and observation, by sharing the fruits of that learning with as many people as she could in as many settings and through as many media as she could, and above all by caring deeply about what she was doing and for those she was doing it for, Barbara Pittard Payne Stancil has truly lived for us gerontology as it should be practiced.

NOTES

1. All statements attributed to Barbara Payne Stancil without citation of another source are from this interview of June 17, 1994, in Decatur, Georgia.

2. "Religion in Gerontological Research, Training and Practice," *Journal of Religious Gerontology* 12/2 (2001): 19.

3. Personal communication from James Ellor.

4. Personal communication.

5. Personal communication.

6. This summary comes from an article I wrote about her keynote: "The Challenge of Caring: Special Conference Report," *Aging & Spirituality* V/2 (Summer 1993): 1, 5-7.

7. "Spiritual Maturity and Meaning-Filled Relationships: A Sociological Perspective," *Journal of Religious Gerontology* 7/1-2 (1991): 37.

Chapter 2

Sex and the Elderly:
No Laughing Matter in Religion

Barbara Pittard Payne Stancil, PhD

SUMMARY. This article provides a brief background for the study of sex and older persons. It examines the prevailing attitudes among older persons and society in general. A number of critical issues regarding sexuality in the latter years of life is addressed. *[Article copies available for a fee from The Haworth Document Delivery Service: 1-800-HAWORTH. E-mail address: <docdelivery@haworthpress.com> Website: <http://www.HaworthPress.com> © 2003 by The Haworth Press, Inc. All rights reserved.]*

KEYWORDS. Sex differences, laughing matter, sexuality, congregations, disparity, gender, heterosexual, marriage, divorce, church/synagogue, lifestyle, co-habitation, homosexuality, affairs, widowed

---

Barbara Pittard Payne Stancil was Director of the Gerontology Center, Georgia State University, Atlanta, GA. She was also a teacher, lecturer, leader, and prolific writer contributing to the development of the field of gerontology and to the body of important literature in the field. Her books and writings were published by a wide range of publishers. She was a leader in the United Methodist denomination and engaged in numerous interdenominational activities regarding ministries with older adults.

This article was originally published in the *Quarterly Papers on Religion and Aging* by the Poppele Center at Saint Paul School of Theology, Kansas City, MO. It is reprinted here by permission.

[Haworth co-indexing entry note]: "Sex and the Elderly: No Laughing Matter in Religion." Stancil, Barbara Pittard Payne. Co-published simultaneously in *Journal of Religious Gerontology* (The Haworth Pastoral Press, an imprint of The Haworth Press, Inc.) Vol. 15, No. 1/2, 2003, pp. 17-24; and: *Practical Theology for Aging* (ed: Derrel R. Watkins) The Haworth Pastoral Press, an imprint of The Haworth Press, Inc., 2003, pp. 17-24. Single or multiple copies of this article are available for a fee from The Haworth Document Delivery Service [1-800-HAWORTH, 9:00 a.m. - 5:00 p.m. (EST). E-mail address: docdelivery@haworthpress.com].

http://www.haworthpress.com/store/product.asp?sku=J078
Digital Object Identifier: 10.1300/J078v15n01_03

When Abraham, a man of 100 years, and Sarah, a woman of 90 years, were told they would have a son, they both laughed–not because of Abraham's age, but because of Sarah's age.[1] In the Old Testament, it is not considered unusual for a man to father a child after he is 100 years of age. It was the limits of the child bearing age for the female that made the possibility of mothering a child at the age of 90 a laughing matter.[2] Perhaps this ancient biblical account is the first recorded incidence of sex differences in aging and the sexual activity of older persons being viewed as a laughing matter.

Given the biblical bases for longevity and continued sexual activity, it seems strange that in 1986 sociologists' research confirming that older people fall in love in the same way that young people do would appear in *Psychology Today* and a syndicated Associated Press article and, that birthday cards, cartoons and jokes would continue to make the sex life of older adults a laughing matter.[3]

Even more difficult to understand is the omission of references to the sexual interests and needs for intimacy of older adults in denominational literature. Although the denominations have responded with programmatic books, they have given little or no attention to the sexuality or sex differences in the age structure of their membership. An exception is Becker's guide for clergy and congregations in ministry with older persons. He induces a short but excellent section on "the masculine-feminine polarity."[4]

While the Bible, science fiction writers and gerontologists treat the sexuality of older persons more positively than many religious writers and denominational leaders, gerontologists have given little attention to the role of religion and participation among the elderly.[5] As a consequence, the two most persistent myths about aging are that sex is for the young and religion is for the old. Contrary to these popular beliefs, adults do not necessarily turn to religion as they age,[6] nor do they lose sexual interest or cease to be sexually active. However, religious sanctions and beliefs about sexual behavior and negative social attitudes about the sexual needs of older persons do affect the way older people respond to their sexuality.

Gerontologists have known for some time that most older people are sexually active. While age has been identified as the most important factor affecting frequency and the form of sexual activity, there is no physiological basis for predicting inevitable sexual dysfunction accompanying aging. On the contrary, the Duke Longitudinal Research study found that, for some older persons, sexual interest and activity actually increased with age.[7] These gerontological research findings need to be utilized by the clergy in their counseling and religious interpretations.

Support for local clergy to address the sexual needs of older members was given in 1974 when the National Council of Churches, the Synagogue Council of America and the United States Catholic Conference issued an Interfaith Statement on sex education affirming that:

> Human sexuality is a gift of God to be accepted with reverence and joy; . . . It is more than a mechanical instinct. Its many dimensions are intertwined with the total personality and character of the individual. Sex is a dynamic urge or power, arising from one's basic maleness or femaleness, and having complex physical, psychological, and sexual dimensions. These dimensions, we affirm, must be shaped and guided by spiritual and moral considerations which derive from our Judeo-Christian heritage. Sex education is not however, only for the young, but is a life-long task whose aim is to help individuals develop their sexuality in a manner suited to their life stage.[8]

As the age of the Church/Synagogue shifts from youth to an adult membership, sex after sixty will no longer be a laughing matter but the reason for life-span sex education and social programs to provide opportunities for heterosexual interaction. The influence of the sheer numbers of the Baby Boomers and their sexual life styles will shape the future direction of these changes. The shift to an older adult membership will make it imperative to rely on retired members to fill the functional lay leader roles in the congregations. This age group, with the most discretionary time and income, will be a major source for recruitment and training for diaconal ministry. The youth-to-adult to older-adult congregations will require a trained lay older adult leadership to carry out the goals and programs for all age members.

Congregations have not only been youth and male oriented, but couple and family oriented. Congregations have been characterized by a "Noah's ark" syndrome in which all are expected to enter two by two. This Noah's ark syndrome is a sex-negativism that places primacy on sexual activity as procreation. Important as this aspect of sexuality is, it is age specific for women and does not represent the total experience of human sexuality.

The disparity of males to females among older adults means that there are fewer married couples. In 1984, 40 percent of adults age 65 and over were married. Twice as many older men (78%) were likely to be married than older women (40%). There were five times (7.8 million) widows as widowers (1.5 million) and the disparity increases at older ages.[9] In 1985, 68 percent of women 75 and older were widowed compared to less than 23 percent of men over age 75. This gender disparity is a consequence of age-specific death rates for adult men and their tendency to marry younger women.[10]

Divorce among older people has increased faster than the older population as a whole in the past 20 years. Four percent of all older persons were divorced–more older women than older men. Furthermore, elderly widowed men have remarriage rates about seven times higher than widows. Among the future elderly (men and women), approximately one-half of the men and women will have been divorced at least once by the time they reach the age of 75.[11] This may seem like a dismal projection, but on the positive side, they (men and women) will know how to enter and exit a single lifestyle. For women, this may be the best preparation for the 8 to 10 years most of them over the age of 65 can expect to be widowed or divorced.

A small number (less than 8 percent) of older persons never marry. Since many young adults are delaying or rejecting marriage, the number of never married older persons may be expected to increase.[12] Studies on marital status and life satisfaction are in general agreement that married persons are happier, healthier and longer lived than the never married, widowed or divorced.[13] Marriage minimizes the negative impact of retirement, reduced income and declining health. This life satisfaction difference may be attributed to the major functions that marriage performs for couples: intimacy, interdependence, a sense of belonging, a shared life history, and continuity of life style.[14]

Marital satisfaction varies among older couples, but most studies of older couples report that older wives and husbands appreciate each other and are highly satisfied whether it is a long or short term marriage. Given the personal investment of time, energy and themselves in the marriage and the alternative of living alone in late life, most dissatisfied older marrieds choose to continue the relationship.[15]

The Church/Synagogue IS challenged to respond to never married, widowed and divorced older members who also have the need to minimize the negative impact of retirement, reduced income and declining health.

Gender differences in marital status are much greater among older age groups and can be expected to continue. Responses to this marital heterogeneity by the Church/Synagogue will include: (1) older singles groups to provide social support and activities that increase morale and life satisfaction; (2) support groups for those experiencing loss of a spouse by divorce or death; (3) marital counseling and adaptation of the marriage ritual for late life remarriages; (4) couple groups for the older newlyweds; and (5) marriage revitalization and enrichment groups for long-lived intact survivor marriages. All of these groups will need leaders, counselors and clergy who are knowledgeable about normal physiological aging and gender changes in sexual functionality.

FROM EITHER/OR TO MULTIPLE CHOICE

Marriage continues to be the most valued state for most Americans. At least 95 percent marry at least once and most who divorce before they are sixty tend to marry again. Although death and divorce reduce the numbers of older marriages, approximately half of the 26 million older Americans are married. Of course, this means that approximately half of these older Americans are not married and that the sex ratio disparity reduces the chance for remarriage, especially for women.

The opportunity for heterosexual activity on the part of the older female, unlike that of the older male or young female, is still more apt to be determined by the availability of a husband and his sexual capability. Unmarried older men maintain sexual activity and interest levels similar to that of married men. Women do not because they lack available and appropriate sexual partners.

The sexual revolution of the past two decades has widened the choices for adults of all ages. The trend has been away from sexual intimacy within marriage or to multiple choices. Although marriage continues to be highly valued by older persons and a life style experienced by most, it can no longer be the only alternative.

The choices other than marriage include: (1) companionship and dating; (2) co-habitation; (3) homosexuality; (4) affairs with married persons; (5) polygamy; and (6) no sexual partner. Marriage and dating may be the only choices sanctioned by the Church/Synagogue. However, the sex ratio disparity among older persons can be expected to influence these limited sanctions in the future. Certainly, the Judeo-Christian faith has an Old Testament precedent for multiple partners. Courtship and dating may lead to marriage or to a "steady relationship." Dating behavior among older persons is reported to be more varied and the pace of the relationship tends to be accelerated. Bulcroft and O'Conner-Roden report that sexual involvement is an important part of the dating relationships for most of the older persons in their study. While sexuality for these dating couples included intercourse, the stronger emphasis was on the nuances of sexual behavior such as hugging, kissing and touching. This physical closeness helped fulfill the intimacy needs of older people, needs that were especially important to those living alone and whose sole source of human touch was often the dating partner. Sex also contributed to self-esteem by making people feel desired and needed. As could be expected, older persons choosing to have a sexual relationship outside of marriage violated the religious values that they have followed. Consequently, older people frequently hide the intimate aspects of a relationship.[16]

Some older persons elect to openly live together. For some this may lead to marriage, but many older people reject marriage as a solution to their need for a sexual relationship because they are not willing to give up their independence, the possibility of deteriorating health and the financial complexities of a legal relationship. Brubaker observes that although the number of people over the age of 65 cohabitating has decreased slightly, cohabitation is increasing in most age groups. This leads us to expect the trend toward cohabitation to gradually increase. The choice of dating with intimacy and cohabitation raise the religious question about the reason for marriage. Do older people have the same reason for marriage as young people? Is the delay in marriage by young adults based on the same rationale that older people use to reject marriage, i.e., the view that marriage is for procreation? This ambiguity about marriage by both young and older adults may stimulate the Church/Synagogues to formulate sanctions and rituals that address age-related sexual expressions and relationships.

Over forty years ago a medical doctor, Victor Kassels, recommended a limited polygamy after the age of 60. He pointed out that this would be a return to a practice that at one time was considered proper in the Judeo-Christian ethic. He argued that:

> marriage enables the unmarried older women to find a partner . . . Most women have an increase in libido after the menopause simply because they lose the fear of pregnancy. A polygynous marriage enables them to express this desire, instead of remaining repressed through a continent widowhood.[17]

As for men, Kassel observed that many sexologists claim the male is polygamous by nature. Furthermore, there is no established age of a male climacteric. Male impotence, not related to disease or medication, may be due to boredom, or an uninterested partner. Polygamous marriage might be a solution to a number of sexual problems of the aged. Kassels may have a good solution, but the strength of the Christian belief in a monogamous relationship, at least serially within and outside of marriage, makes it unlikely that this choice will be sanctioned in the future.[18]

More likely to increase are affairs outside of marriage. As partners within a long term marriage experience changes in health, interests, and compatibility, discrete affairs that protect the marriage partners may be a choice for some older persons.

Always open as a choice is no sexual partner. Many widowed persons find a new freedom without sexual relationships. They focus their energy and interests on other activities and relationships. The importance that Americans of all ages place on sex suggests that this will not be the voluntary choice of most older adults in the future.

The need and requests for counseling related to these choices can be expected to increase. Consequently, the professional training for clergy and other counselors will include not only the sexual needs, choices, socio-psychological problems unique to older persons, but also the religious conflict and dilemma older persons experience.

Church/Synagogue rituals related to marriage and sexual practice will need to be adapted to the non-procreative stage of life so that the joy of intimacy, experiencing one's sexuality and sexual identity will be extended to older members. The inclusion of older' persons in all religious matters related to sex, sex roles and sexuality will destroy the basis for making sex and the elderly a laughing matter.

NOTES

1. "Genesis," Chapter 17:17; 18:12-13. The Holy Bible revised standard version (New York: Thomas Nelson and Sons, 1953).

2. Frank Stagg, *The Bible Speaks on Aging*. (Nashville: Broadman Press, 1981).

3. Kris Bulcroft & Margaret O'Connor-Roden, "Never Too Late," *Psychology Today* June 1986, pp. 66-69; "Old Folks Who Fall in Love Still Teenagers at Heart," The Atlanta Journal/Constitution, May 29, 1986.

4. Arthur H. Becker, *Ministry With Older Persons: A Guide for Clergy and Congregations* (Minneapolis: Augsburg Publishing House, 1986).

5. Barbara Payne, "Religiosity." In Mangen, David J. & Warren A. Peterson (eds.), *Social Roles and Social Participation*, Vol. 2 (Minneapolis: University of Minnesota Press, 1983), pp. 343–388; Fecher, Vincent. *Religion and Aging: An Annotated Bibliography* (San Antonio: Trinity University Press, 1982).

6. Jon P. Alston and Ray Wingrove, (eds.). "Cohort Analysis of Church Attendance, 1936-69." In ~ 1949, September, pp. 59-67.

7. Erdman Palmore, "Sexual Behavior." In *Social Patterns in Normal Aging: Findings from the Duke Longitudinal Study* (Durham, North Carolina: Duke University Press, 1981); Butler, Robert & Lewis, Myra. Sex after sixty (New York: Harper & Row, 1976); Peterson, James A. & Payne, Barbara, *Love in the Later Years* (Association Press, 1975).

8. "Interfaith Statement on Sex Education" (National Council of Churches, Synagogue Council of America, United States Catholic Council). In Gordon, S. & Libby R. *Sexuality Today and Tomorrow* (North Sctuate, Mass: Duxbury Press, 1976), pp. 154-56.

9. Paul C. Glick, "Marriage, Divorce and Living Arrangements of the Elderly: Prospective Changes," _____ *Journal of Family Issues*. 5:7-26, 1984.

10. "Developments in Aging: 1985," Volume 3 (Washington, D.C.: Special Committee on Aging, United States Senate, 1986).

11. Timothy Brubaker, *Later Life Families* (Beverly Hills, California: Sage, 1985).

12. *Psychology Today* (see footnote #3).

13. Russell A. Ward, "The Never Married in Later Life," *Journal of Gerontology* 34: 861-869, 1979; Jay F. Gubrium, "Being Single in Old Age," *International Journal of Aging and Human Development* 6: 29-41, 1975; Charles Longino, and Aaron Lipman Aaron, "The Married, The Formerly Married and The Never Married: Support System Differentials of Older Women in Planned Retirement Communities", 1982; Glenn Norvel, "The Contribution of Marriage to the Psychological Well–Being of

Males and Females", *Journal of Marriage and the Family 37* (3): 594-601; Brubaker, 113–116 (see footnote #18); P. Uhlenberg, and M. Myers, "Divorce and The Elderly" Gerontologist 21 (3), 276–82, 1981.

14. Robert Atchley, *Social Forces and Aging* (4th Edition) (Belmont, California: Wadsworth Press, 1985).

15. Rosalie Gilford, "Marriages in Later Life," Generations (4): 17-21, 1986; A. Skolink, "Married Lives: Longitudinal Perspectives on Marriage." In Eichorn, David et al., (eds.) *Present and Past in Middle Life* (New York: Academic Press, 1981).

16. Atchley, op.cit.

17. Victor Kassels, "Polygamy After 60," Geriatrics 21, No. 4, April, 1966.

18. Ibid.

Chapter 3

A Practical Theology for Aging

Derrel R. Watkins, PhD

SUMMARY. After a brief look at contemporary liberal and evangelical approaches to the formation of theology, this paper suggests implications for constructing a practical theology of aging utilizing a *praxis* approach. Issues such as the life course, mental health, physical health, and spiritual formation are highlighted along with implications for the field of gerontology. *[Article copies available for a fee from The Haworth Document Delivery Service: 1-800-HAWORTH. E-mail address: <docdelivery@haworthpress.com> Website: <http://www.HaworthPress.com> © 2003 by The Haworth Press, Inc. All rights reserved.]*

KEYWORDS. Theology, traditional, doctrines, praxis, systematic, deontologists, liberal, enlightenment, conservative, liberation, process, practical, life course, physical health, mental health, spiritual formation

---

Derrel R. Watkins is Adjunct Faculty, The Institute for Gerontological Studies, School of Social Work, Baylor University, Waco, TX; Professor of Social Work Emeritus, Southwestern Baptist Theological Seminary, Fort Worth, TX; and Oubri A. Poppele Chair (Gerontology) in Health and Welfare Ministries (retired), Saint Paul School of Theology, Kansas City, MO.

[Haworth co-indexing entry note]: "A Practical Theology for Aging." Watkins, Derrel R. Co-published simultaneously in *Journal of Religious Gerontology* (The Haworth Pastoral Press, an imprint of The Haworth Press, Inc.) Vol. 15, No. 1/2, 2003, pp. 25-38; and: *Practical Theology for Aging* (ed: Derrel R. Watkins) The Haworth Pastoral Press, an imprint of The Haworth Press, Inc., 2003, pp. 25-38. Single or multiple copies of this article are available for a fee from The Haworth Document Delivery Service [1-800-HAWORTH, 9:00 a.m. - 5:00 p.m. (EST). E-mail address: docdelivery@haworthpress.com].

http://www.haworthpress.com/store/product.asp?sku=J078
© 2003 by The Haworth Press, Inc. All rights reserved.
Digital Object Identifier: 10.1300/J078v15n01_04

I can only imagine how Professor Donald Browning felt in 1974 when Seward Hiltner asked him to write a paper on the subject, "a practical theology of aging." The task called for him to reflect on Erik Erikson's concept of *generativity* and develop a practical theology of aging. The product of his study is included in the proceedings of a conference on the Theology of Aging that was sponsored by the National Retired Teachers Association and the American Association of Retired Persons in 1974. Human Sciences Press published the proceedings in 1975.[1] Now, at the beginning of the 21st century, I am attempting to address a similar subject and feeling the same frustrations I imagine Browning felt. The subject is too large for one paper and there are too many facets to even come close to being comprehensive. All I can logically do here is provide a framework for the articles that follow.

Any theology that addresses the everyday-lived-lives of older persons is potentially practical. I am fond of saying that all good theology is practical and any theology that is not applicable to the everyday lived lives of human beings is not good theology.

Traditional Jewish and Christian theologies, when properly addressed, have significant practical meaning for the everyday lived-lives of older persons. Basic doctrines such as the attributes of God, creation, anthropology, soteriology, ecclesiology, Christology, and eschatology do, in fact, affect the spiritual, physical, and mental wellness of older persons in their everyday lives.

Contemporary theological discussions have shifted from a quest for universal abstractions to the clarifying of situation-specific expressions of faith and faithfulness.[2] Practical theology recognizes that what we may know about God is first known through our everyday life experiences. For example, early in our lives we learn that there is someone or something that much more powerful than us. We experience the wonder and awe of mountains and oceans. We experience the warmth of the sun and marvel at the stars. We come to know love from our relationship with parents and others. Through experiences such as these we have our first understandings about who God is and what God is about.

Many attempts to establish a practical theology begin with constructs derived from the behavioral and social sciences. Theologians then attempt to overlay traditional doctrinal teachings. Some discover that there are significant conflicts. Often these conflicts are the result of rigidly interpreting church doctrines and scriptural teachings. Sometimes these conflicts are the result of trying to impose culture-specific scriptural and theological examples to contemporary issues in people's lives. This has lead to at least two responses: (1) Throw out the traditional teachings and/or reconstruct a "new theology" that addresses the everyday-lived-lives of older persons; or (2) ignore the conflicts and utilize behavioral and social science paradigms to explain the aging phenomenon and to work with older persons at the expense of theological reflection. I want to offer a third approach. I wish to begin with the essential teachings of traditional theologies as the foundation and draw insights from the behavioral and social sciences that will enable contemporary explanations and applications regarding the everyday-lived-lives of senior adults. For me, the scripture, when properly interpreted, is the basic authority for all theology. The Bible, however, does not specifically deal with every aspect of the modern everyday-lived-lives of older people. To be viable any theology and/or scientific theory must be consistent with principles that are derived from the revealed Word of God.

It is important to recognize that life is lived according to a dynamic, progressive, and circular paradigm rather than a linear one. This means that many things are happening simultaneously. Life is constantly changing. You cannot step into the same river twice and you will never again be the same age (chronologically, physiologically or psychologically). The only entity we know that does not drastically change is God. What we know and understand about God and how God works with and through us changes with each change in our experience. Practical theology recognizes and works with this dynamic paradigm.

PRAXIS AND PRACTICAL THEOLOGY

One of the clearest understandings about how practical theology is different from systematic theology is in the concept, *praxis*. Praxis is a methodological construct that seeks to pursue theology based upon the dialectic of theory and practice.[3] When applied to older persons in the community and in the church this model offers significant insights that enables the minister (professional or lay) to theologically reflect on the everyday-lived-lives of senior adults. Most existing systematic theologies are inadequate when attempting to explain the aging experience. The *praxis* approach includes developing theory and practice simultaneously. Practice illustrates theory and theory explains practice. *Praxis* is a much more viable way of understanding aging when it utilizes the theological reflection process.

Praxis, as the basic concern of practical theology, suggests that we understand that there is a duality in its meaning: *praxis* is both normative and transformative.[4] Anderson's *Christopraxis* model, for example, attempts to demonstrate that God was in Christ engaging human experience while illustrating a comprehensive approach to theology. Christ was intimately involved with humankind while at the same time teaching humans, by word and action, about God's unique attributes (theology). Indeed, while Christology was being developed, it was being lived out in everyday life.[5]

SYSTEMATIC THEOLOGY

In reality, a great deal of theological reflection and writing has utilized an Aristotelian approach to theology rather than a praxis model. Aristotle's *poises* addressed the need to develop a systematic theory and then explain phenomena using that model.[6] Practical theologians insist that it is only after engaging in reflection on life experiences that we may be able to discuss our spiritual relationships in the abstract. These abstract formulations attempt to understand God in logical, and orderly ways. This process is called "systematic theology."

Theological explanations of God and human experiences have taken a number of forms throughout history. There continues to be a tension between those who wish to take a deontological approach and those who prefer a more flexible or liberal one. Deontologists initially identified what they believed to be normative attributes for how humans were to understand God and they orally passed them on from generation to generation. As languages became more sophisticated and vocabularies were standardized, they wrote them down. Strict sanctions were imposed upon those whose behavior deviated from the norms.

On the other extreme were those who chose to explain God in terms of human reason and experience. Their doctrines were fluid and changed with human circumstances. Truth about God tended to be very subjective and therefore changeable with the political atmosphere and the emotional state of the scholar at the time. This was possibly a reaction to the perceived rigidity of the deontologists. This more liberal approach appeared to offer more freedom and less guilt and shame.

Modern deontologists tend to be found in both extremes. Those who declare a belief in the "fundamentals of the faith" and the inerrancy of scripture form one group. The other extreme is made up of "liberals" who will not tolerate anyone who does not agree with their position or take their particular approach to the study of theology. Conservative deontologists treat theology as a set of unchangeable rules. God is perceived as a rigid creator whose rules never change irrespective of the physical or sociocultural situation. Most senior adults were taught a version of these doctrines during their most sensitive, formative years. Although they may have changed their basic approach to theology, what they learned during their formative years remains their reference ideology.

Liberal deontologists reject the rigid creator and rigid unchanging rules concept but impose a rigid standard for a fluid systematic theology that excludes any believer who embraces an evangelical or conservative view. A minority of senior adults grew up with a theological understanding that was based primarily on human logic, reason, and experience. Scripture and tradition were a part of the mix, but did not form the complete foundation for their understanding of God's work in everyday life.

These contemporary liberal theologies grew out of the 16th century Enlightenment movement in Europe and then spread to America. The philosophies of Emanuel Kant and more recently Alfred North Whitehead have been major forces in the development and sustenance of contemporary liberal theologies.

The enlightenment inspired theologies developed an understanding of God that is based on reason and experience. Mystical attributes of God and God's relationship to human beings were basically rejected or minimized. Scientific methods of discovering truth and the nature and work of God were embraced.

Conservative theologians embraced enlightenment methodologies for interpreting scripture and explaining theological formulations. Evangelical theologians utilize the scientific method in analyzing texts and doctrines. They assume that the scriptures are inspired by God and therefore infallible or without error. They use enlightenment methodologies to explain the meanings of scripture and/or to defend against attacks on the authenticity of scripture. For Evangelicals, all doctrine is based upon biblical principles and therefore scripture and theology are two sides of the same coin.

TRADITIONAL THEOLOGIES

Traditional views of God prior to the Enlightenment embraced both mystical and experiential views of God. Problems arose when theologians and religious leaders developed rigid rules, laws, and regulations that led to unbending judgments regarding how human beings experienced God's pleasure or wrath. Theologians generally embraced these instructions as normative. They often ignored, however, how God actually interacted with those who violated this and other laws.[7] For example, the Law of Moses required that the people kill a person caught committing adultery (Lev. 20:10). King David was not stoned to death nor was the woman, Bethsheba (cf. II Samuel 11-12). God's judgment of David was not on his adultery but on the murder of Bethsheba's husband. God continued to use David and chose Bethsheba to be the person through whom Jesus Christ would be born.

Jesus himself violated rabbinical law regarding how the Sabbath was to be observed. The rigid legalist wanted to kill Jesus for his behavior. Jesus interpreted the law of the Sabbath, however, in light of a higher value, the well being of persons (cf. Mark 2:27). Some Practical theologians have observed that, "God never restricts anything that is good for us nor encourages us to do anything that is bad for us."

Roman Catholic theologies are based in scripture and tradition and interpreted in light of the way God is perceived to work in nature. Catholic Theologies are often referred to as "natural theologies" because an attempt is made to synthesize doctrine, authority, and practice with the "natural order." Issues such as birth control, abortion, homosexuality, and euthanasia are prominent sources of tension with liberal segments of the church and society, when leaders, basing their arguments on the natural order, speak in opposition to them.

LIBERAL THEOLOGIES

On the other end of the continuum are the more liberal theologies. Instead of ascribing absolute authority to scripture and tradition, they give more weight to reason and experience. They do not ignore scripture, but they do not give it the same absolute authority as conservatives. Liberal theologians are more likely to stress social issues and raise questions regarding traditional beliefs.

Alfred North Whitehead's philosophy led to the formulation of a contemporary theological movement identified as *Process Theology*. According to "process" thought, God is evolving along with humanity and other parts of creation. This theology does not consider the God who is described in the Bible to be the God of today. It teaches that God changes with creation and is in the dynamic process of revelation and creation.

Liberation theologies such as South American, Black, Feminist, Womanist, and Mujarista stress the shared experiences of oppressed populations. These experiences form the basis for defining who God is and how God relates to humanity. Each of the above mentioned Liberation Theologies focus on the unique life experiences of a particular group and interpret God's attitude toward sin and redemption in light of those experiences.

IMPLICATIONS FOR PRACTICAL THEOLOGY

Theological purists have difficulty accepting practical theology's tendency to eclectically draw insights from all of the above theologies and apply them to explanations of human lives and draw implications from them for use in ministry. Practical theologians may hold personal beliefs that are more compatible with one of the standard theological positions mentioned above, but most will not hesitate to utilize insights from other theologies, religions, psychologies, and/or social theories when dealing with persons who need their help.

When practical theologians encounter problematic issues that are resident in a particular set of beliefs they attempt to simultaneously understand the theological, philosophical, and experiential base for the difficulty. This praxis approach suggests that the action or situation and the *telos* (final meaning and character of truth) work together to enable understanding of the issue.

Systematic theologians, on the other hand, begin with a set of assumptions that are then used to explain the situation. They use a conceptual schematic overlay to determine the degree to which certain events, behaviors, or actions can explain the final meaning of truth (*telos*).[8]

PRACTICAL THEOLOGY AND THE LIFE COURSE

For a *praxis* model to be effective it is important that practice and theory be anchored, though not totally restricted, to a theoretical framework. Postmodern approaches that are open to recognizing a number of ways of getting at truth can be helpful as well. Erik Erikson's psychosocial stages of development, Maslow's hierarchy of needs, along with other developmental theories have made significant contributions to a workable construct for discussing the processes of aging. Social gerontologists, in addition, choose to discuss the process of aging in terns of the *life course*. Persons, families, and groups process through the *life course* at different rates, times, and in different ways depending upon their particular sociocultural environments. Persons who are identified among the young old, for example, may be fifty years of age or they may be seventy, depending upon their personal perceptions and life circumstances. Some persons may seem old at forty while others are still young at age seventy-five. Such issues as careers, health, family, life goals, and outlook on life are just a few factors considered when determining the place of an older person in the *life course*.

The way older persons live their everyday lives, the challenges they accept or reject, the goals they choose to pursue, and their reaction to physical, emotional, and social changes in their lives have spiritual implications for what some theologians call the *human vocation. Human vocation* and *life course* are compatible terms. Both attempt to describe the lived-lives of persons. The term *vocation* has been traditionally used by many Christian theologians to describe the totality of the life lived by persons who are followers of Christ. In recent years secular society has used the term to describe the public *life course* of persons in occupations, careers, or professions. Theologian James Fowler links the concept of *human vocation* [spiritual life course], in a more traditional way, to practical theology:

> Vocation must not be reduced to occupation, profession, or career. It has to do with the response persons make to God's call to partnership and with the way that response exerts ordering power in a person or community's priorities and investments of self, time, and resources. . . . My ap-

proach to pastoral care is based on the conviction that the Christian faith offers us a determinant conception of the *human vocation* [italics mine]–the human calling or destiny. This is taken to be the calling to partnership with God in God's work of ongoing creation, governance, redemption, and liberation.[9]

PRACTICAL THEOLOGY AND PHYSICAL HEALTH

One facet of the life course of older persons is the constant presence of physical decline. We simply can't do the things, physically, that were at one time took for granted we could do. This calls for a process of scaling down our expectations and adjusting our physical, mental, and social activities to what we can actually accomplish. While there is a strong correlation between physical, emotional, and social wellness to spiritual wellness, spirituality does not have to decline. Statistical analysis may show a strong correlation between one's physical condition, for example, and one's church or synagogue attendance. It does not, however, prove to be an essential causative factor. A regression analysis might more likely discover that a physical illness that affects the mental capacities of a person can be linked directly to the spiritual health of a person.

Indeed, my hypothesis is that persons who have clear minds have the capacity to grow spiritually, even if their physical conditions prohibit significant social interaction. Practical theology might suggest that private and small group worship such as prayer, Bible reading, devotional reading, listening, and/or viewing may actually be, for many, more helpful to one's spiritual nurturance than attendance at formal worship services. The inability to receive or participate in the Eucharist (Communion or Lord's Supper), for example, is a crucial element of worship to many and offers an opportunity for *ecclesial praxis*.[10]

The role of the church as a community of faith engaged in the "ecology of vocation"[11] suggests a practical theological approach to enabling the spiritual nurturance of persons who are members of faith communities. This includes those who are physically unable to attend formal worship and educational services. Many churches adapt their ecclesiastical methodologies and seek ways of meeting the spiritual needs of all the members of their faith communities. A large percentage of churches from all denominations offer regular worship experiences in nursing homes for persons who are unable to attend services at a church building. Many have teams made up of lay and clergy who take the Eucharist (Communion or Lord's Supper) to the home bound and nursing home congregants.

Another dimension of practical theology's praxis includes addressing the needs of persons who are victims of accidents and severe physical traumas. We have probably all heard of persons who experienced a severe illness or accident where rehabilitation was possible and they heroically worked through their situations and were restored to some degree of health. We may have also heard of others who simply perceived their condition to be hopeless and never recovered. Their perceptions may have been wrong, but the consequences were real nevertheless. Practical theologians may enable persons to reflect on the presence and will of God in such circumstances. Enabling persons to utilize the strengths and gifts God has provided for them can prove to be of inestimable value to individuals and families in crisis.

When older persons (and younger ones as well) become frail and experience significant physical difficulties they, or their family members, often ask, "Where is God? Why is God allowing this to happen?" Practical theologians are often at a loss, attempting to answer these questions. Any attempt to defend God is most often an exercise in futility. Yet, the feelings of frail older persons and their families call for some type of theological response. Becker suggests that the questions being asked may have a deeper meaning. They may be feeling that God has abandoned them in their time of greatest need and they are seeking to be assured that God is not displeased with them. Pastoral care workers may wish to assure these persons that their suffering is not the result of God's displeasure and that God is walking with them through the journey. God is involved with them in every experience and will see them through even the most painful times.[12]

PRACTICAL THEOLOGY AND MENTAL HEALTH

A few years ago I was invited to participate in a post-graduate seminar on spirituality and dementia among the elderly. One of the primary questions we attempted to address was "In the final stages of Alzheimer's Disease the person can no longer talk or give any response. Their bodies are continuing to function but their minds seem to be gone. Is there a soul present? Or, is there only a soul present when persons can know and interact in some way with family, friends, and care providers? When does the soul leave the body?" My thought was, "These are some heavy questions being asked by professional health care providers." I was not sure that theologians could adequately answer those questions. I went to Robert Davis' book, *My Journey Into Alzheimer's Disease*[13] and gained some insights, but no definitive answers. I then read carefully a book entitled *God Never Forgets*.[14] It gave me some additional insights. My conclusion was that the issue is more dependent on God than on the person/patient. The soul is not just mental activity; it is body *and* spirit (Genesis 2:7). Therefore, as long as there is breath "there is still a person in there"[15] and God may be the only one who knows for certain when the soul leaves the body.

I believe that this same principle applies to all forms of mental and emotional confusion. God is always present and involved in the mental as well as the physical suffering of persons. Reflecting on the mind of Christ while working with a confused mind of a woman or man is where the *praxis* of practical theology is at its best. In the not too distant past people assumed that Satan or one of his demons possessed the demented person. When Jesus Christ encountered persons with such a condition he didn't avoid them; he immediately dealt with the situation. Contemporary ministers and laypersons today often avoid persons who are diagnosed as mentally ill. Practical theology, however, suggests that mental illness should be just as much the purview of the ministry of the church as physical illnesses.

PRACTICAL THEOLOGY AND SPIRITUAL FORMATION

Jane Thibault suggests that many older persons may be bored with life and the church because they have not developed a deeper love relationship with God.[16] They may have been very active in their church life, but they plateaued spiritually.

Many older persons are more vibrant in their faith expressions today than they were when they were in their 40s or 50s. Many others, however, seem to be bored with their church and with God. They have heard all of the bible stories and can almost outline the sermons young pastors are going to preach as soon as the text is announced. Those who appear to be more vibrant have most likely continued to develop their spiritual lives. They are not content to rest on the past and be content with the present. They have an eschatological view of the future that offers them something more and they want it.

Those who are bored are probably content with things the way they are and have been, and don't believe that there is that much more for them. They are quietly disengaging from their spiritual lives and church activities. Often they are disengaging in other areas of their lives as well. They may have already retired from active employment or they are approaching retirement.

Practical theology, with its emphasis on *praxis*, offers one of the most promising approaches to dealing with the spiritual formation of older persons. Since there are more of us now than any time in human history and we are living longer and more healthy lives we can also look to God for those promises of a richer and more fulfilling life here on earth as a foretaste of what is ahead in eternity with complete union with our Savior. Jane Thibault challenges older persons with the promise of a greater gift at this time in our lives,

> For there is always more–much, much more to which you are constantly being invited. Your Father has called you into being to experience, to share an incredible, perpetually expanding abundance of life–God's own life lived in loving unity with the Son and the Spirit . . . God's great anguish comes from your barriers–your inability or refusal to become aware that these gifts exist for you.[17]

Even when our memories and our pilgrimages have not always been pleasant, we can grow in our love relationship with God and others. Roberta Bondi, reflecting on her life experiences and the lessons she learned from studying the ancient masters she called her "teachers," says:

> I am not looking forward to losing physical strength, nor having the people I love die. Still, none of the gifts that have come to me as I have aged have been imaginable to me in advance. As little as I may know what is ahead of me, I am able to believe from my own experience what my ancient teachers have been telling me all these years: love in God, in whatever form it takes, is continual growth in love that never comes to an end.[18]

A few years ago I shared insights such as these with a church in southern Missouri, and challenged older persons and younger ones, as well, to seek and accept this great gift of an ever-growing love affair with God. A woman came by after the worship service and said, "Today, for the first time, I am proud to be 78 years old. I now understand that old age is not a curse, it is truly God's wonderful gift. I am excited about what is ahead for me."

Although many feel that they know what the terms spiritual, spirituality, and spiritual well-being mean, it is difficult to find an adequate definition. The National Interfaith Coalition on Aging, in 1975, attempted to address this issue. Many of us have used the definition of spiritual well-being that was developed at that meeting in Chicago. Tom Cook, the Director of the NICA Research and Development Project, after listening to the discussion by members of almost all of the faith bodies in America, wrote out this succinct definition: *Spiritual well-being is the affirmation of life in a relationship with God, self, community, and the environment that celebrates wholeness.*[19] The assembled representatives approved the definition with the understanding that each could translate the key words according to their own traditions. It was pointed out that "*spiritual* is not one dimension among many in life; rather it permeates and gives meaning to all life."[20] Each of the key concepts: affirmation of life;

relationship with God, self, community and environment; and celebration of wholeness, forms the basis for discussions regarding spirituality that space does not allow us to cover.

There is a growing body of literature that seeks to address issues of spirituality among older persons. Harry R. Moody's book, *The Five Stages of The Soul,* is very insightful and helpful to students of practical theology and the spirituality of older persons. The five stages of the soul are: the call; the search; the struggle; the breakthrough; and the return. He discusses each of these stages in order in 353 pages.[21]

Harold G. Koenig and Andrew J. Weaver provide very insightful practical theological guidance in their book, *Pastoral Care of Older Adults.* They suggest four specific actions clergy can take to encourage the spiritual growth of older persons: (1) Address the meaning of pain and loss in sermons, making sure to address the specific issues faced by specific older persons in their congregations; (2) plan and implement educational programs that enable congregants, especially senior adults, to understand the role of faith in coping with everyday struggles of lived lives; (3) when counseling with older persons who are struggling with life crises, encourage them to bring God into the picture as a part of the solution; and (4) encourage older persons to use their gifts, talents, and wisdom to serve God by meeting the needs of others.[22]

IMPLICATIONS FOR GERONTOLOGY

Gerontologists from all academic and professional disciplines can benefit from an understanding of the role of practical theological *praxis* in understanding and working with the spiritual issues of older persons. The study of religion, spirituality, and aging is receiving a great deal of attention by researchers and educators in almost all of the gerontological venues. Research is suggesting that older persons who have a vital relationship to a faith group tend to be healthier and live longer.[23] Thus, it stands to reason that more of the older persons whom gerontologists encounter will be people with a viable belief in God. Those older persons will expect that those professionals who propose to help them understand their basic faith issues.

This does not mean that all gerontologists should become theologians as well. It might suggest, however, that gerontological social workers, psychologists, nurses, and medical doctors become aware of persons with knowledge and abilities in theological praxis and learn to access their expertise. Social Gerontologist David Moberg's edited volume, *Aging and Spirituality: Spiritual Dimensions of Aging Theory, Research, Practice, and Policy*, might prove to be a valuable resource for most, if not all, gerontologists.[24] Another book that might prove helpful to many is *Religion and Aging: An Anthology of the Poppele Papers.* This volume includes some insightful practical theology articles from a variety of perspectives.[25]

For a number of years encyclopedic handbooks on such subjects as *The Psychology of Aging, The Sociology of Aging, The Biology of Aging,* etc., have been available. In 1993, Professor Melvin Kimble of Luther Seminary in St. Paul, Minnesota, brought together a large number of scholars to deal with the subject Religion, Spirituality, and Aging. They produced A Handbook on Religion, Spirituality and Aging that follows the same encyclopedic model as those listed above.[26] It is an invaluable comprehensive resource for gerontologists, physical and mental health professionals, and professors of gerontology in colleges, universities, and schools of theology.

NOTES

1. Donald S. Browning, "Preface To A Practical Theology of Aging," in Seward Hiltner, editor, *Toward A Theology of Aging* (New York: Human Sciences Press, 1975), 151-167.
2. David Polk, "Practical Theology," in Donald W. Musser and Joseph L. Price, eds. *A New Handbook of Christian Theology* (Nashville: Abingdon Press, 1992), 375.
3. Ismael Garcia, "Praxis," in Musser and Price, 377.
4. James W. Fowler, *Faith Development and Pastoral Care* (Philadelphia: Fortress Press, 1987) 16.
5. Ray S. Anderson, *The Shape of Practical Theology* (Downers Grove, IL: InterVarsity Press, 2001).
6. Ibid., 48-49.
7. See, for example, John 8:3-11.
8. Ibid., 49.
9. Fowler, 21.
10. Ibid., 19.
11. Ibid., 21.
12. Arthur H. Becker, *Ministry With Older Persons* (Minneapolis: Augsburg Publishing House, 1986), 96-100.
13. Robert Davis, *My Journey Into Alzheimer's Disease,* (Wheaton, IL: Tyndale House, Publishers, 1984). Rev. Davis was the pastor of a large Presbyterian church in Miami, Florida, when he was diagnosed with Alzheimer's Disease at age 48. The book was the result of his journal and completed by his wife after his death.
14. Donald McKim and James W. Ellor, eds., *God Never Forgets: Faith, Hope and Alzheimer's Disease* (Louisville: Westminster John Knox Press, 1998).
15. Michael Castleman, Delores Gallagher-Thompson, and Matthew Naythans, *There's Still A Person In There* (New York: Berkley Publishing Group, 1999).
16. Jane Marie Thibault, *A Deepening Love Affair: The Gift of God in Later Life* (Nashville: The Upper Room, 1993). 13-20.
17. Ibid., 38.

18. Roberta C. Bondi, "Smoke, Tears, and Fire: Spirituality and Aging," in Andrew J. Weaver, Harold G. Koenig, and Phyllis C. Roe, *Reflections on Aging and Spiritual Growth* (Nashville: Abingdon Press, 1998), 21-27.

19. James E. Thorson and Thomas C. Cook, *Spiritual Well-Being Of The Elderly* (Springfield, IL: Charles C. Thomas, Publishers, 1980), xiii. This definition appears in the Preface that was written by Thomas C. Cook.

20. Ibid.

21. Harry R. Moody and David Carroll, *The Five Stages of the Soul* (New York: Anchor Books, Doubleday, 1997).

22. Harold GT. Koenig and Andrew J. Weaver, *Pastoral Care of Older Adults,* (Minneapolis: Fortress Press, 1998), 21-23.

23. A number of publications in medical journals and books such as those published by Harold Koenig of the Duke University Medical School, have reported strong correlations between religion, faith and health.

24. David O. Moberg, ed., *Aging and Spirituality* (Binghamton, NY: The Haworth Pastoral Press, 2001).

25. Derrel R. Watkins, ed. *Religion and Aging* (Binghamton, NY: The Haworth Pastoral Press, 2001).

26. Melvin A. Kimble, James W. Ellor, Susan H. McFadden, and James J. Seeber, eds., *Aging, Spirituality and Religion: A Handbook.* (Minneapolis: Fortress Press, 1995).

Chapter 4

Needing to Make Room for Change:
A Theology of Aging and Life

Brian McCaffery, DMin (PhD abd)

SUMMARY. Building upon concepts drawn from Process Theology, this article suggests a practical theological approach to aging that recognizes the changing patterns of life, especially among older persons. Insights drawn from literature, philosophy, psychology, and scripture are included. *[Article copies available for a fee from The Haworth Document Delivery Service: 1-800-HAWORTH. E-mail address: <docdelivery@haworthpress.com> Website: <http://www.HaworthPress.com> © 2003 by The Haworth Press, Inc. All rights reserved.]*

KEYWORDS. Change, changelessness, natural process, love, process, worldview, Quantum Theory, Chaos Theory, modernist, post-modernist, mystery, experiences

---

Brian McCaffrey is presently enrolled in the PhD program in Pastoral Care at Luther Seminary. A 1997 graduate of the Gerontological Pastoral Care Institute and a 1981 graduate of Luther Seminary, Brian has served as a chaplain and pastor in long term care, hospital and parish settings.

[Haworth co-indexing entry note]: "Needing to Make Room for Change: A Theology of Aging and Life." McCaffery, Brian. Co-published simultaneously in *Journal of Religious Gerontology* (The Haworth Pastoral Press, an imprint of The Haworth Press, Inc.) Vol. 15, No. 1/2, 2003, pp. 39-54; and: *Practical Theology for Aging* (ed: Derrel R. Watkins) The Haworth Pastoral Press, an imprint of The Haworth Press, Inc., 2003, pp. 39-54. Single or multiple copies of this article are available for a fee from The Haworth Document Delivery Service [1-800-HAWORTH, 9:00 a.m. - 5:00 p.m. (EST). E-mail address: docdelivery@haworthpress.com].

Since the "Enlightenment" much of western science and theology has shared a worldview with an underlying faith in changelessness. This faith held a hope that with enough knowledge of the laws of nature and the nature of God one could answer the questions of life with certainty. A focus on objective systematic truth with a belief in its singularity has so narrowed our cultural perspective that we as "people of faith" are ill prepared to value or even hear stories of God within the unique constellation of the experiences of an individual. Thus individuals are ill prepared by the Church for recognizing and responding to the presence of the Divine in their processes of aging and life. Questions and times of confusion need to be lifted up and valued as much as answers and certainty within the Church.

The underlying premise of my theology of aging is that aging is a natural process set within the context of life. This process involves more than a set of biochemical and sociological interactions. Within the complex blend of nature and nurture there remain variables that are unpredictable. Unpredictability and change have always been part of life. Adaptability and resiliency in the face of change have been identified as significant factors in determining personal satisfaction. This ability to adapt and to bounce back can have a developmental component, yet is itself often unpredictable. Viktor Frankl in *Man's Search for Meaning* witnessed that survival was not directly linked to physical or intellectual strength but to one's ability to make meaning.[1]

I do not look upon aging as a mistake that needs to be corrected, a disease that needs to be cured, a detour that needs to be avoided at all costs, nor as a problem that needs to be solved. Life itself is a process of change, with ebb and flows; birth-death-birth. As Ecclesiastes says, "to everything there is a season" (Eccl. 3:1).[2] Even though change is natural it can be most unsettling. At times I have heard Ecclesiastes' proclamation that "all is vanity" as a word of cynicism and despair.

"Vanity of vanities! All is vanity. What do people gain from all the toil at which they toil under the sun? A generation goes, and a generation comes, but the earth remains forever. The sun rises and the sun goes down, and hurries to the place where it rises. The wind blows to the south, and goes around to the north; round and round goes the wind, and on its circuits the wind returns. All streams run to the sea, but the sea is not full; to the place where the streams flow, there they continue to flow. All things are wearisome; more than one can express; the eye is not satisfied with seeing, or the ear filled with hearing. What has been is what will be, and what has been done is what will be done; there is nothing new under the sun." (Eccl. 1:2b-9)

Life and aging bring loss. The fear and the experience is that in looking back we will find that so much of what we've built on, trusted, hoped in, and lived for, is simply a puff of smoke. The presentation in Ecclesiastes is that of an objective observer. But within the observations and the questions is there something deeper than mortality? I find a word of grace in our being part of something beyond our control, something greater than our understanding. All of life; including death, strivings, achievements, failings, apparent stability and change stand within the context of the presence of mystery in life. Even knowledge and understanding are fleeting. It was true for Ecclesiastes; it seems even truer on the information highway of today, whose bumper sticker reads, "You snooze, you lose." I find that I no longer hold too tightly to any understanding or belief beyond our connectedness to the Divine, the Divine's inclusive love for the Creation, the significance of Mystery, and that Easter is a concrete historical manifestation of God's love.

Two corollaries to the above are that we are invited to share the Divine's perspective of love for Creation; and secondly life and all creation are sacred. This sacredness is derived through the on-going relationship of the Divine with life and the creation.

Although I can speak my theology of aging and life with conviction and integrity based upon experience and reflection, which lend to it a level of concreteness. It is yet a statement of this moment. It will always remain a work in progress, shaped less by any systematic set of answers than by the questions that are being raised in relationship to life itself. I conceive of Life, Age, the Divine, Faith, Hope, and Love more in terms of "verbs," which reflect movement, change, and relationship, than "nouns" signifying concrete, static, and an identifiable singularity. Spending time working in Long Term Care has convinced me of the great wisdom in Paul's words:

> Love never ends. But as for prophecies, they will come to an end; as for tongues, they will cease; as for knowledge, it will come to an end. For we know only in part, and we prophesy only in part; but when the complete comes, the partial will come to an end. When I was a child, I spoke like a child, I thought like a child, I reasoned like a child; when I became an adult, I put an end to childish ways. For now we see in a mirror, dimly, but then we will see face to face. Now I know only in part; then I will know fully, even as I have been fully known. And now faith, hope, and love abide, these three; and the greatest of these is love. (1 Corinthians 13:8-13)

We objectify much of the world around us, whether it is things, people, or life itself. I suspect we do this because an object is more concrete, definable, and controllable than a relationship. Whether we train ourselves to see this way or it is an unconscious perception, it is the way that many of us interact with the world around us. The scientific method has been the standard of this Age of Reason. Physics having been a part of my training, I am intrigued by the implications of Quantum Theory, which has led to Chaos Theory. Chaos Theory suggests that the Universe has a beginning and an end, is never static, and is predictable only within limited parameters. Left to themselves, things break down; entropy is a law of nature–perhaps another way of saying, "all was vanity and a chasing after wind" (Eccl. 2:11).[3]

Scientific certainty, in which I was trained, also began to break down. As scientists experienced more data that fell outside of the preconceived box of their training, they came to question the models of the past. The machine-like universe that Newtonian physics described is no longer an adequate metaphor. Modernist and some Post-Modernist thinking has looked at this as implying that everything truly is relative, fragmentary, chaotic, and a matter of the roll of the dice. There are scientists who in their work with the theory of Quantum Mechanics find signs of there being a greater underlying unity to everything than the sensory-perceived fragmentation; that separation itself may be an illusion. Through great acrobatic feats of mathematics and reasoning, some are suggesting that intuition as well as reasoning is now a necessary part of the scientific method. Some scientists have made connections to spiritual traditions of both the East and the West that emphasize the Oneness and unity of everything, a perspective that I believe is shared by a number of mystic traditions which have cut across time, cultures, and religions. Most representative of this would be such books as *The Tao of Physics* and *Turning Point* by Fritjof Capra,[4] *The Dancing Wu Li Masters* by Gary Zukav,[5] *The Universe Is A Green Dragon* by Brian Swimme[6] and the writings of people like Dr. Deepak Chopra[7] and Matthew Fox.[8] Rather than Chaos, the truth is a greater–Complexity.

The underlying worldview of physics and the natural sciences is shifting. Within the western Christian Church we have done much of our pastoral care and theology within this older framework. As within the scientific community there is much that we've assumed, which will not stand the test of time. We have tried to find answers within our discipline's understanding of persons and of God. This reminds me of Frankl's laws of dimensional ontology[9] example where the same shaped shadow is cast upon a flat screen by a cone, sphere, or cylinder. Our understanding could be considered flat, two-dimensional, missing the greater complexity of the whole and thus inadequate to the task. We've tried to respond to human needs by finding universal truths. This response has been based on a kind of faith that one size really would fit all. The "answer" because of its timeless, changeless connection to God became seen as more important than the person with the question. As a chaplain in Long Term Care I have witnessed the pain inflicted on families and individuals when traditional religious answers were applied to their situations: such as when behavior brought on by dementia has caused them to fear for the individual's salvation. I have heard clergy question the value of visiting or bringing sacraments to residents with Alzheimer's disease. I've sat in support groups with cancer patients who express what it feels like in church to be treated as if they were contagious. And I have heard family members tell their loved ones who are HIV positive that they were going to hell. In pediatric units I have stood by the bedside of dying children and heard well meaning people say, "that God needed another little angel" or that "we must accept God's Will."

I suggest that the Church is better served by theologies of aging and life, which allow for complexity, chaos and change, while trusting in a God who is beyond our understanding. The categories of experience, relationship and love are more helpful (albeit nebulous) ones, than attempting to determine black and white unchanging truths. The questions that arise out of the innumerable situations of life will often outgrow the answers. This is poignantly portrayed in the Hasidic story:

> When the great Rabbi Israel Baal Shem-Tov saw misfortune threatening the Jews it was his custom to go into a certain part of the forest to meditate. There he would light a fire, say a special prayer, and the miracle would be accomplished and the misfortune averted.
>
> Later, when his disciple, the celebrated Magid of Mezeritch, had occasion, for the same reason, to intercede with heaven, he would go to the same place in the forest and say: "Master of the Universe, listen! I do not know how to light the fire, but I am still able to say the prayer." And again the miracle would be accomplished.
>
> Still later, Rabbi Moshe-Leib of Sassov, in order to save his people once more would go into the forest and say: "I do not know how to light the fire, I do not know the prayer, but I know the place and this must be sufficient." It was sufficient and the miracle was accomplished.
>
> Then it fell to Rabbi Israel of Rizhin to overcome misfortune. Sitting in his armchair, his head in his hands, he spoke to God: "I cannot even find the place in the forest. All I do is to tell the story, and this must be sufficient." And it was sufficient.
>
> God made man because he loves stories.[10]

The importance of this for me is the placing of life and aging within the context of a Universe/Creation which is not perceived as inert matter, nor a functioning machine, nor a dualistic tension between spirit and matter; but that each unique individual with his or her strengths and limitations (body, mind, spirit) is a significant and valuable member of a greater whole. This relationship within this greater context is of more value than having the right answers. "The sabbath was made for humankind, and not humankind for the sabbath" (Mark 2:28).

Developmental theories such as Piaget, Kohlberg, Erikson, Kegan and Fowler suggest that with every step of the journey of life, opportunities have arisen for us to learn lessons, which we get to carry with us. However even in saying this I wish to avoid the stages-of-development language with its hierarchical images. As many have named in working with Kubler-Ross's stages of death and dying, the descriptions of the individual elements and the process are helpful, but placing them within a rigid structure can be detrimental. Instead of an image of stages and climbing, I prefer an image of steps in a dance.

Ancient traditions spoke of Maiden, Mother, Crone, Sage or Elder. These aboriginal traditions pointed to the later stages of life as having great value. Old age was understood as a period of life marked by service, in which the community was strengthened and guided by the wisdom obtained through experience and the passing on of the stories. The holding and the telling of the stories was a trust. The elders were the keepers and the teachers of the wisdom; the teller often shaped the story, a mark of the individual would become a piece of the communal identity. Viewing Bill Moyers' interview with Joseph Campbell, on Public Broadcasting's *The Power of Myth*,[11] opened me to a whole new level of respect for story which has been reshaping me and my theology ever since. I have also be similarly touched by the book *Yellow Woman* by Leslie Marmon Silko.[12]

The statement "It takes a village to raise a child," is not broad enough, for it takes a village to bring us through every stage of life. The valuing and the telling of the stories is part of the community identity. The stories of the Church are a prime example. The Book of Genesis establishes a consortium of world-views, which will be in dialogue throughout the Bible, but which all agree that God is the one true Creator, that this God is both transcendent and imminent and in relationship to the creation. Issues of identity and redemption appear throughout but most strongly through the stories Abraham, Isaac, Jacob, the Book of Exodus, and the Gospels. Parameters of socially acceptable behavior are established through the Deuteronomic texts and New Testament Letters–giving codes of ethics for parents, children, husbands, wives, slaves, owners, hospitality to strangers, care for widows and orphans and worship. Guidance is offered through wisdom literature. These stories continue to be acted out as Holidays and rites of passage (Passover, Circumcisions, Baptism, Communion, Confirmation, Mitzvahs, Weddings, Funerals). My understanding of the function of remembering and story within the Judeo-Christian tradition is that it keeps the event alive; participating in the story is participating in the event.

However as Berger and Luckman describe in their *The Social Construction of Reality*,[13] experience is easily transformed into a tradition, into a doctrine, into a truth to which we must rigidly adhere. The common phrase "we've always done it this way" carries an implied and often unconscious–because this is the only right way. So that any experience which falls outside of the accepted parameters of truth is likely to be denied or attacked, much as Job experienced with his friends. What happened to Job threatened his friends' whole system of theology. This still happens both within the Church and the culture.

There will almost inevitably be periods of chaos intruding in each person's life, overwhelming the tried and true answers. For example the process of aging often brings an individual to places to which we had not planned on coming. One could say that this journey brings us beyond the charted map we've been given–*"beyond here there be dragons."*[14] The situations require us to make choices even without answers. Arthur Frank in his book *The Wounded Storyteller*[15] spoke of how interviewers of Holocaust survivors frequently directed the conversation toward an acceptable conclusion. Somehow the individual's story must be able to be heard and interpreted outside of these restrictions. But the value is not in the story alone.

I've heard it suggested that, at the time of his public ministry, Jesus would have been considered an elder. I see Jesus using stories to challenge the perspective of the status quo and common wisdom. Jesus was confronted with a worldview of fear. The Gospels take place in an occupied country. Although the portrayal of the Pharisees shows them as a small elite segment of the Jewish community, they probably represented the most popular position, a mixture of life within the Roman rule while maintaining a Jewish identity. They believed that the structure of Life was maintained through a rigid adherence to the Law. My understanding of the Pharisaic tradition and much of the canonization of the Old Testament is that they were attempts to make sense of a war-torn world for a people who felt threatened by Chaos or Punishment. What Life was bringing them didn't fit their expectations of Life as the People of God–the Chosen. The emphasis was placed upon holiness–being able to clearly identify right from wrong, acceptable from not acceptable, those who belong from those who stand outside. This emphasis allowed for a sense of control–the creation of a sanctuary-refuge. The Holy of Holies is a good symbol for this tradition: It is set apart, has clear boundaries, limited access is allowed, it is easily profaned, and there are clearly defined negative consequences for stepping beyond the limits. Holiness was perceived as fragile; there was much that threatened it. Jesus threatened it.

Yet, in so doing Jesus was standing firmly within the Jewish tradition. The confrontation was not about the Jewish faith, but about what was being done with it:

> My house shall be called a house of prayer for all the nations, but you have made it a den of robbers . . . . woe to you Pharisees! For you tithe mint and rue and herbs of all kinds, and neglect justice and the love of God. (Mt. 21:13; 23:23)

Instead of an emphasis upon separateness, Jesus emphasized connectedness–the love of neighbor and enemy. Instead of pointing to the Temple he pointed to the everyday world–birds of the air, lilies of the field, shepherding, times of planting and harvest, "the Kingdom of God is in your midst." Instead of a strict obedience Jesus pointed to mercy, forgiveness, flexibility–the Sabbath was made for us not us for the Sabbath. Instead of an emphasis on tradition alone Jesus claimed equal authority– "They were astounded at his teaching, for he taught them as one having authority, and not as the scribes." Instead of sacrifice an emphasis upon the direct relationship with "the Father" and our capacity for repentance-turning toward, returning to God–the parable of "the prodigal son" or, as Helmut Thielicke called it the parable of "the waiting father."[16] One might also say that Jesus took the focus from the "Fear of the Lord" being the beginning of wisdom, and instead lifted up trusting in a loving God. As the writer of 1 John puts it:

> There is no fear in love, but perfect love casts out fear; for fear has to do with punishment, and whoever fears has not reached perfection in love. (1 John 4:18)

The motivation behind knowing the stories may be a linking to the past, which provides a place to stand–an identity–a rootedness, in which to face the present and the future. Our Judaic-Christian heritage arose out of an oral tradition; long before we became people of "The Book" we were tellers of "the old old story." We have probably all known them, those elders who in their humble way speak with authority concerning the Divine, an authority which, using Buber's phrase, has developed through the intimacy of an I-Thou relationship.[17]

Sr. Miriam Therese Winter, who spoke at the 1995 Re-imagining Conference,[18] was eloquent and imaginative in her stories. She suggested that we have done a real disservice to our Scriptures by attempting to concretize letter and word into the literal Word of God. When we can "know" what the stories mean it can feel like a solid ground upon which to stand. It becomes easier to identify the "right" answers; life may be simplified into black-white, yes-no, in-out, right-wrong, Us–Them–again what I have referred to as a one-size-fits-all mentality. But I believe that there is a price to pay for such a handling of the Word, a rigidity that the Scriptures and tradition would challenge. In codifying the meanings of "the Word" we now have a monologue to be passed on, carved in stone, rather than a dialogue that engages the listener. For many today what they've heard from the church is irrelevant, because they are expected to accept rather than become engaged. What get offered are answers, old answers, without the kind of dialogue that values the questions and the questioners. We, both in and out of the church, need to hear the real questions and the emotions behind them, not in order to pose solutions, but to stand in solidarity. The "space between" is the place of the Divine Presence.[19]

Today's world is marked by such rapid change, both technological and informational, that there is little value placed upon knowledge from the past. I have found numerous writers from psychology such as Viktor Frankl, Mary Pipher,[20] Clarissa Pinkola-Estes,[21] Rachel Remen[22]; philosophy such as Sam Keen[23] and Robert Bly[24]; comparative mythology such as Joseph Campbell; and theology such as John Hoffman[25] and Sr. Jose Hobday,[26] who are pointing to the loss of overarching stories and traditions as a significant mark of our time.

> . . . Until recent years the keystone of personal identity was participation in the shared stories, legends, and myths of a tribe, nation, cult, or church. The past, present, and future of the individual were bound together by the memories and hopes of a people to which he [sic] belonged. With the birth of secular, pluralistic, technological society, a new type of man [sic] has emerged–the man without a story, the rootless, protean man living without the stability of a tradition which he remembers with pride or a future he awaits with longing.[27]

My theology of life is that there is a Spirit that hovers over the void. The Word becomes flesh and dwells among us. But this is a living Word. This Incarnational Word then is not dead or changeless, but rather a Word that responds to, shapes, and is shaped by the relationships and experience of life. Sr. Winter spoke more in terms of the "Words of God." Stories and Words that remains open to interpretation–an understanding that is being shaped by those participating in the speaking and the hearing of the Words.

I come back to an old distinction made in an Education class in college between "Instruction" and "Education"–the one being a pouring into a passive learner, while the other requires the student to actively participate in the process-drawing out of themselves.[28] I have observed, in the last couple of years, that much of the power I find in the stories of Jesus and his parables lie in their being open-ended. They invite engagement, a drawing out, a response. The similes of the Kingdom invite us to search out interpretations from our own life experience–not, what have I been instructed as to its meaning?–rather, how do I understand the comparison to a wedding feast, or to planting, or to finding that which has been lost? Can there be such a thing as a wrong answer, if the focus itself is not on the answer but on the process of the relationship? If we feel that the stories are personally addressing us we will continue to search for connections in the world around us. Compare the teaching parables of Jesus to the stories of the Desert Fathers and Mothers, Sufi stories, Hasidic stories and Zen koans. Their power is not in their reasonableness or connection to tradition, but rather in their requiring a letting go, an internal movement to a new perspective. Any particular life is filled with stories. These stories are placed within the context of space and time. Yet they also exist within the context of a story greater than any particular space and time. I remember at a time of great upheaval in my life–my mother's death, my divorce, and a move to a new parish–that the story of Jacob wrestling with the angel, and stories of "exile," spoke loudly to me, engaging me in dialogue with God. Every life is filled with stories of crises and opportunities, choices made, moments of brokenness and healing, sin and grace. These lives and their stories are as sacred as any in Scripture.

As infants and children, we are deeply affected by the ability of those who care for us to offer a caring and nurturing relationship. The ability of the face we look into to mirror love and acceptance has been shown to impact our ability to look at others and ourselves with love and acceptance. Socialization requires us to continue to broaden our world, first beyond our own fingers and toes and the presence of our primary caregivers, to the familiar faces of our family, then beyond the familiar and into the world. Each step was probably met by a corresponding separation anxiety. Each new phase brought a new lesson or a deepening of an old lesson. Neither our parents nor their love for us ceased to exist when they left the room, nor when we left the house. How much life do we need to experience before the depth of God's connectedness sinks into our bones:

> Who will separate us from the love of Christ? Will hardship, or distress, or persecution, or famine, or nakedness, or peril, or sword? No, in all these things we are more than conquerors through him who loved us. For I am convinced that neither death, nor life, nor angels, nor rulers, nor things present, nor things to come, nor powers, nor height, nor depth, nor anything else in all creation, will be able to separate us from the love of God in Christ Jesus our Lord. (Romans 8:35, 37-9)

Children are incredible models of this witness of love. With time and hormones, passion is added to that love. But only the experience of longevity can provide glimpses of how love grows and changes. Hopefully we've known people whose time together has withstood the ravages of life and who stand up on their 50th or 75th Anniversary to say, "We love each other more now then we ever could have imagined then."

I resonate to the idea in John McCutcheon's song and Robert Fulghum's book, that we learned much of what we needed in Kindergarten:

> Of all you learn here remember this the best: don't hurt each other, and clean up your mess, take a nap everyday, wash before you eat hold hands, stick together, look before you cross the street. Remember the seed in the little paper cup first the root goes down and then the plant grows up.[29]

I take the leap of faith to say that what we learn about psychologically healthy, nurturing, loving relationships can be transposed into our spiritual lives as well. It is a part of my theology of aging that only time will tell how the lessons will grow in our lives; what kind of roots they will put down, what shape the lessons will take in our lives, and how they will change us. All that we experienced as children was not healthy, nurturing or loving. There were times when we reached out into the world and were hurt. We may spend a considerable amount of time and energy trying to build something that can protect us–good defenses, good answers, good fences, and good armies. But no matter how hard we try, life is not safe. Many of our values could be used as examples of answers needing to be held loosely. Early on we learn the difference between right and wrong, good and bad. There is a strength in these lessons that serves us well and gives us a standard by which to live. But the lessons also have their limits. Some of the lessons included racism, sexism, ageism to name just a few. As Gloria Steinem has said, "The first problem for all of us, men and women, is not to learn, but to unlearn."[30] One can surprised to learn that love and forgiveness can be more powerful than right or wrong, and in the process an I-it relationship is transformed into an I-Thou. While at the same time many a marriage or relationship has not survived conflict because a standard of right and wrong, good and bad, imposed a perspective which transformed an I-You relationship into an I-It.

I remember a children's book about persons who built a fence or wall around themselves and later discovered that they could take the same material and build a bridge. It takes some real skill (experience) and imagination to take the same material, which has always been used to build a fence, and use it to build a bridge. The experiences of life are the raw material we have with which to build our lives and our identities. How we put that material together determines the stories we tell and the life we lead. What we build changes with our ability to reflect on what has been. We need to be able to search out meaning beyond the ones imposed from outside, which often cannot withstand the test of time. We need to be able to deconstruct the familiar in our lives, in our traditions, and in our cultures in order to risk building something new.

Viktor Frankl pointed to the fact that people entering the concentration camps had the same experience, yet there were a variety of responses. Frankl posits that the human spirit is one variable that makes us unpredictable. Even if an individual has responded to a stimulus the same way one hundred times the fact remains that the 101st could be different. I've grown to appreciate the spirit and depth of a little piece called: "Autobiography in Five Short Chapters" by Portia Nelson. She speaks of walking down a street and falling in a deep hole. This experience is repeated several times. She attempts different solutions until finally she avoids the hole and takes another street.

I hate to compare old-old age or life in a nursing home to a concentration camp, but that is how many people see it. It is a time marked by feelings of worthlessness and suffering. I was deeply struck by Frankl's writings, and how apropos they are for the experience of many of the Residents. So what is left when everything (or so much) has been ripped away? Where is God in the Holocaust, or in dementia? This truly is the place of Mystery for me. In the midst of suffering, when someone wonders, "Where is God?", I can join both in the question and in the belief that God is present. But what that really means is still a mystery to me. When I was doing my CPE Residency I stumbled upon a group that I came to call "Scandinavian Farm Wives." These were mostly women whose life stories included a litany of woe that I found overwhelming:

> We got married during the Depression and didn't have much; I had to do the farming and look after the kids while my husband left to look for work; the drought of the dust bowl years was devastating; we lost the farm; we lost the baby to influenza; another son died in WWII; my husband died a couple years ago after a long illness; this is my fourth operation–but GOD IS GOOD, LIFE HAS BEEN GOOD.

These people knew the "theology of the Cross" from the inside–God is present even in the Chaos and suffering. But I don't think that it is a theology or head knowledge that has survived. I think it is the experience of the relationship over time, through good and bad, that nurtures the beliefs. There is a connectedness or perception of the original blessing that "it is good." There is an experience of the underlying unity and complexity, which goes beyond the limits of theology.

Listen to me, O house of Jacob, all the remnant of the house of Israel, who have been borne by me from your birth, carried from the womb; even to your old age I am he, even when you turn gray I will carry you. I have made, and I will bear; I will carry and will save. (Isa. 46:3-4)

The books that have recounted the stories and witnessed to the Presence are too numerous to count here, but I'd like to mention a few in recommendation: *Having Our Say, The Delany Sisters' Book of Everyday Wisdom,* by Sarah and Elizabeth Delany with Amy Hill Hearth; *On My Own At 107* by Sarah Delany with Amy Hill Hearth; *Final Time: A Husband's Reflections on His Wife's Terminal Illness* by Robert G. Esbjornson; *Kitchen Table Wisdom* by Rachel Remen (founder of Commonweal).

I have found myself also comparing entering a nursing home to entering a religious order. It becomes a place and time of letting go of much of the world that we have known–letting go of home, family, and identity while taking what amounts to vows of poverty and celibacy. I take great delight in those people whose spirit flourishes in old age. People whose relationship with The Divine is "a deepening love affair"[32] (as Jane Thibault describes in her book of that name). Those people who

> . . . have this treasure in clay jars, so that it may be made clear that this extraordinary power belongs to God and does not come from us. We are afflicted in every way, but not crushed; perplexed, but not driven to despair; persecuted, but not forsaken; struck down, but not destroyed; (2Cor. 4:7-9). So we do not lose heart. Even though our outer nature is wasting away, our inner nature is being renewed day by day. For this slight momentary affliction is preparing us for an eternal weight of glory beyond all measure, because we look not at what can be seen but at what cannot be seen; for what can be seen is temporary, but what cannot be seen is eternal. (2Cor. 4:16-18)

I've always found meaningful this anonymous quote, "The only God there is, is the God above God." The experiences of Life will continue to fall inside and outside of the box of our expectations. Our God will frequently, as J. B. Philips[33] said, be too small. So it becomes a challenge to keep the dialogue open, to let our God, our understanding of God, and ourselves grow and change. Many of the Sunday School lessons that seem so simple, like Jesus Loves Me, John 3:16, Psalm 23, 1 Corinthians 13, or "Love God and Love neighbor," may take a lifetime to absorb. The passage of time, the gaining of experience, the ability to reflect moves our perspective, offering us a new view, perhaps a deeper understanding. With Long

Term Care I have found that many of those lessons are the ones that we return to–not solely because of their being simple, but because of a lifetime of experience, which has reinforced them. Part of my understanding of what aging offers to us is the opportunity to grow into ourselves in relationship to the One who loves us.

> The wise Rabbi Bunam once said in old age, when he had already grown blind: "I should not like to change places with our father Abraham! What good would it do God if Abraham became like a blind Bunam, and blind Bunam became like Abraham? Rather than have this happen, I think I shall try to become a little more like myself."[34]

NOTES

1. Viktor Frankl, *Man's Search for Meaning* (New York: Simon & Schuster, 1959) p. 56 passim.

2. All Biblical quotes are taken from *The New Revised Standard Version Bible,* (Nashville, TN: Thomas Nelson Publishers, 1989).

3. Three examples of scientists who ask questions around the existence of God in the universe and find nothing that points to any Divine involvement in existence are Stephen Hawking, *A Brief History of Time* (New York: Bantam Books, 1992), Steven Weinberg, *Dreams of a Final Theory* (New York: Pantheon Books, 1992) and Carl Sagan, *Cosmos* (New York: Random House, 1980).

4. Fritjof Capra, *The Tao of Physics* (Berkeley: Shambhala; [New York]: distributed in the U.S. by Random House, 1975) and *The Turning Point: Science, Society, And The Rising Culture* (Toronto: New York: Bantam Books, 1983).

5. Gary Zukav, *The Dancing Wu Li Masters : An Overview Of The New Physics* (New York : Morrow, 1979).

6. Brian Swimme, *The Universe Is A Green Dragon : A Cosmic Creation Story* (Santa Fe, N.M.: Bear, 1985).

7. Deepak Chopra, *Ageless Body, Timeless Mind : The Quantum Alternative To Growing Old* (New York: Harmony Books, 1993), *Boundless Energy: The Complete Mind/Body Program For Overcoming Chronic Fatigue* (New York: Harmony Books, 1995), *Creating Health: Beyond Prevention, Toward Perfection* (Boston: Houghton Mifflin, 1987), and with David Simon *Grow Younger, Live Longer: 10 Steps To Reverse Aging* (New York: Harmony Books, 2001).

8. Matthew Fox, *The Coming Of The Cosmic Christ: The Healing Of Mother Earth And The Birth Of A Global Renaissance* (San Francisco: Harper & Row, 1988), *Creation Spirituality: Liberating Gifts For The Peoples Of The Earth* (San Francisco : HarperSanFrancisco, 1991), *Original Blessing: A Primer In Creation Spirituality, Presented In Four Paths, Twenty-Six Themes, And Two Questions* (Santa Fe, N.M.: Bear, 1983), with Rupert Sheldrake, *Natural Grace: Dialogues On Creation, Darkness, And The Soul In Spirituality And Science* (New York: Doubleday, 1996).

9. Viktor Frankl, *The Will to Meaning: Foundations and Applications of Logotherapy* (New York: Penguin Group, 1969) pp. 22-25.

10. Elie Wiesel, *The Gates of the Forest as quoted in the Preface to John Shea's Stories of God: An Unauthorized Biography* (Chicago: The Thomas More Press, 1978) p. 7.

11. *The Power of Myth* (New York, NY: Mystic Five Video, 1988) Campbell discusses with Bill Moyers the archetype of the hero and the heroic quest in mythology and literature and the transformations of consciousness which they represent.

12. Leslie Marmon Silko, *Yellow Woman* (New Brunswick, N.J.: Rutgers University Press, 1993).

13. Peter Berger and Thomas Luckman, *The Social Construction Of Reality; A Treatise In The Sociology Of Knowledge* (Garden City, N.Y.: Anchor Books, 1967).

14. A phrase found on maps of antiquity to note the edge of the known world.

15. Arthur Frank, *The Wounded Storyteller: Body, Illness, and Ethics* (Chicago: The University of Chicago Press, 1995) p. 101. I highly recommend reading this book particularly chapter five *The Chaos Narratives.*

16. Helmut Thielicke, *The Waiting Father: Sixteen Parables of Jesus Interpreted for Today* (New York: Harper & Row, 1959) pp. 17-40.

17. Martin Buber, *I and Thou* (New York: Charles Scribners and Sons, 1959; second edition translated by Ronald Gregor Smith, New York: Collier Books, Macmillan Publishing Company, 1987). At the heart of Buber's theology is the Jewish tradition is the message of Yom Kippur: that anyone at any time can return to God. We stand in a direct relationship to God and require no mediator.

18. An international conference exploring feminist expressions of Christianity held at the Minneapolis Convention Center in 1995.

19. Ruthellen Josselson, *The Space Between Us: Exploring the Dimensions of Human Relationships* (San Francisco: Jossey-Bass Publishers, 1992).

20. Mary Pipher, *Reviving Ophelia: Saving The Selves Of Adolescent Girls* (New York: Putnam, 1994); *Another Country: Navigating The Emotional Terrain Of Our Elders* (New York: Riverhead Books, 1999).

21. Clarissa Pinkola-Estes, *Women Who Run With The Wolves: Myths And Stories Of The Wild Woman Archetype* (New York: Ballantine Books, 1992).

22. Rachel Naomi Remen, *Kitchen Table Wisdom: Stories That Heal* (New York : Riverhead Books, 1996).

23. Sam Keen, *Your Mythic Journey: Finding Meaning in Your Life Through Writing and Storytelling* (NY: St. Martin's Press, 1989).

24. Robert Bly, *Iron John* (Reading, Mass.: Addison-Wesley, 1990).

25. John C. Hoffman, *Faith-Full Stories: The Narrative Road to Religion* (Toronto: The United Church Publishing House, 1994).

26. Sr. Jose Hobday, *Finding God In The Ordinary [Sound Recording] : Feeding Our Hunger* (Simi Valley, CA : Convention Seminar Cassettes, 1994).

27. Sam Keen, *To A Dancing God: Notes of a Spiritual Traveler/Rediscovering the Sacred Through Personal Mythology* (San Francisco: Harper & Row, 1970) p. 71. This is a book that every pastor should read.

28. Paulo Friere, *Pedagogy Of The Oppressed.* Translated by Myra Bergman Ramos. (New York: Herder and Herder, 1970) p. 57 passim. Chapter 2 explores "the banking" concept of education.

29. John McCutcheon/Appalsongs ASCAP *Kindergarten Wall* from C.D. *Water From Another Time* (Rounder C.D. 11555).

30. Gloria Steinem *New York Times* 1971 (also seen as a poster slogan).

31. Ingrid Dilley, OTR, Carol Troestler, M.S.W., and Josiah Dilley, PhD *Renewing Life: Ideas and Techniques for Making the Most of What Life Hands You–Facilitator*

Manual (Madison WI: Self Published 1991 updated 2000) p. 71. A program for those touched by life-threatening illness, their support persons, and staff persons.

32. Jane Thibault, *A Deepening Love Affair: The Gift of God in Later Life* (Nashville, TN: Upper Room Books, 1993). This is a wonderful book exploring spiritual development in later life.

33. J. B. Phillips, *Your God Is Too Small* (New York: Macmillan Publishing Company Inc., 1961).

34. Martin Buber, *Heart Searching and the Particular Way* in *Modern Spirituality: An Anthology* ed. by John Garvey (Springfield, IL: Templegate Publishers, 1985).

Chapter 5

The Kyrios Christos as Ultimate Hope: A Response to Pain and Suffering

Kellie A. Shantz, MSN, MDiv

SUMMARY. This article addresses suffering from a practical theological perspective. It recognizes the realities of God's own suffering along with God's understanding of human suffering. It relates the suffering of humanity to Christ's suffering on the Cross, and the ultimate hope that persons of all ages have as a result of the resurrection of Christ from the dead. *[Article copies available for a fee from The Haworth Document Delivery Service: 1-800-HAWORTH. E-mail address: <docdelivery@haworthpress.com> Website: <http://www.HaworthPress.com> © 2003 by The Haworth Press, Inc. All rights reserved.]*

KEYWORDS. Suffering, crucifixion, resurrection, attitude, self-sufficiency, spirituality, reality, affliction, *imago dei*, prayer, empathy, core beliefs, protest, transformed

God lets himself be pushed out of the world on to the cross. He is weak and powerless in the world, and that is precisely the way, the only way in which he is with us and helps us. Matt. 8:17 makes it clear that Christ

---

Trained as a psychiatric nurse, Kellie A. Shantz also studied theology in order to better understand how to deal with the spiritual issues her patients confront.

[Haworth co-indexing entry note]: "The Kyrios Christos as Ultimate Hope: A Response to Suffering." Shantz, Kellie A. Co-published simultaneously in *Journal of Religious Gerontology* (The Haworth Pastoral Press, an imprint of The Haworth Press, Inc.) Vol. 15, No. 1/2, 2003, pp. 55-67; and: *Practical Theology for Aging* (ed: Derrel R. Watkins) The Haworth Pastoral Press, an imprint of The Haworth Press, Inc., 2003, pp. 55-67. Single or multiple copies of this article are available for a fee from The Haworth Document Delivery Service [1-800-HAWORTH, 9:00 a.m. - 5:00 p.m. (EST). E-mail address: docdelivery@haworthpress.com].

Digital Object Identifier: 10.1300/J078v15n01_06

helps us, not by virtue of his omnipotence, but by virtue of his weakness and suffering . . . only the suffering God can help. (Bonhoeffer)[1]

THE SUFFERING OF GOD

These words were put to paper shortly before the execution of Dietrich Bonhoeffer at Flossenburg camp in April, 1945. They capture my attention in part, because they doubtless reflect the deep meditations of one who knew all too well what it was to experience suffering firsthand: spiritual, emotional and ultimately physical suffering to the point of death. In addition, Bonhoeffer's words reflect the poignant struggle to the many who in the midst of their torment, long to discover what kind of God exists that would permit such suffering.

Over a span of approximately twenty-five years, I have been in service to suffering persons of all ages, races and creeds in a variety of health-care settings. My years of nursing service have included work with alcoholics and addicts, emotionally and physically abused persons, the mentally and terminally ill, and those suffering from a variety of physiological illnesses. Engagement with such enormous, seemingly relentless suffering pushes one to confront questions of a theological nature. As I listened to my own questions, those of the patients and their families, and my fellow health care workers over time—one, central question began to repeat itself: "Where is God in the midst of all this suffering?" This is the question that in its persistent demand for an answer drove me to seek a seminary education. The beginnings of a response to this question can be found in the reflections of Dietrich Bonhoeffer: through the cross of suffering, God is with us in the midst of our pain. Only the suffering God can help . . .

The magnitude of suffering I have witnessed over the years has resulted both in my need to develop a theology of care which adequately addresses and is relevant to such suffering, and a deep and abiding concern with a larger question: "What does it mean for theology to take suffering seriously?" Jesus' cry to God as he died on the cross was "Eli, Eli, lama sabachthani?" "My God, My God why hast thou forsaken me?" (Mat. 27:46, KJV). This is so frequently the heartfelt cry of suffering persons that I have heard echoing through the hospitals, clinics, hospices, drug and alcohol treatment centers, nursing homes, and psychiatric institutions across the years.

It is my contention that for suffering persons whose cry often seems to emulate the cry of the crucified Jesus, a ministry of true hope must begin *in the midst* of the crucifixion experience, itself. It is precisely this cry of Jesus in his forsakenness that places him in hope-filled solidarity with all suffering persons. The suffering God, argued Dietrich Bonhoeffer, is one to whom suffering does not have to be explained: Such a God knows and understands our cries and moanings, and hears the grief-filled sighs of the forsaken ones.[2]

KYRIOS CHRISTOS AND SUFFERING

Over against this crucifixion experience however, the triumph of the Resurrection must stand: The promise that *assures* those of us who serve in the health care professions where suffering abounds, and the patients and their family members who are its reluctant victims–that *suffering shall not have the last word!* The ultimate response of suffering is the *Kyrios Christos*–the Risen Lord. Our ability to confront suffering, to be with those afflicted with AIDS, alcoholism, addiction, and mental illness is possible *only* in light of the Resurrection. Jesus the Christ saves; the Resurrection happened in history. The question for us as faithful, confessing Christians become, "How are we to get ourselves involved in the ongoing process of the resurrected life which Jesus Christ promised in full through the Resurrection?" Greater still, how do we begin that ministry of care at the cross–the place where suffering begins and hope must be found?

In this essay I seek to address how a theology of the empty cross informs the practice of health care ministry. At the heart of such a ministry is a concern for developing strategies of care which support and assist the afflicted persons with whom I work and discover the strength and endurance to take up the cross of their own lives.[3] The cross is "revelatory of the life of the Christian community that is not confined to liturgical assemblies and official pronouncements but goes on continuously and interpersonally as part of the web of daily events."[4] Crucifixion is an inevitable part of the life experience–but the resurrection is not far off. Any attempt to articulate such a theology must necessarily include a bit about the personal context out of which my commitment to work with suffering persons emerged. I write as a white, middle-class, educated female whose life-long call to service and stewardship was shaped in large part by my attendance in Catholic schools during my early elementary education, and my upbringing in the Catholic Church. It was in both of those settings that I first heard Jesus' call that we are to live out the expectations of our Lord; we are to focus our love for our neighbor in service to "the least of these" (Matt. 25:40. NRSV).

STRUGGLE AND PROTEST AGAINST SUFFERING

A greater part of my call to care for and advocate on behalf of suffering persons emerged as a protest of sorts–against the overwhelming amount of pain and suffering I encountered in my own family life. My struggle to develop a theology which adequately addresses suffering is not merely an exercise in the pursuit of academia. I do not write from the midst "of a society in which certain forms of suffering are avoided gratuitously, in keeping with middle-class ideals"—the charge leveled by Dorothee Soelle against a class which is largely apathetic to the suffering in its midst.[5] Rather, I write as one who once knew what it was like to be a helpless victim: Of child abuse so severe and relentless that I was eventually removed from my home and sent away to live with a grandmother so that my life might be spared; of alcoholism so ruthless that it robbed me of a mother and her of her life, at an age when she was much too young to die. I write as one forced to watch in helpless desperation as drug addiction threatened to destroy my younger sister—a sister who had once been as close to me as my own heart. I write from somewhere near the margins of that middle-class society—grateful to be alive and a part of all the privileges that such a life has to offer, but unwilling to fall into the somnolent, forgetful apathy that such privileges might permit. I write as one who remembers, and who has spent years of healing and serving—while standing at the foot of the cross in protest of suffering.

POSITIVE ATTITUDE AND SUFFERING

Out of this protest has emerged a praxis of health care ministry that might best be described by the words of Saint Paul: "For see what earnestness this godly grief has produced in you, what eagerness to clear yourselves, what indignation, what alarm, what longing, what zeal, what punishment!" (2 Cor. 7:11). An aspect of care that arouses a great deal of indignation in me is the amount of emphasis placed by contemporary persons on *positive attitude*. By this I refer to the contemporary trend toward the belief that outcomes can be controlled by and are based largely upon one's state of mind. It is a profoundly optimistic view that draws upon a long heritage of American self-sufficiency and self-help. As part of what has been termed the *New Age* spirituality movement, its tendency is to view personality as shaped by "dynamic forces of the unconscious, it emphasizes multiple realities, it aims toward an understanding of extraordinary states of consciousness and expanded human potential."[6]

Those who fall short of its focus on growth and potential are seen as somehow lacking. The problem with such a view is that it promotes another form of *individualism* under the guise of *spirituality*. In so doing, it merely perpetuates the American story of success that says that if we just try hard enough or just have a positive enough attitude, poverty, disaster, illness and any number of tragedies that impact human lives can be overcome. The problem with living into such a story is that those who ascribe to it are generally not willing to view the pain and suffering their lives and this reality as anything other than temporary; neither do they recognize its intolerability and the need for real intervention.

For Christians this is often an over-emphasis placed too soon on the resurrection experience in an attempt to offer hope to suffering persons. In reality, there is a time to be lifted out of suffering and a time to be comforted in its midst. Out of sincere desire to provide solace, I have too often witnessed the tendency of myself and others to bypass the experience of suffering in an effort to reach the consolation of the Resurrection. In truth, this may do more to comfort us in our experience of powerlessness when faced with insurmountable pain of another whose suffering we desire to alleviate, but cannot.

True hope must be discovered in a present that, even in its experience of suffering, is alive with possibilities. For those whose present is imbued with pain and torment, the message of hope must begin in the immediacy of the crucifixion experience. Such hope must be grounded firmly in the knowledge that in the cross of Jesus Christ, God assumed all suffering, and in the Resurrection, God has overcome all suffering. Individuals can summon the strength to carry their own cross of suffering when they have the assurance that "while God does not preserve us *from* all suffering he does preserve us *in* all suffering."[7] Any refusal or failure on our part to acknowledge the *present* reality of suffering and any attempt to banish it prematurely disempowers persons and constitutes false hope. Likewise, any attempt to find sanctuary in the Resurrection of Christ and by pass the suffering of Jesus on the cross is to trivialize and distort the harsh reality of those who are suffering, and to overlook the hopeful message that emanates from the cross as it is cast in the light of the Resurrection.

GOD RELATES TO SUFFERING

A critical question for suffering persons is, "How does God relate to our suffering?" The answer, and the fundamental source of hope for those who suffer lies in the knowledge that God, out of infinite love for the created, suffers with us.[8] The cross signifies that God *never* directly inflicts suffering. In the cross, God accepts the suffering that befalls God. Thus, we have a glimpse of the depth of God's love for us in the suffering of his Son on the cross. The cross is the extent to which God is willing to go to reconcile humanity to God's self. That God suffers with us and knows us fully means that we can bring our suffering to a God that *knows*; we do not have to explain or beseech a God who doesn't know suffering. While the suffering of God in solidarity with us is made known through the cross of his Son, the protest against such suffering is delineated in the Biblical witness to the life of Jesus–the first century, Palestinian Jew. Jesus' entire history was one of suffering in solidarity with human-kind, a history that culminated in his own agony on the cross. His life was shaped by and lived in response to the suffering he saw around him. He was personally involved in pronouncing love and healing for those who were suf-fering: the sick and lame, the sinful and the guilty, the poor, the marginalized, and even the enemy.[9]

His suffering however, was by no means the suffering of a desperate man who was unable to escape his fate. It was instead, an act of perfect obedience to the One he called 'Aba'; an act by one who refused to let the cup of suffering pass him by, but instead *freely* acknowledged, "For this I came into the world" (John 18:37, NRSV). His was an act of the *utmost* surrender, out of boundless love for God and human persons. It is this One who surrendered himself in ut-ter and perfect obedience, who was crucified, died and buried, to be resur-rected for all eternity to sit at the right hand of God as the Kyrios Christos. This is he who is in solidarity with us in our suffering. This is he who demonstrated with his very life and in his death and resurrection, that suffering shall not have the last word. The historical life of Jesus that issued in our redemption is the basis for all declarations of hope for suffering persons. He, who shared our lot in life in all aspects, announced by his life the nearness of the reign of God.

The task of continuing in our own historical time and place, Jesus' mission of announcing and demonstrating the coming of the reign of God becomes the daily challenge in the work of health-care ministry. As Christians who are gifted with the Spirit of Christ, we are called to discipleship with a mission pat-terned on the way of Jesus Christ. Jesus asked us again and again to love one another as he had loved (John 13:34). Out of love for us he went to the cross. He continues to suffer in solidarity with us. We are called to do likewise in his memory: "As often as you do this, do it in remembrance of me" (1 Cor. 11:24). Human suffering cannot be abolished or explained away or dismissed–but it can be endured. The assurance of this must come from those of us who are charged as Christians with preserving the knowledge of suffering persons–par-ticularly when they cannot, that in the face of Jesus' cry of forsakenness from the cross he maintained the certainty "I and the Father are one" (John 10:30).[10] With this assurance, the possibility of a new perspective emerges: If God is fully present with us in our suffering, then we are not consigned to mere endur-ance. The transforming, transfiguring power of Spirit becomes a real and pres-ent hope.

The cross illustrates and illuminates God's salvific will for us; it is an end to suffering and a revelation of the salvation already in place for all. In the cross Jesus has done something we cannot do for ourselves. His was an act of vicarious atonement; a passion so divine that in him our reconciliation is complete. In Christ, God goes out of God's-self to be in solidarity with the afflicted. Christ brings God's companionship to people who feel forsaken and abandoned. Christ's suffering is not exclusive–it is inclusive of ours, and our suffering is inclusive of Christ's. Thus, there is no affliction, no amount of suffering that can ever cut us off from Christ. Jesus is in brotherly solidarity with suffering, but atones fy taking the consequences of sin upon himself, and reconciliation is the result.[11] "God was in Christ reconciling the world to himself" (2 Cor. 5:18-19). God *does* take on our suffering through God's Son, Jesus the Crucified One. This has clear implications for discipleship and service in health care ministries. If God is to be made immanent in the world for the afflicted and the marginalized, we must be willing to go out of ourselves to care for the mentally ill, comfort the dying, hear the confessions of the addicts and child abusers, and hold the hands of AIDS patients who have been abandoned by society. Lochman identifies the critical need for forgiveness in our lives: "The essential lines of the gospel in the words, deeds, and destiny of Jesus meet at the focal point of the forgiveness of sins . . . The forgiveness of our debts must prove to be a necessity of existence even more urgent and more radical than the necessity of daily bread." It seems that this aspect of care is often lost in the focus of health and welfare ministries on meeting the material needs of persons.[12] Our *actions* of service and care assure that the healing love of God continues to be made incarnate in the world.

A theology of service that takes seriously the charge identified in Matthew 25:31-46 calls upon us to love God through *all* our neighbors–particularly those considered to be "the least of these" among us. In my work with those who are truly society's marginalized, those who are considered its deviants, I must work with both the victimizers and the victimized–this is not always an easy task. It requires the willingness on my part to grapple constantly with the painful awareness of just how far out of God's grace we have fallen, and how desperately we are all–predator and prey alike–in need of God's grace to recover. In so many of the faces of the people to whom I give care on a daily basis, I am forced to confront the distortions of the *imago dei.* The personal stories of those who come into my care are filled with episodes of child abuse, family violence, rape, incest, abandonment–the list is long. The deformed, oftentimes shattered lives become in turn generational mirrors reflecting the chaos which came before, and sadly enough, the chaos that will continue for generations.

PRAYER AND SUFFERING

The misuse of our freedom to choose for God confronts me daily in these stories. It would be less than truthful of me if I failed to admit to the significant amount of inner turmoil which must be stilled in an effort to provide a true ministry of presence which the care of such persons demands. In my struggle to do so, I often turn to prayer. In the historical Jesus who prayed in the Garden of Gethsemane and assented to the cup of suffering so that we might find the strength to endure our own, we are taught about prayer. Prayer is transformative: " . . . every prayer changes the one who prays, strengthens [us] . . . , it pulls [us] together and brings [us] to utmost attention, which in suffering is forced from us and which in loving we ourselves give."[13] Prayer allows me to suspend judgment in a way that I am not able to accomplish of my own devices. It facilitates my ability to be with afflicted persons and accept *their* reality; not my version of what I think their reality should be. This is an *absolute necessity* in a profession that charges me with the delivery of good nursing care regardless of my personal feelings towards a person. As a Christian servant in the health-care field, prayer assists me to accept the *realness* of another's life and the suffering and torment that might be a part of such a life–if only by allowing me to come to grips with the understanding that is real for them in ways that I can never know.

Imago Dei and Empathy

In the face of such an understanding, sometimes I can only sit in compassionate and empathic silence, listening to the story of the afflicted one. Soelle would argue that in our ability to do just that, the possibility of attaining the *imago dei* lies. We must first, however, desire Christ's image: "To attain the image of Christ means to . . . remain with the oppressed and the disadvantaged. It means to make their lot one's own."[14] In the face of suffering persons, we glimpse the *imago dei* through God's Son, Jesus Christ. The restoration of the *imago dei* seems to depend in part on our willingness first to attain Christ's image . . . Christ the One who suffered and died, and Jesus, the man who sided with the afflicted and the marginalized. It means that we must remain with those who are suffering, and stand in solidarity with the victims by sharing their fate. There are no short-cuts to the restoration of the *imago dei*; it must be lived proleptically in the *now* of time and history. It demands our willingness to remember the suffering of Christ as we co-endure one another's burdens.

An ability to co-endure the pain and suffering of the afflicted requires an awareness that theirs is the sort of pain that manifests itself not just physically or psychologically, but socially as well. Their suffering is that which "threatens every dimension of life: time to await what is promised, freedom of movement and opportunity for development, vital association with others, food and health and living space as one's share of the land of promise."[15] It is this kind of suffering which not only afflicts one physically and mentally, but in whose grip one must also bear the brunt of isolation, loneliness and social ostracism as well.[16]

This is particularly true to a *devastating* degree with the patient population that I serve. The only way to break through this isolation and loneliness is to spend time with these patients and to listen to their stories, ultimately to lend visual witness to the power and presence of God's imminent love in their lives. Watkins speaks to the necessity of this incarnational love in health and welfare ministries: "God's love and the Christian's incarnation of that love is the primary cornerstone for all ministry . . . If we had no concept other than the love of God as a motive for social ministry, it would be sufficient . . . Incarnation carries with it the idea of embodying the concept. Thus the social minister becomes the embodiment of the love of God in relationships with other human beings, in grateful response to God's love."[17] Failure to do so is to consign the afflicted ones to the role of social leper. To the extent that any affliction tends to shape existence and determines relationships, including touching at the very deepest level one's relationship with God, abandoning persons to such a role becomes a threat to life itself. Tragically enough, we are too easily prone to do just this in our world today.

Core Beliefs and Suffering

It has long been my observation that people's deepest feelings about God will heavily influence, if not outright determine, any sense of emotional well-being and mental health. Cooper-Lewter and Mitchel refer to such feelings as *core beliefs*. The state: "Some core beliefs help people survive and cope, in the deep and abiding faith that God is good and life will always turn out right, no matter how terrible it may seem at a given time. Other core beliefs confer no such competence, so the believer . . . finds it impossible to persevere and thus gives up. Emotionally balance persons depend on the providence of God, holding therefore that life is always worth living."[18] I find this statement to be true in general, and most poignantly true when it is applied to those who attempt to succeed in committing suicide: Such persons have usually lost all sense of the providence of God, and theirs becomes an extreme act of giving up.

This is most important in the face of chronic illnesses such as those addressed in nursing homes and convalescent facilities where emotional balance is a critical determinant of long-term coping and compliance with cumbersome treatment regimens. The truth of the Word cannot be demonstrated if it exists only as some abstract revelation that stands outside of human experience. It must be made available to people where they live their lives; its meaning and impact can only be evaluated insofar as it addresses pain and suffering in context. If the living Word of Jesus is to find meaning in the human struggle it must be brought into the lives of the drug addicts, the AIDS patients, and those suffering from mental illness such as dementia. A theology of service which seeks to address and respond to their suffering, and the social isolation and degradation that results from such afflictedness, must testify to the conviction that we live and move in a world which can be changed. The willingness to work on suffering with others is an acknowledgement that the process of the resurrected life can, and must be, a daily occurrence–demonstrated by our continuing commitment to be present to one another on a continuing basis.

Language and Suffering

The ability to move from a mere endurance of suffering, to a suffering that can serve to potential growth in a productive way, can be found through language and the gift of speech. Nellie Morton speaks to the critical need for "hearing to speech" those whose voices are lost or go unheard. Morton tell the story of a well-meaning counselor who succeeds only in squelching another's speech by interjecting her own misguided comments. She cautions, "Clever techniques seen as positive agents for creation and change are not good for the kind of hearing that brings forth speech."[19] I believe this caveat applies to my own profession, and might well be passed on to many pastors and other ministers.

Soelle speaks to the isolative aspects of suffering that accompanies the inability to name one's pain: " . . . one of the fundamental experiences about suffering is precisely the lack of communication, the dissolution of meaningful and productive ties. To stand under the burden of suffering always means to become more and mores isolated."[20] This is *most particularly true* in the population with whom I work. The diagnoses of AIDS, addiction, dementia, and mental illness can throw up a societal wall around which those in front are afraid to peer, and over which those behind are unable to climb. To be rendered speechless in the experience of suffering and affliction is to lose one's ability toward relatedness: the victim becomes further victimized; the "helper" becomes helpless. A theology of care that includes a strong emphasis on a ministry of presence requires first and foremost the skill of careful, attentive listening–perhaps the most critical step in establishing relatedness. The story that initially pours forth often reveals the hidden anguish that life for the suffering one is a prolonged experience of the cross. Hearing one another into speech is often the first step toward release from that cross: personal resurrection becomes a hopeful possibility.

SUFFERING AND THE RISEN LORD

The ultimate source of hope that calls those of us to service in the face of all suffering is the hope of the promise of the Kingdom of God; the *Kyrios Christos*–the risen Lord. I have spoken through this article of the strength this promise lends to patients and those receiving care; the assurance of this promise is *no less critical* for those of us that work in the field of health-care ministries. Even if in the midst of acute pain, chronic and terminal illness, and grieving families we cannot always see the alternative future as promised in the resurrection, we can begin from the other end of God's promise.

In the eschatological hope in whose light we find the courage to struggle with afflicted persons through the daily darkness in which they labor, it is possible to discover our own source of strength and to live out a hope that is strong enough to transform the present. This willingness to live as if the future, eschatological promise has already broken into our midst is critical if we are to make the confessional statement, "I believe in Jesus Christ." There has been many times through the years where, if I did not have the assurance of the wondrous future to come, I would not have the ability to shape hopeful presents in the face of the overwhelming amount of suffering I encounter in my work. Without the promise of the Kingdom breaking into this present–and the many presents over the years I have served in health-care, I would be unable to continue confronting the kind of suffering I encounter day in and day out, year after year. I can rise to the demands of life, and I can summon the strength to protest *only* because I *know* in the deepest parts of my being, that my Lord rose before me. I continue to keep my eyes on the empty cross in front of me . . .

GOD PROTESTS SUFFERING

Thus the cry of abandonment by suffering persons finds its answer in the living Word of Jesus first from the experience of the cross, always however, cast in the light of the promise of the resurrection. No only is God present in suffering, but God protests against suffering. The experience of the cross can only be understood– and tolerated–in light of the assurance of resurrection. We understand that God protests suffering, actively contending against the principalities and powers of sin and death through the resurrection. God worked with death in a transformative way. The ultimate hope for suffering persons is: the loving power of God is even stronger than death. God raised the crucified Jesus to life. "The resurrection is the strongest possible sign that God really can be trusted to have the last word which is life. In the crucified and risen Jesus Christ, the arrival of the reign of God, the fullness of salvation, and the reconciliation of God and the world finally became fully possible."[21]

As disciples of Jesus Christ, we are called to be the "instrument[s] of the reign of God in history."[22] Jesus Christ saves. As Christians we live in obedient response to the discipleship required of us by suffering with those who suffer. The process of moving from the cross of Jesus to the resurrected life must involve a living response to the decisive action of God through Jesus–the daily resurrection to a changed, transformed life, in faithful response to the ultimate, heavenly resurrection to come.

CONCLUSION

Those who, like myself, have lived and worked with a significant amount of suffering through the years often come to acquire a rather weary kind of wisdom: Oftentimes suffering cannot be explained. This essay made no attempt to do so. When all is said and done, it appears that there is such a thing as "meaningless" suffering–the kind of suffering that defies explanation. Sometimes suffering just is. There is no amount of theorizing or theodicy-making that can ever really provide an adequate accounting for this sorrowful phenomenon. I find myself in agreement with Kenneth Surin who dismisses as superfluous the attempts of any human thinker to "justify God vis a vis the fact of evil": "The Christian who takes the atonement seriously has no real need for theodicy."[23]

This being said, even in the face of seemingly *meaningless* suffering, we are called to be in solidarity with suffering persons, wherever and whenever possible, as God is with us in our suffering through the cross of his Son. This is perhaps where suffering finds its meaning: Each time we are willing to be with our neighbor to care and comfort and to protest with them their suffering, we do this in memory of Christ. This is health care ministry in light of the empty cross.

NOTES

1. Dietrich Bonhoeffer, *Letters and Papers From Prison* (New York: Macmillan and Company, 1971). 369f.

2. Ibid.

3. The term *affliction* is employed by Soelle but originally used by Simone Weil. Originally cited in "The Love of God and Affliction," *Waiting for God,* trans. Emma Craufurd, (New York: G. P. Putnam's Sons, 1951), 117.

4. Elizabeth Johnson, "Redeeming the Name of Christ," in *Freeing Theology: The Essentials of Theology in Feminist Perspective.* Catherine Mowry Lacugna, ed., (New York: HarperCollins Publishers, 1993), 116.

5. Dorothee Soelle, *Suffering,* (Philadelphia: Fortress Press, 1973), 38.

6. Eugene Taylor, "Desperately Seeking Spirituality," in *Psychology Today,* Nov/Dec, 1994, 62.

7. Hans Kung, *CREDO: The Apostles Creed Explained for Today* (New York: Doubleday, 1992), 92.

8. Elizabeth Johnson, *Consider Jesus: Waves of Renewal in Christology* (New York: Crossroad, 1993), 115.

9. Kung, *CREDO,* 53-54.

10. Soelle, *Suffering,* 134-141.

11. Inspiration for this paragraph came from a lecture delivered by Dr. Young Ho Chun on 10/28/1994, at Saint Paul School of Theology, where he identified the "Solidarity Christology Approach" as directly reflective of his own Christology.

12. Jan Milic Lochman, *The Lord's Prayer,* Geoffrey W. Bromiley, trans., (Grand Rapids MI: Wm. B. Eerdmans, 1990), 118.

13. Soelle, *Suffering,* 86.

14. Ibid, 132.

15. Soelle, *Suffering,* 16. Originally in Christopher Barth, *Die Errettung vom Tode in den individuellen Klage–und Dankliedern des Alten Testaments,* (Zollikon: Evangelischer Verlag, 1947).

16. Ibid.

17. Derrel R. Watkins, *Christian Social Ministry,* (Nashville: Broadman and Holman Publishers, 1994), 57.

18. Nicholas Cooper-Lewter and Henry H. Mitchell, *Soul Theology: The Heart of American Black Culture,* (Nashville: Abingdon Press, 1991), 155.

19. Nelle Morton, *The Journey Is Home,* (Boston: Beacon Press, 1985) 202-206.

20. Soelle, *Suffering,* 75.

21. Johnson, *Consider Jesus,* 76.

22. Ibid., 77.

23. Kenneth Surin, *Theology and the Problem of Evil,* (Oxford: Basil Blackwell Ltd., 1986), 143.

Chapter 6

Biblical Foundations for a Practical Theology of Aging

DeeAnn Klapp, DMin

SUMMARY. This article reviews Biblical sources pertaining to the elderly, particularly the frail elderly. Founded on these sources, implications for elderly with Alzheimer's Disease and other forms of dementia are addressed through a personal perspective informed by writings of Christian mystics. *[Article copies available for a fee from The Haworth Document Delivery Service: 1-800-HAWORTH. E-mail address: <docdelivery@haworthpress.com> Website: <http://www.HaworthPress.com> © 2003 by The Haworth Press, Inc. All rights reserved.]*

KEYWORDS. Reason, self-transcendence, body, *soma, sarx,* Alzheimer's, community, neurological, respect, decalogue, covenant, salvation, pastoral, relationships, dehumanization, grace, soul, personality, mysticism, validation, communication

ELDERLY IN THE HEBREW SCRIPTURES

The Hebrew Bible contains at least 250 references to old age.[1] From the texts emerge recurrent themes and valuations of the elderly as esteemed and

---

Dr. Klapp is a United Methodist Pastor in Iowa. She works with nursing homes in her region to provide worship services for residents, especially those suffering from Alzheimer's Disease. She is a Graduate of Garrett Theological Seminary (MDiv) and Saint Paul School of Theology (DMin).

[Haworth co-indexing entry note]: "Biblical Foundations for a Practical Theology of Aging." Klapp, DeeAnn. Co-published simultaneously in *Journal of Religious Gerontology* (The Haworth Pastoral Press, an imprint of The Haworth Press, Inc.) Vol. 15, No. 1/2, 2003, pp. 69-85; and: *Practical Theology for Aging* (ed: Derrel R. Watkins) The Haworth Pastoral Press, an imprint of The Haworth Press, Inc., 2003, pp. 69-85. Single or multiple copies of this article are available for a fee from The Haworth Document Delivery Service [1-800-HAWORTH, 9:00 a.m. - 5:00 p.m. (EST). E-mail address: docdelivery@haworthpress.com].

http://www.haworthpress.com/store/product.asp?sku=J078
© 2003 by The Haworth Press, Inc. All rights reserved.
Digital Object Identifier: 10.1300/J078v15n01_07

useful members of the community. Age is generally considered as a blessing, or favor of God; certainly not something to resent, deny or dread. Wisdom is often attributed to the elderly, but in the candor of the Hebrew Bible, it is not always automatic or assumed with the simple passing of years. It is earned through righteous living and faithful obedience. Job voices this attribute, "Wisdom is with aged men, with long life is understanding" (Job 12:12). Throughout the Scriptures there is tension and balance of principle and exception. However, on some issues, there is no variance. Some of the principle affirmations concern the inherent worth, role and care of the elderly–especially the infirm.

The first principle is pronounced upon the first breath of the first man and woman: "And the Lord God formed man of dust from the ground, and breathed into his nostrils the breath of life; and man became a living being" (Gen. 2:7). I believe that the meaning of being created in the "image of God" includes the human capacity for reason, self-transcendence, freedom of choice (the will), moral responsibility, and creative constructive purpose: in short, an aspect of spirit.

The cognitive ability to be creatively constructive, the capacity for reason, even the direction and strength of the will may be altered by the degenerative aspects of Alzheimer's disease, but the God-breathed life remains. At the deepest level of human existence, deeper than intellect and personality which are debilitated by the disease and outwardly less approachable by human means, the inward spirit, the God-breathed life remains.

The second principle, also related to creation, is that human beings have physical substance, a body, formed from the dust of the earth, as well as mind and spirit. The only Hebrew word for body means corpse; a conglomeration of orderly biological and physiological events from which emanate psychological and emotional activity.[2] In the Gospels, the body as physical existence is not deemed as the whole of life. Bodily death is to be less feared for the body will be raised in the Resurrection. Of much greater concern is eternal death of the soul by sin (Luke 12:4).[3]

In the Greek of the New Testament, the apostle Paul makes distinctions between *sarx*, which refers to the whole person distinct from God, and *soma* to redefine the meaning of body, mind and spirit before God. *Sarx* refers to the whole person distinct from God, subject to infirmity and mortality.[4] *Soma* describes the human, in relation to creation and God, as being in fellowship with the Creator. Paul explains that *soma* and not *sarx* will inherit the Kingdom and share in the resurrection of Christ.[5]

> Now I say this, brethren, that flesh and blood cannot inherit the kingdom of God nor does the perishable inherit the imperishable. Behold I tell you

a mystery, we shall not all sleep, but we shall all be changed, in a moment, in the twinkling of an eye, at the last trumpet: for the dead will be raised imperishable and we shall be changed. For this perishable must put on the imperishable, and this mortal must put on immortality. (I Cor. 15:50-53)

The concept of *soma* has hopeful implications for the Christian stricken with Alzheimer's disease. The believer with Alzheimer's, despite deteriorating cognitive ability and physical limitations, is joined heart, mind, body and soul in relationship with Creator God in Christ Jesus. As the disease progresses, the conscious will decrease and concerns of the "flesh" (sarx) are no longer subject to the resident who becomes increasingly dependent upon others. The person becomes more dependent upon *God's will and not one's own.* With interfering defenses weakened or breached, I believe *soma* becomes a radical means (i.e., circumventing normative channels of reception and expression) through which God's Spirit works in and through the person.[6]

Furthermore, as all human beings have the common origin of being created in God's image, no one person can be valued simply on the basis of either positive or negative physical attributes alone. Nothing in Scripture indicates that advancing age diminishes the "image of God."[7]

A third principle is that of community. The account of Creation attests that human beings do not exist in solitary confinement. We are created for interaction and interrelationship with God and with one another. God deemed that "it is not good for man to be alone" (Gen. 2:18). The creation of all animals, and ultimately, a suitable human mate was a divinely creative exercise toward the ordination of community as an essential aspect of human existence.

The Hebrew Scriptures are resplendent with affirmations of the community's senior members. Into the hands of the eldest generation was entrusted the recitation of the Commandments and the might acts of God to the younger generations.[8]

The Shema lived and walked and spoke through its oldest devotees: God's best advertisement for its effectiveness. They embodied a living memory of Truth exemplified in past experience, and they ministered to the present generations as a constant living witness to the call and task of preserving the community of God's chosen people.

The Bible glorifies its elderly heroes is by attributing them with good health and vigor in their later years. For example, Abraham and Sarah are gifted with Isaac when they are "beyond childbearing years" (Gen. 18:11-14). Abraham dies "at a ripe old age" (Gen. 25:8). In all his 120 years, Moses never suffered blindness nor "abated strength" (Duet. 34:7). Gray hair, "the hoary head," is the "crown of a life of righteousness" (Prov. 16:31)." At the age of 365, Enoch took a faith walk with God straight into eternity without tasting death (Gen.

5:22-24: Heb. 11:5). Rewarding promises are found in Psalms. For example: "Because he has loved Me, therefore I will deliver him: I will set him securely on high, because he has known My name. He will call upon Me, and I will answer him: I will be with him in trouble; I will rescue him, and honor him. With a long life I will satisfy him. And let him behold My Salvation" (91:14-16). By contrast, an early death implies an element of judgment. "The fear of the Lord prolongs life, but the years of the wicked will be short" (Prov. 10:27).

Even though the Hebrew Scriptures laud its heroes and the glowing virtues of long life, it also candidly acknowledges the reality of human frailties and finitude. Aging is viewed as inevitable and accepted as part of God's plan for life. Our days are determined, irreplaceable, and therefore precious (Ps. 139: 16:90:12). Among the expectations of advanced years are the loss of vitality, powers, and some diminution of the quality of physical life. However, life is not unbearable as attested by Psalm 71. It is decidedly a period of physical deterioration. Abraham and Sarah had suffered depression for want of a son (Gen. 27:1-4). Isaac suffers blindness (Gen. 27:1-4). The tremors he experiences when angry may indicate some neurological disability (Gen. 27:33). Other ailments noted are clumsiness and obesity (1 Sam. 4:18), poor circulation and loss of sexual desire and/or potency (1 Kings 1:1-4), inability to conceive (Gen. 18:13), and problems with feet (1 Kings 15:23). However, Psalm 71 affirms hope, "But as for me, I will always have hope; I will praise You more and more" (vs. 14).

Finally, the principle that weaves from humanity's common divine thread is: All people are created in the image of God. Faithful reverence to the Almighty entails dutiful responsibility toward one another with particular regard to the weak, the oppressed and the infirm. The elderly qualify. Respect for elders is a prominent theme in the Scriptures. The Holiness code closely links respect for elders with reverence for God: "You shall rise up before the gray headed, and honor the aged and you shall revere your God: I am the Lord" (Lev. 19:32). Lack of respect incurs God's judgment. Disrespect towards Elisha resulted in the death of 42 boys mauled by bears (2 Kings 2:23ff.).

The clear message is: God expects respect of elders regardless of appearance, circumstance, and personality. Even when God was angry with the chosen people, a heavy indictment was charged against Babylon because "You did not show mercy to them, on the aged you made your yoke very heavy" (Is. 47:6). Heavy judgments are born from God's great compassion for the oppressed, the afflicted, and the needy.

In practice, the Hebrew's care for the elderly was unique at a time when sick aged persons were often killed or left to die. Nowhere is this more clearly evident than the commanded respect and care for parents in the Decalogue. The previous commandments directly pertain to one's relationship with God that is prime of all relationships. These are followed by the pivotal commandment, which links worship of God with moral responsibility toward others. It is the only commandment with a promise clause: "Honor your father and your mother, that your days may be prolonged in the land which the Lord your God give you" (Ex. 20:12). The term "honor" comes from the root *kabad*, which means "giving weight to" and commonly referred to glorifying God.[9] One must honor parents with demeanor worthy of their divinely ordained authority. The commandment implies personal service including attentiveness, obedience, and provision of needs. That might entail sharing possessions, shelter, and literally feeding them.[10] The Mekilta de Rabbi Ishmael, a rabbinic commentary on Exodus states, "The honoring of one's father and mother is very dear in the sight of Him by whose word the world came into being."[11] Keeping faith with parents is correlated with keeping the Sabbath: "Every one of you shall reverence his mother and father, and you shall keep My Sabbaths; I am the Lord your God" (Lev. 19:3).

Failure to honor parents is more than filial irresponsibility. It is treated as an assault on God; "If one curses his father or his mother, his lamp will be put out in utter darkness" (Prov. 20:20). Cursing, understood as the antithesis of honor, is deserving of the death penalty (Duet. 21:18-21).

When God's love and command is violated, judgment follows. God fights for the poor: "Do not rob the poor because he is poor or crush the afflicted at the gate; for the Lord will plead their case, and take the life of those who rob them" (Prov. 22:22-23). The disabilities suffered by the elderly are afflictions deserving divine attention and intervention. God exerts the same passion for ravaged parents, condemns their mistreatment, and supports their deliverance.

THE NEW TESTAMENT AND THE ELDERLY

The Hebrew Bible, the history of a chosen people living under the covenantal canopy of their true living God, creates the foundation, context, and the climate for the New Covenant revolution. In spirit, the Law of Moses remains, but with the Gospel the human-devised game rules drastically change.

Unlike Genesis in which age is a major issue,[12] the dawn of Christianity seldom addressed the specific concerns of the elderly or the respect due them by divine decree. Nevertheless, the opening chapters of the Gospel according to Luke gracefully portray the dignity and crucial role of older people anticipating and helping the promised Messiah. In their advanced age, Zechariah, a priest, and his wife Elizabeth conceive a son destined to become the "voice in the wilderness" (Luke 1:7, 13; 3:4). Age did not disqualify Zechariah from ministering to the Lord before the altar of incense (Luke 1:8-9). Silenced by the angel Gabriel, Zechariah is unable to speak until he inscribes the baby's appointed name, "John" (Luke 3:36). Elizabeth's pregnancy bears striking similarities to that of Sarah, Abraham's wife; a lovely intimation of the continuity of faith woven from the Old Covenant into the New.

After Jesus' birth Simeon, a devout and righteous man filled with the spirit, enters the temple. He has clung to life in a faith-driven search for the "consolation of Israel" (Luke 2:25). Holding the Infant Jesus, he thanked God that his life was filled and complete: "Now Lord, Thou dost let Thy bond-servant depart in peace, according to Thy word; for my eyes have seen Thy salvation" (Luke 2:29). Likewise, neither Anna's widowhood nor age of 84 years prevented her from serving "night and day with fasting and prayer" in the temple (Luke 2:37).

Jesus' life and teachings serve as the foremost example of Godly love and duty toward the aged and infirm. Some of His teachings and bantering with the elders of the established religious institution might call to question His filial respect and regard for the venerable vessels of tradition. For example, Jesus has a sharp retort for the man who would follow Him, but first requested "Let me first bury my father" (Mt. 8:21). Jesus demands His disciples to forsake and even "hate" their own relatives, which presumably include elderly members (Matt. 10:34-39, Luke 9:59-62; 14:25-27). When Jesus was told that His own mother and brothers stood outside seeking to speak to Him, Jesus responded in a manner that would seem to deny His own family:

> "Who is my mother and who are my brothers?" And stretching out his hand toward his disciples, He said, "Behold, my mother and my brothers! For whoever does the will of my father who is in heaven, he is my brother and sister and mother." (Matt. 12:48-49)

Therein is revealed a clue to Jesus' apparent unexplainable demeanor. It was not that His family was unimportant, or that aging parents were insignificant. It is His uncompromising, obedient love for God, and the urgency of His mission for the Kingdom, that take precedence over all other relationships, social amenities, and irrelevant occupations.[13]

Jesus' great empathy for the poor, the plight of widows, the infirm in body, mind, and spirit attest to the infinitely broad horizon of His love, call and anointed ministry. Early in His preaching tour, Jesus declared His life's purpose during service at the synagogue in His own hometown of Nazareth.[14]

That was the prime directive by which Jesus met the widow of Nain and restored the life of her son (Luke 7:12). The focus of His empathy, the widow offering God all she had, prompted an object lesson for contented self-righteous Pharisees (Mark 12:42). He casts the singular object of His undivided devotion and obedience as a compassionate, merciful Father welcoming the return of a wayward son (Luke 15:20). Poor, captive, intellectually blind, and emotionally downtrodden, the nursing home resident with Alzheimer's disease meets all the requirements which Jesus proclaimed would qualify recipients of His ministry.

Jesus defends the plight of elderly parents as more sacred than the vow of Corban in the faces of the Pharisees (Mark 7:9-13). When the rich young ruler asks what he might do to inherit life, the Master recites all the commandments pertaining to human relationships including the command to honor one's parents (Luke 18:18-20). When aging, night wandering Nicodemus came to call, Jesus met his longing soul with its greatest need: to see the kingdom (John 3:3). By the transforming power of the Holy Spirit, an old man can be born anew. What greater life-affirming gift is there than to love the elderly as self, and to assure them by willing sacrifice of their priceless worth to God?

The gentle manner of Jesus with the afflicted, and His moral outrage against oppressive hypocrisy of the religious elite, bespeak of both God's tender mercy and righteous judgment. Perhaps at no time during His ministry, is Jesus' matchless care for the widow and aging parent more revelatory than in His dying hour as He tenderly entrusts His mother Mary to the care of the beloved disciple (John 19:26-27). In response to the Master's last request, John immediately takes Mary into his household. Even in the agony of His death, Jesus honors His aging mother by amply providing a means for her care. The deaf, the blind, the lame, the stooped, the epileptic, the insane, the poor, the abandoned, the widowed, and the aged receive His attention, compassion, empathy, and grace which restored to them dignity and self-worth. This is the biblical model for ministry among persons with Alzheimer's disease.

Paul, the apostle, says little about the aged in his epistles, but passionately demands human dignity, unity, justice, and above all, love for the brethren. By the time the epistles to the Colossians and Ephesians were in circulation, the Gospel had attained considerable success and "the Way" was settling down to the beginnings of formulated doctrine. No longer were all of its followers living as itinerant preachers, but as responsible family members. Marriage and family relationships were reinterpreted in the context of Jesus' relationship with the Church (Eph. 5:22-23, 6:1-4). A new definition of conduct and Christian relationships are reflected in the house-tables or "station codes."[15] The continuity with the Law of Moses remains as the commandment to honor mother and father, intact and complete with its unique promise, is transferred into the New Church.

Concerning pastoral relationships, Paul advises young Timothy not to "sharply rebuke an older man, but rather appeal to him as a father . . . the older women as mother . . . Honor widows who are widows indeed [having no one to care for them]" (1 Tim. 5:1-3). Adult children, even grandchildren are charged to care for their aged and widowed family members (vs. 4). Paul lists qualifications for a "true" widow eligible to receive assistance from the Church:

> She must be over sixty, the widow of one husband, one who is known for her good works, has raised children, has shown hospitality, has washed the feet of the saints, has relieved the afflicted, and has devoted herself to doing good in every way. (1 Tim. 5:9-10)

As stringent as these qualifications are, notice that they reflect the work of her life that is past. Infirmity, forgetfulness, or disabilities are not conditions that disqualify eligibility. Frailty of old age or debilitating disease summons respect and care, not ridicule, condemnation, nor abandonment. The letter to Titus spells out what is expected of the elderly with the same candor as the Hebrew Scriptures:

> Older men are to temperate, dignified, sensible, sound in faith, in love, in perseverance. Older women likewise are to be reverent in behavior, not malicious gossips, not enslaved to much wine, teaching what is good, that they may encourage the young women to their husbands, to love their children, to be sensible, pure, workers at home, kind, being subject to their own husbands that the word of God may not be dishonored. (Titus 2:3-5)

Nowhere does this job description specify glowing perfect health, 20/20 eyesight, a marathon physique, or unimpaired hearing. It does require heart and soul. Review of the Scriptures asserts that by virtue of their losses, their utter helplessness, and impoverished quality of life, the elderly infirm qualify as a particular concern for the protection, guardianship, and care of God as exemplified by Jesus Christ. As such, they are certainly a pastoral concern for the Church. For the person suffering Alzheimer's disease, soundness of mind and body do not define the receptivity of faith, but rather the God-breathed spirit, the heart and point of need.

THEOLOGICAL QUESTIONS AND IMPLICATIONS

For a biblically based theology to adequately serve as foundation for ministry with the elder suffering from Alzheimer's disease, I perceive five difficult theoretical and practical problems that must be addressed: (1) The progressive dehumanization through the symptoms of the disease in its early stages and diagnosis raises questions of sin and guilt by the patient and the family. "What terrible thing did I do to deserve this?" (2) Eventually, the person's severely impaired and declining mental faculties deny the passage of spiritual insight through normative means such as intellectual comprehension, self-reflection, verbal expression and volitional ascent. Without these faculties how does the resident worship, praise, repent, confess, receive forgiveness, and offer devotion and service? (3) Progressive memory loss and failing abilities diminish the person's sense of self-worth, eventually robbing the mind of personal history, present orientation, the sense of God's presence, and one's own identity. How does one relate to God to Whom there seems to be no perception of access? (4) The inability to reason leaves the person very vulnerable to the influence of random thoughts, unbidden memories, irrational fear, sudden impulses, delusions and hallucinations. These may seem very real and may evoke physiological reactions. A theological framework for pastoral care must deal with these "demons in legion." (5) The erratic behavior and vulnerability of the person necessitates close supervision, consistent routine, familiar surroundings, and restricted mobility. These limitations contribute to social isolation and physical absence from the Church as the locus of the community of faith.

How can a theology bear the burden of all those contradictions of practiced religion? Where does one begin? In His book *Forgetting Whose We Are: Alzheimer's Disease and the Love of God,* David Keck addresses this very concern:

> What happens in Alzheimer's? What becomes of a person and her memories? Is there a metaphysical basis for the human person which this disease does not destroy . . . How is it possible to speak of a personal relationship with God, when there seems to be no person left? Does the Holy Spirit depend on a conscious subject in order to be present or provide comfort to a person?

From the beginning, the Hebrew Scriptures attest that humanity was created in the image of God. In the Gospels, the Incarnation, God in the flesh, is clearly the most profound affirmation of the invaluable worth of human beings. Therefore, we can esteem the person with Alzheimer's disease to be deserving of compassion and care in the emulation of the love Christ. Karl Barth states:

> On the basis of the eternal will of God we have to think of every human being, even the oddest, most villainous, or miserable as one to whom Jesus Christ is a Brother and God is Father; and we have to deal with him on this assumption.[16]

The very fact that God took the drastic measure of offering the Son to cancel sin bespeaks of its all-pervasive, destructive, infectious and lethal nature (Rom. 6:23). Jesus dealt squarely with sin in His ministry of forgiveness and healing. He emphasized the nature of the whole person and downplayed the distinctions between the body, mind and spirit. Likewise, in some instance, He treats infirmity as iniquity. To the paralytic man Jesus gave absolution. The scribes were skeptical. Which was easier, to heal the body or to forgive sins? To demonstrate that He has the power to forgive sins, Jesus commanded the man to rise, take up his bed, and go home cured, and forgiven (Matt. 9:6)!

On the other hand, Jesus attributes no guilt to the man whom He heals of blindness. The disciples asked whether it was his parents' sin or his own that caused the man's affliction. Jesus tell them neither was responsible, but that it was permitted so "that the works of God might be displayed in him" (John 9:1-7). During an object lesson on repentance, Jesus frankly asks His listeners if they thought that the eighteen people who were crushed by the falling tower of Siloam were worse sinners than all the men in Jerusalem. Of course not! He tells them, "I tell you no, but unless you repent, you will all likewise perish" (Luke 13:5). Sometimes evil indiscriminately befalls undeserving victims.

These narratives attest to the reality that sin, which brought death into the world, is the cause of sickness. However, an individual may suffer illness because of sin operative in the world, or indiscriminate evil, and not some particular sin personally committed. Like the man born blind and the experience of Job, that evil may be allowed to serve a purpose known only to God. This is a word of peace for the Alzheimer's patient crying out, "What terrible sin did I do to deserve this?"

Scripture is replete with examples of ways in which people suffered, endured, and sustained losses and intense emotions. To name a few: Moses, Naomi, and her daughters-in-law, Joseph, Jonah, Job, Hannah, Elijah, Isaiah, Jeremiah, David, and Apostle Paul. Jesus, however, is unique. As the Incarnation, Jesus embodied the life of God. In Christ we see how God lived as a human being.[17] In Him we see perfect willing obedience. We see the love of God willing to innocently suffer our sin which breeds sickness and reaps death. The redemptive power of the crucifixion transforms the curse to the infinite blessing of salvation. Estrangement from fellowship with God, and death in the body is transformed to Life incorruptible. In the power of the Cross of Christ, even the loss of personality may have a redemptive purpose!

Christ was pre-existent with God from the beginning of creation (John 1:1). To be born as a human being, under the finitude of the flesh, would entail reduction of personal being beyond our comprehension. Is it not possible that Christ, through His descent and embodiment on earth, sustained losses cosmically comparable to the reduction and debilitation of a person Alzheimer's disease? Did Jesus' identification with humanity, publicly demonstrated in the baptismal waters of the Jordan (Matt. 3:13-15), begin with a depletion of His former glory as His very conception, that was ratified through the waters of

Mary's womb? One might speculate that an implication of such cosmic reduction might be an inborn empathy for those who suffer such losses during earthly existence.

Christ's Incarnation, Crucifixion, and Resurrection accessed the means of grace sufficient to restore humanity's relationship with God. Jesus said, "If any one would come after Me, let him deny himself, take up his cross, and follow Me" (John 16:35). Graced by God, one way in which suffering enhances faith is by enabling the sufferer to acknowledge dependence upon God. A suitable theology for the framework for ministry with the Alzheimer's patient must include grace to surrender to God all control and accept each moment as it comes. The patient unwittingly experiences what many able-minded persons fail to learn: absolute dependence upon the unmerited grace of God. The loss of control over faculties, and the inexpressible grief, frustration, as well as muted cries might well become the avenues of God's grace. Compare the patient's sufferings with Apostle Paul's internal wrestling with warring principles:

> For good that I wish, I do not do; but practice the very evil that I do not wish. But if I am doing the very thing that I do not wish, I am no longer the one doing it, but sin which dwells in me. I find then the principle that evil is present in me, the one who wishes to do good. For I joyfully concur with the law of God in the inner man, but I see a different law in the members of my body, waging war against law of my mind, and making me a prisoner of the law of sin which is in my members. Wretched man that I am! Who will set me from the body of this death? Thanks be to God through Jesus Christ our Lord! (Rom. 7:19-25)

The "warring principle" affecting the members of the body for the Alzheimer's patient is the ravaging disease, a corollary to the "principle of evil" which dwells in the patient and over which the patient has no control. How far does the grace of God extend when there is no will left to receive that grace?

Grounded in the belief of a triune God, a theology applicable to the unique spiritual needs of the person with dementia must see God's self-expression through means which are not primarily intellectual, cognitive, or verbal. It must ask: "If never abandoned nor forsaken, at what level and through what means does God relate to a soul who is prisoner to a fading mind?" Scripture offers the first clue:

> Oh Lord, Thou hast searched me and known me. Thou dost know when I rise up: Thou doest understand my thought from afar. Thou dost scrutinize my path and my lying down, and are intimately acquainted with all my ways. Even before there was a word on my tongue, behold, O Lord

Thou dost know it all. Thou has enclosed me behind and before, and laid Thy hand upon me. Where can I go from the Spirit? Or where can I flee from Thy presence? (Ps. 139:1-7)

This Psalm beautifully expresses utter confidence and complete dependence upon the faithfulness of God's Spirit, gracious mercy, guardianship, protection, and intimate relationship even without the person's conscious awareness of God's presence. Even darkness, mental midnight, is not beyond the luminous glory of God. The Psalmist's soul is never beyond the sight or the reach of God (Ps. 139:11-12).

Through the image of the Good Shepherd, Jesus elicits our assurance of God's absolute trustworthiness: "My Father, who has given them (the sheep) to Me, is greater than all; and no one is able to snatch them out of the Father's hand. The Father and I are one (John 16:13-14). The same Spirit bears witness that the person who has confessed Christ, regardless of diminution of power and personality, has the Son. "He who has the Son has life" (John 5:12a).

Robert Davis' wife completed his manuscript after he succumbed to the terminal stage of Alzheimer's disease. His last notes tell of a miraculous spiritual insight that relieved his soul and released his vanishing control into the loving arms of God:

One night in Wyoming, as I lay there in the blackness silently shrieking out my repeated prayer, there was suddenly a light that seemed to fill my very soul. The sweet holy presence of Christ came to me. He spoke to my spirit and said, "Take my peace. Stop your struggling. It is all right. This is all in keeping with My will for your life. I now release you from the burden of the heavy yoke of pastoring that I placed upon you. Relax and stop struggling in you r desperate search for answers. I will hold you. Lie back in your Shepherd's arms, and take my peace."[18]

A THEOLOGY OF UNION:
A REINTERPRETATION OF CHRISTIAN MYSTICISM

An anonymous fourteenth century English writer referred to the intimate experience of God as the "Cloud of Unknowing." The mind of Augustine was arrested "in a flash of a trembling glance to Absolute Being–That which is."[19] Jan van Rysbroeck writes in Flemish of Darkness, Nakedness, and Nothingness.[20] Contemporary theologian Jurgen Moltmann, gazing intently upon the mystery of God in relation to the Church, writes glowingly of the union of God through Christ, glorified by the Holy Spirit.[21] The interior castle toured by St. Teresa of Avila, the Dark Night of the Soul navigated by St. John of the Cross, the immensity of God's love impressed upon the heart of Mother Julian of Norwich, raptures in soul-deep silence, prophetic visions, agony of the spirit and ecstasies in unutterable grace that map the pilgrimage of the loved to the Beloved.

PERSONAL PERSPECTIVE

Why would I, the wife of the same devoted husband for twenty-seven years, mother of four children, pastor of three very small rural congregations, burdened with a calling to minister among institutionalized elderly, have inclination (much less time or temperament) to pursue the theology and spirituality of the Christian mystic? There are four reasons:

First, I understand all aspects of my life in terms of calling and relationship. With my relationship with Christ, all others are ordered, informed, sustained, graced and fulfilled. The primacy of that relationship has drawn me to increasingly deeper and more intimate fellowship. The fruit of that fellowship has been the single desire to be faithful, to will and to do the will of God for the love of Jesus Christ.

The second reason is that the energy expended for the level of activity required by the tasks and demands of my calling finds its source, stamina and direction in the power of the Holy Spirit. In Christ, God calls. Through Christ, God empowers. I take to heart the words of my Lord, "Apart from Me, you can do nothing" (John 15:5).

The third reason is that the experience of overwhelming gratitude has spawned longing within me that only intimacy with Christ can encompass. Christian Mysticism provides a context for the formation, interpretation, and expression of faith within the Prime Relationship that informs, inspires, corrects, and enhances my relationships with others and the material world as well as my inmost being.

The fourth is my concern for the institutionalized older adult. Ministry among persons in the third and fourth stages of Alzheimer's disease intrinsically demands of the pastoral caregiver an other-mindedness and sensitivity not solely dependent upon what is visibly seen or audibly heard. There is, of necessity, reliance upon the Holy Spirit of God who infinitely loves them, a setting aside of oneself, and an outreaching love in order to minister to souls incapable of awareness and communication of their needs. Spiritual sensitivity, self-renunciation, detachment, and outpouring love are notable attributes of the Christian mystic.

In his volume *The Varieties of Religious Experience,* William James delineates four traits of the mystical experience as being ineffability, integrative insights and knowledge, passivity, and transience (meaning that experiences are intermittent temporary states).[22] The English word "mysticism" is derived from the Greek word *mysterion* by which the Church Fathers denoted the secret or hidden dimension of Scripture, the mystery of the sacraments, and the knowledge of God in Christ.[23] Succinctly stated by Teresa of Avila, the heart of Christian mysticism is "making my will one with the will of God."[24]

Repeated throughout the works of the mystics like a refrain of a many versed hymn is the haunting soulful melody of passionate longing for God and ultimate, dispassionate self-surrender. St. Catherine of Sienna espouses her ardor for God:

> Grant that my memory may be capable of retaining thy benefits, that my will may burn in the fire of thy charity, and may that fire so work in me that I give my body to blood, and that by that blood given for love of the blood, together with the key of obedience, I may unlock the door of heaven.[25]

St. Catherine prays that God preserves her memory of acts of Grace and that she will be overwhelmed and consumed by God's love. Even if the resident with Alzheimer's disease has little cognitive memory intact, the Holy Spirit can stir and rekindle the benefit of God's grace received earlier in life. The Psalmist pleads, "For You have been my hope, O Sovereign Lord, my confidence since my youth . . . Do not cast me away when I am old; do not forsake me when my strength is gone" (Ps. &1:5,9).

St. Teresa of Avila explains the necessity of self-renunciation: "Without complete self-renunciation, the state is very arduous and oppressive, because, as we go along, we are laboring under the burden of our miserable nature, which is like a great load of earth, and has not to be borne by those who reach the later Mansions."[26] She adds, "Perfection consists not in consolations, but in the increase of love; on this too, will depend our reward, as well as on the righteousness and truth which are in our actions."[27]

According to Naomi Feil, author of *Validation: The Feil Method,* one of the four emotions which remain in tact even to the last stages of the disease is love. St. Teresa of Avila emphasizes the necessity of self-renunciation which is evident in persons with progressed Alzheimer's disease as they lose control of cognitive and physical ability. Love, however, remains. Quaker mystic from the 19th century, Hannah Whitehall Smith extends the mystical experience out of the cloister into the mainstream of life in Christ. She writes, "All dealings of God with the soul of the believer are in order to it bring into oneness with Himself, that the prayer of our Lord may be fulfilled; 'That they may be one; as thou, Father art one in me, and I in thee, that they also may be one in us . . . '"[28]

Hannah Whitehall Smith reminds us that God's intention, poignantly expressed in Christ's high priestly prayer, is to bring all believers into oneness. That oneness includes both the spiritual caregiver and the one among the "least of these"; the resident with Alzheimer's disease.

St. John of the Cross describes utter subjection to God as the "dark night of the soul" in which "He leaves them so completely in the dark that they know not wither to go with their sensible imagination and meditation . . . their inward senses being submerged in this night."

The truth of this insight has been borne in my own spirituality. Just prior to entering seminary, my spiritual sensibilities were jettisoned by a fresh awareness of the overwhelming love of God and immediate presence of Christ. Prayer was punctuated with ecstatic praise, instant in the awareness of continual companionship of the Lord, graced by visions, insights and spiritual vitality flowing in devotion to Christ, and through Christ to those around me. Then I entered a season of aridity, which St. John of the Cross describes as the Dark Night of the Soul. What had I done to so offend my Lord that He would withdraw His presence, hide His love, and seemingly take His Spirit from me? Never before had I felt such abandonment, nakedness, or fear of being utterly lost. Desperate for God, having lost hold of everything else, I clung to the printed word of Scripture as would cling to flotsam in the wake of shipwreck. I woodenly rehearsed the promises for which I felt no reality, no fulfillment, only emptiness:

> (Nothing) can separate us from God in the love of Christ Jesus (Rom. 8:39). Lo I am with you always, even to the end of the age (Matt. 28:20). I will not leave you as orphans, I will come to you (John 14:18). If anyone loves Me, he will keep My word; and My Father will love him and We will come to him, and make Our abode with him. (John 14:23)

One by one the veils like gray mist evaporating in the rising sun of a bright morning leaving only dew behind to refresh the grass. From then on I knew perfect love is to love God for God alone. Even the best gifts of God, if cherished more than the Giver, can become distractions that partition the soul its first Love.

Leander Keck observes that dementia shares a common element with the dark night of the soul described by St. John of the Cross: "perhaps that dementia-like states and a seeming isolation from God are not alien to the purgation trials of mysticism." If that is so, God is nearer to those so seemingly "isolated" than to the hearts of those able in body and mind who ignore, reject, and denounce God's presence.

The author of *The Cloud of Unknowing* reiterates St. Augustine's observation that all of one's life is to be one of longing for God, and all else forgotten. It is expressed in prayer directed to win not the favors, but the very heart of God's Self:

> Lift up thine heart unto God with a meek stirring of love, and mean himself and none of his gods.[29] This perceptible state of longing, as real as the pangs of hunger or throb of a pounding heart, can be attributed to the sorrow of separation.[30] It prepares the soul for any touch God might impart.[31]

Ignatius of Loyola believed, "union is union-in-service, the involvement of the human person in the redemptive work of the Trinity in the world."[32] The mystery of redemption through the Cross and oneness with God is actualized and lived in the service of mankind for the sake of Christ. It is a social mysticism: contemplation that incarnates the passion of Christ in substantiated service. How does the resident in a locked Alzheimer unit become "involved in the redemptive work?" One answer is to offer that resident the opportunity for prayer, worship, service, and participation in the Body of Christ through Sacrament and fellowship using perceptible means and medium: i.e., Validation methods of communication.

Contemporary mystic Thomas Merton also gazed upon the Unknowable with fervor for the peace of Christ to reign in this world. Jane Marie Thibault, author of *A Deepening Love Affair: The Gift of God in Later Life* recollects the powerful influence exerted on her life by Merton's writing *Seeds of Contemplation.* "I took it home and in its pages found what I had been seeking for so long but, didn't know it–a statement that God dwells within each of us, that God is able to be known by experience, and that God actually craves an intimate relationship with all God's children."[33]

The experience of God is not one of knowing all about God, but simply knowing God; knowing God by emptying oneself and waiting in stillness, by negation of attributes, by inspired action, passivity, ecstatic joy, and soul-filled sorrow. The nameless visionary of *The Cloud of Unknowing* entreats us:

> Try to understand this point. Rational creatures such as men and angels possess two principal faculties, a knowing power and a loving power. No one can fully comprehend the uncreated God with his knowledge, but each one, in a different way can grasp him fully through love.[34]

So it is through love, not intellect, the soul may embrace the fellowship and eternal love of Almighty God. This is a word of infinite hope for the patient with Alzheimer's disease.

NOTES

1. Stephen Sapp, *Full of Years* (Nashville: Abingdon Press, 1987), 22.

2. John L. McKenzie, S.J. *Dictionary of the Bible* (New York: Macmillan Publishing Co. Inc., 1965), 100.

3. Ibid.,100.

4. Sapp, 1987, 102.

5. I Cor. 15:50-53.

6. Sapp, 103.

7. Ibid., 72.

8. Duet. 6:7.

9. Gordon J. Harris, *Biblical Perspectives on Aging* (Philadelphia: Fortress Press, 1987), 61.

10. (Sapp, 1987, 83).

11. Harris, 1987, 124.

12. Frank Stagg, *The Bible Speaks on Aging* (Nashville: Broadman Press, 1981), 9.

13. Harris, 1987, 82.

14. Luke 4:18-19.

15. Sapp, 1987, 21.

16. Sapp 1987, 185.

17. Ibid., 101.

18. Davis, 1984, 54-55.

19. Hugh T. Kerr, ed., *Readings in Christian Thought* (Nashville: Abingdon Press, 1993), 81.

20. Cheslyn Jones, Geoffrey Wainwright, Edward Yarnold S.J., ed., *The Study of Spirituality* (New York: Oxford University Press, 1986), 318.

21. Jurgen Moltmann, *The Church in the Power of the Spirit,* (Minneapolis: Fortress Press, 1993), 60.

22. Melvin A. Kimble, Susan H. McFadden, James W. Ellor, James J. Seeber, ed. *Aging, Spirituality, and Religion* (Minneapolis: Fortress Press, 1995) 88.

23. Ibid., 89.

24. Jones, Wainwright, and Yarnold, S.J. 1986, 370.

25. Kerr, 1996, 127.

26. St. Teresa of Avila, *Interior Castle* (Garden City: Image Books, Doubleday, 1986), 66.

27. Ibid., 68.

28. Hannah Whitehall Smith, *The Christian's Secret of a Happy Life* (Waco: Word Books, 1985), 142.

29. Jones, Wainwright, Yarnold S.J. 1986, 333.

30. William Johnston, ed. *The Cloud of Unknowing* (New York: Image Books, Doubleday, 1973), 12.

31. Jones, Wainwright, Yarnold, S.J. 1986, 333.

32. Ibid., 361.

33. Jane Marie Thibault, *A Deepening Love Affaire: The Gift of God in Later Life* (Nashville: UpperRoom Books, 1983), 16.

34. Johnston, 1973, 52.

Chapter 7

The Dilemma of Aging

Julie A. Gorman, DMin

SUMMARY. Our minds and hearts search for meaning in this relentless process of constant change that began when we were born. By intentionally reflecting on this aspect of life in the light of our faith and from the perspectives revealed in Scripture, this query moves into a theological arena. Does our aging have meaning for God? In what ways does the nature of God help us understand this phenomenon? What does the biblical perspective on persons contribute to our insight? To follow this path leads to realignment of views and to newness in awareness of God's purpose in this march toward further maturity. *[Article copies available for a fee from The Haworth Document Delivery Service: 1-800-HAWORTH. E-mail address: <docdelivery@haworthpress.com> Website: <http://www.HaworthPress.com> © 2003 by The Haworth Press, Inc. All rights reserved.]*

KEYWORDS. Mortality, throwaway, personal dignity, independence, desirability, realized gains, cultural view, stamina, commitment, theology, character, value, change, unconditional, munificence, respect, justice

---

Julie A. Gorman teaches Christian Formation and Discipleship at Fuller Theological Seminary, Pasadena, CA. Dr. Gorman served fifteen years as Pastor of Adults and Families in a number of churches in the Los Angeles area. She has authored a number of books and served as editor of Baker Books, *The Dictionary of Christian Education*.

[Haworth co-indexing entry note]: "The Dilemma of Aging." Gorman, Julie A. Co-published simultaneously in *Journal of Religious Gerontology* (The Haworth Pastoral Press, an imprint of The Haworth Press, Inc.) Vol. 15, No. 1/2, 2003, pp. 87-105: and: *Practical Theology for Aging* (ed: Derrel R. Watkins) The Haworth Pastoral Press, an imprint of The Haworth Press, Inc., 2003, pp. 87-105. Single or multiple copies of this article are available for a fee from The Haworth Document Delivery Service [1-800-HAWORTH, 9:00 a.m. - 5:00 p.m. (EST). E-mail address: docdelivery@haworthpress.com].

http://www.haworthpress.com/store/product.asp?sku=J078
Digital Object Identifier: 10.1300/J078v15n01_08

" . . . Every Member of the Human Race Ages Daily."[1]

This is not news. But is it good news? Or bad news? While reading this article you will participate in the process of aging. There is only one escape from having birthdays. And that option doesn't appeal to us either.

A classic moment from the film "City Slickers" is Billy Crystal's soliloquy of angst given before his son Danny's grade school class in the course of their exploring "What does your dad do?" Facing the reality of his fortieth birthday with increasing gloom, he gets caught up in his own desperate advice.

"Value this time in your life, kids, because this is the time in your life when you still have your choices. And it goes by so fast.

When you're a teen-ager you think you can do anything and do you.

Your twenties are a blur . . .

Thirties . . . you raise your family. You make a little money. And you think to yourself, 'What happened to my twenties?'

Forties . . . you grow a little potbelly. You grow another chin. The music starts to get too loud. One of your old girlfriends from high school becomes a grandmother.

Fifties . . . you have a minor surgery—you call it a 'procedure' but it's a surgery.

Sixties . . . you'll have a major surgery. The music is still loud but it doesn't matter because you can't hear it anyway.

Seventies . . . you and the wife retire to Fort Lauderdale. You start eating dinner at two o'clock in the afternoon. You have lunch around 10, breakfast the night before. You spend most of your time wandering around malls looking for the ultimate soft yogurt and muttering, 'How come the kids don't call? How come the kids don't call?'

In the eighties you'll have a major stroke. You end up babbling at some Jamaican nurse your wife can't stand but whom you call, 'Mama.' Any questions?"

The class of grade schoolers sits in shock as their dismal future has just flashed before them.

Is aging to be viewed only as a liability? Is loss the unqualified result of adding years? Is depreciation the only realistic evaluation of this creeping but relentless reality we all face?

A recent best seller, *Tuesdays With Morrie*, speaks to an issue we all face—our own mortality. Why would a book that so clearly ends in death hold such a fascination in a culture that does everything it can to live in denial of this march toward an inevitable end? The Scriptures put it frankly, "It is appointed to every person who lives to die." Aging reminds us that we're headed that way. "Growing old" doesn't make our list of Top Ten Favorite Things To Do, and "older persons" are frightening mirrors. As Nouwen writes, " . . . Without the presence of old people we might forget that we are aging. The elderly are our prophets, they remind us that what we see so clearly in them is a process in which we all share."[2] Indeed they are "prophets without honor" because we would rather forget.

With few exceptions–such as wine and cheese–aging is definitely not a plus. Our throwaway society sees old as synonymous with useless and our "old" items fill junkyards to such a degree we are becoming alarmed over the magnitude of our discards. Will we be consumed by the old? Even in education we follow the trendy Athenians in Paul's time valuing the "newest," while disregarding the older. "Older books" go out of print rapidly today. Newer versions replace our "outmoded" systems with regularity.

While geriatrics is increasingly becoming a focus of attention in the medical and commercial-economic world because of the inevitable march of the "Baby Boomers" in this direction, Christians have been slow to pursue this concept of aging to reclaim it theologically.[3] Christian thought has produced several works of significance on how to deal with certain stages of the life span and such occasions as "mid-life crisis" but dealing with the theological frameworks behind the aging process has been sparse. Most of our efforts in the realm of "Aging" have gone into providing pastoral "ministries" to the elderly or church "programs" in which Seniors are involved. How are we as Christians to "think Christianly" about aging?

Why did God establish the process of getting older? What does the act of aging reflect to us of the person and ways of God? If we have a "changeless God," why a "changing creation?" What is the role and function of old age? . . . of allowing persons to reach old age, especially as science is adding increasingly numerous years to the life span? . . . of years far beyond the necessary service of bearing and raising offspring to keep the race going? . . . or extended living beyond the years of "productivity" and "contribution to society?" Is God promoting "golf" and "cruises," or "rocking chairs and nursing homes?" The very presence of so many aged persons promotes competition between generations for limited goods and services. How should we rule on a decision that diminishes or creates burdens for one segment of humanity in order to preserve another? What are the theological dimensions of this dilemma? These threads lead to a theological reframing of related issues such as work, retirement, leisure and others.

The purpose of this paper is to look at prevalent views of aging, to survey representative biblical data that refers to this subject, and to propose some "collected" theological propositions for seeing this phenomena with a God-centered perspective.

WHAT ARE WE TALKING ABOUT–DEFINITION

"Aging" and "old" are difficult to tie down. When do I begin aging? One author suggests "we begin to 'age' while we are still in our late teens."[4] Another observes that "a person is aging" as based on evidence of physical and mental decline, thus referring to such perceivable factors as increasing wrinkles or forgetfulness or decreasing energy levels–circumstances that usually occur in later adulthood. Indeed, aging or aged is often synonymous with the "elderly." They are the aged ones.

When does a person become old? This question was asked as far back as the early sixteenth century.[5] Do we "age" for four to five decades (years 50 to 90+) of our life span? Was Picasso, who at ninety-plus, had more energy than most persons at mid life, aged? If we elect to retire at 47 or 52 are we then considered "aged?" American Association of Retired Persons (AARP) begins membership mailings to persons turning 50. Or do we become aged when we are eligible to collect social security?[6]

If we explain aging as "moving from beginning to end of life," then a person begins to age from birth onward.[7] How far must we go in life to be considered "aged"? In a survey of 1700 "elderly" one of six considered themselves old between 54 and 69, while one in three selected ages 70-79 and 40% claimed 80 plus was old. One of seven never considered themselves to be old.[8] For most of us there was a time when anybody over 30 was old, then "old" moved to 40, then 50, then 65, etc. Eighty-two year-old Florida Scott-Maxwell encapsulates this question we have all asked at different ages, "Am I old yet?"

"We wonder how much older we have to become, and what degree of decay we may have to endure. We keep whispering to ourselves, 'Is this age yet? How far must I go?' For age can be dreaded more than death . . . It is waiting for death that wears us down, and the distaste for what we may become."[9] "Aging," we tell ourselves, "is only a state of mind."

Thus, the terms aging, aged, old, older are relative, ambiguous, imprecise and based on many variables. In this paper "aging" will refer to the passage of chronological time with accompanying responses in the life of a person regardless of number of years accrued. "Aged" will follow its most common usage as defining those considered at the higher end of the scale in number of years lived regardless of physical or mental condition. That scale will vary in different contexts from a three phase span to a five stage category. In any case, "aged" refers to the last phase of the total span of life.[10]

Harris, along with many ecclesiastical and scientific bodies today, breaks down the last stage into three phases: the young old (65-74), the middle old (75-84) and the older old (85 onward). He also culls some "constants" that cut across the divisions–common factors that create a basis for understanding the "aged" as described in biblical and Near Eastern cultures. These "constants" identifying "old age" are the mention of "white hair" (wool), and the usage of the word, "elder" (the Hebrew cognate connects this period with that of the stage when a male would grow a beard). The word used as "elder" also became common to identify "leadership or head of family." These two aspects help to distinguish (in biblical literature) this season of life. Other descriptive signs of having reached this stage were centered on having passed the age for producing children, change in ability to handle responsibility of work and the experiencing of failing health due to number of years.[11]

A definition of aging is integrated with how that process is viewed. For example: if aging is GROWING, how is growth impacted by different years or seasons? If we define aging as COMING OF AGE, then privilege and duty help to identify what we are saying. Should we see aging as MATURING, we tend to view the process as moving toward becoming "ripe." Of course there follows the consecutive phases of "over-ripe" and "rotting," which leaves our perspective in disarray and brings us back to the "throw-away" image. If aging is explained as GETTING ON IN YEARS, we may view this time period as being one of wisdom valued over physical activity.[12] So what are common Views of Aging with arrival at the stage of Being Aged?

VIEW AND VALUE OF AGE

Valuations of the aging process run the gamut. Famous are Browning's romanticized lines from "Rabbi ben Ezra," "Grow old along with me, the best is yet to be, the last of life for which the first was made." Others would identify more with the question a nursing home resident put to his rabbi, "Rabbi, Why does the Torah state a curse as the reward for fulfilling a Mitzvah?. . . . Why does God punish those who keep His commandments by promising to make them old?"[13] Birthday greeting cards lean toward the latter accenting the limitations that accompanying the aging process. From a study of persons 18-64 Lou Harris came up with the following stereotype of persons over 65: ". . . the portrait of senior citizens drawn by younger people is that of unalert, physically inert, narrow-minded, ineffective, sexually finished old people deteriorating in poor health and suffering the miseries of loneliness."[14]

The most common perception in vogue is that life has a peak, flanked by an ascending and declining slope on each side, a Bell curve rising and falling after reaching an apex. Whether aging is viewed as the "play, work, play" linear model, the commercial "consumer, producer, consumer" economic version or the crawling baby rising to become an erect, walking adult who goes on to become the stooped, shuffling and finally stationary elderly.[15] What creates these images?

Loss

Most individuals are aware of the losses that come with aging and these are viewed as overwhelmingly negative. Chief among those loses is a loss of *personal dignity*. Who hasn't winced at the word that bifocals are now needed if one wants to continue to see clearly. A popular president resisted the wearing of a hearing aid in his ear because he felt it demeaned his image. The indignity of not being able to remember is laughed off as a "senior moment" but chalked up to a growing list of fears which include being seen as not being able to keep up or moving toward the first stages of Alzheimer's disease. The loss of *remunerative work* feeds into this loss of dignity. With it goes not only a tightening of the financial belt but often the loss of a framework for reality testing and of structures of time, space and conversational content. Having to be "at work" at a particular time, being able to talk about one's work gives a sense of order and importance. Loss of *independence*, the quintessential mark of being American, making your own decisions, handling your own affairs, not needing to depend on another–is an undermining of our confidence. "Becoming dependent on gadgets and aids, pills and rest periods, memory props, and special transportation arrangements, we feel we are losing our independence and do not like it."[16] Finally, a sense of loss of *time left*–the future is no longer endless–causes agitation, drivenness, worry and hurry. Mid-life crisis, facing the fact that youth is gone forever, creates fears and desperate actions to prove worth and assure satisfactions. With any loss comes a feeling of unlovability–with decline in assessed worth comes a lessening of *desirability* and the accompanying feeling that we have less to give in loving others.[17]

And "age" is the thief that is robbing us blind without our being able to apprehend and restrain the pillaging. Perceiving aging as "loss" turns hoped for dreams into spoilage. How could a Creator who is good engineer this "rape" of His creation?

But not everyone looks at aging with the aforementioned lens. Well known author Pearl S. Buck articulates a different view shared by many aging persons: "Would I wish to be 'young' again? No, for I have learned too much to wish to lose it. It will be like failing to pass a grade in school. I have reached an honorable position in life because I am old and no longer young. I am a far more valuable person today that I was 50 years ago, or 40 years ago, or 30, 10, or even 10. I HAVE LEARNED SO MUCH SINCE I WAS 70 . . . This, I suppose, is because I have perfected my techniques, so that I no longer waste time in learning how to do what I have to do."[18,19] Some view aging through the lens of gain.

Realized Gains

What compensations structure this view that even causes some to describe their later years the happiest?

- There is the pleasure of increasing *discovery of some good and healthy adult dependencies.* The "empty nest" can become a time of rediscovering how much one needs and enjoys his/her spouse or enjoys the family they took for granted. As retirement looms ahead one can realize how much work is enjoyed.
- Satisfaction is found in *redefining one's status*–often in terms of personal satisfactions–choosing to do what she really likes to do or starting a new venture or assuming more responsibility in shaping her own role. There is new identity formation growing out of integration.
- *Relaxation of fears and defenses.* There may come more openness to face realities without fear of being overwhelmed. Protective stances and hyper vigilance can become less. "Learn how to pick your battles" rather than becoming upset over every infraction is a plus. Greater openness to talking to strangers or to sharing emotions with greater congruence evidence this relaxation.
- Choosing or creating *work that gives personal satisfaction* and creates a feeling of personal worth is part of the freedom and the new lease on life.
- *Living in the present* becomes an asset rather than driving toward an expected and worrisome future that depends on them. In the framework of spirituality, writes de Caussade, it is a focus on seeing "the sanctity of the present moment."
- For persons of faith, there is an abandonment to *living out of the reality of the faith* they claimed to profess all their lives.
- Aging can promote new *freedom for revealing innermost thoughts.* There is a new candor, lessening of fear about what another will think, greater courage to communicate heart as well as reason.

Each of these gains that bring the person more in sync with who he/she really is or gives the person opportunity to develop newness in line with interior desires frees up energy and positive feelings about themselves and their living.[20] Popular writer Gail Sheehee identifies this phenomenon as The Age of Integrity, where the person is released to be who he/she really is, after spending years of conforming to others' expectations and agendas as he/she sought acceptance and identity.[21]

Cultural View

One of the strongest influencers of our views of aging is cultural factors. Certain societies condition their members to live by their traditional views. The Greeks prized both youth and old age while discounting mid life.[22] Other cultures elevate the elderly and ancestors to highest honor.

What is communicated through scripture as a Jewish view of aging? Walter Brueggemann offers a cautioning word in this regard, "It is not always easy to distinguish what is theologically intentional in the Bible and what is sociologically taken for granted. At some points the Bible is surely intentional in its theological concern about the elderly, as in the fifth commandment of the decalogue. But at many other points, the Bible appropriates and practices what is common in ancient Near Eastern culture, and it likely does so without great intentionality or reflectiveness."[23]

Even a cursory reading of the first book reveals that the Old Testament is careful to record the number when it came to the years of the primeval Methuselahs. Skagg summarizes, "Genesis is very age conscious, with special attention to a man's age at the time of his marriage, his fathering of his first son, and his death. Longevity is clearly viewed as positive, if not actually normal."[24] To this Clements comments, in view of such numbers being mythological, "More important is the view of the biblical genealogists . . . for whom these numbers meant human life in its fullness, specifically symbolized by an enormously high age. . . . These heroes finally died, but more important than that, the texts emphasize how long they had lived."[25] (Note: Rachel Dulin comments that the phrase "that you may fare well and have a long life" found in Deuteronomy was not reward for a person's action but a logical consequence of conservation. A wish for "length of days" became a hope of long and good life, living on the land God had given.[26])

Care for the aged was endemic to the Jewish community. The required solidarity of the family supported this goal as each member of the community took responsibility to protect, resource, and look out for each other, especially honoring those who were "elders." It was they who were the custodians of tradition, interpreting and handing it down to succeeding generations.[27]

In particular there was intensive emphasis on caring for and showing respect toward parents (whose years were naturally greater than one's own). This is spelled out in numerous warnings for mistreatment (e.g., Exodus 21:15; Deut. 27:16; Prov. 19:26; Prov. 30:17 addressed to adults in their treatment of old parents).[28] To dishonor a parent was considered a capital offense (Deut. 21:18-21).

The inclusion the positive admonition as one of the ten requirements highlighted in the Decalogue adds clout to this concern in Israel's history. Rabbi Blech makes interesting distinction between Exodus 20:12 which utilizes *kabed* for "honor" and the same command in Leviticus which is translated "You shall revere every man his mother and his father." The latter employs *tira-u* instead of *kabed*. He explains that the former requires a person to provide for the physical needs of parents while the latter term requires the child "not to stand or sit in their place nor to contradict them." These two fall under our present day headings of "Social Security" and "Personal Security." Jewish law gives priority to the latter.[29] Interestingly Jesus treats harshly the conduct of adult Pharisees in their use of "corban" when it came to responsibility for parents.

Older men appear as valued counselors and advisors to those in authority (I Kings 12:6-11) and were given significant role as elders in the city gates (Ruth 4:1-12). They were those handing on the legacy of blessing, possessions, and the heritage of tradition to those of the next generation. (e.g., Gen. 47:29-49:33).[30] (Note: Just being "old in years" was to promote some respect but the Israelites used different adjectives for the "aged, decrepit" (yasis in 2 Chron. 36:17) and "aged, venerable" (yasis in Job 12:12; 15:10, etc.).[31]

Speaking of New Testament perspectives, Harris comments, "Aging in the Christian community did not necessarily bring a loss of status or responsibility. In some way responsibilities increased as physical stamina decreased. Older members were challenged to live exemplary lives for the younger members to imitate. Christian letters . . . deal . . . with overcoming social problems associated with growing old. These epistles commanded all generations to care for one another and to accept reciprocal responsibilities toward each other."[32] Family responsibilities are balanced with an emphasis on mutual care and support. . . .The Johannine materials reaffirmed the dignity of old age and elevated elders by promoting respect for them and praising their leadership."[33]

How did Israel's view of accumulating years compare with other social systems? What is unique to her common theology:

- Compared to data found in other literature the biblical texts exhibit greater fervor for this concern.
- Contrary to surrounding societies biblical commands and teachings affirm equity in treatment of both father and mother rather than favoring harsher treatment of one over the other. Both merit equal respect.
- Intergenerational concerns in Israel's laws are connected with their response to God. Again Harris states, "Biblical passages equate support for

the rings of Israel's society with loyalty to the God of Israel and the concern for a separated religious community. The Holiness Code directly suggests that respect for the elderly arises out of concerns rooted in the nature of God. Wisdom literature in its more theological instruction associates fear of God with listening to parental teaching." Note Lev. 19:32: "You shall rise up before the gray head, and honor the face of an old person and you shall fear your God; I am the Lord."

Thus concern for welfare of the aging and equal treatment of both male and female reflects God's commitment to justice and his salvation of the powerless in the Exodus. Commitment to both God and parents mirrors a central principle of our faith and a basis for God's response to his people.[34] And this reflection on our views of the connection between God's character and his rules for how we are to act toward one another propels us toward the realization of theological axioms that shape our view of aging. It offers to us in our present cultural melee the uniqueness that comes from responding to Romans 12:2 in regard to this subject: "Don't let the world around you squeeze you into its mold–BUT LET GOD TRANSFORM YOUR PERSPECTIVE from your heart. . . ."[35]

Toward a Theology of Aging

Probably most persons in the Old Testament or even the new never considered asking the question, "Why do we age?" The phenomenon was simply taken for granted. Today, however, with increasingly successful attempts to prolong life and to counteract diseases that often cut short the life span we face issues (mid-life crisis, empty nest syndrome, Medicare and euthanasia ethical issues) never imagined by our predecessors and must take into account the increasing significance of aging in our lifetime experience. While a passage of scripture must take into account the author's primary intent and the textual context, it may be required to shed light on addressing new issues arising out of current attitudes and circumstances of aging. The other side is that a theology of aging "recognizes in aging potential contributions to theological understanding."[36]

While taking into account all that the experience of humanity that science and reasoning can supply, theology itself "can be described as systematic reflection on human life and experience in the light of faith."[37] Taking into serious consideration all that the Bible conveys, "Christian theology remains convinced . . . that the basic question of human existence itself, including the fundamental questions of human nature and destiny, are not matters of human discovery and control . . . The ultimate questions are answered only by a 'revelation,' which comes to us from outside our own 'existence.' "[38] It is most fitting, therefore, that the questions of aging such as "Who am I as an aging person?" "Why am I still here?" "What is purpose/value in my getting old or older?" should be addressed not only by gerontology, psychology, sociology, anthropology, etc., but most especially and ultimately by theology. Note: Interestingly it is probably the faith perspective, more than other disciplines, which will cause persons in society to respond differently to issues in bioethics.

It is foundational to accept that "aging is God's intentional plan for human existence." It goes with being created human. Genesis 1:28 calls upon our Garden predecessors to "be fruitful and multiply, and fill the earth and subdue it." Van Tatenhove, in writing on the evangelical view of aging, interprets the significance of this verse to imply "a sequence of conception, birth, and growth. Aging, then, is not to be viewed as another negative outcome of the fall. However, the fall does indeed influence the aging process."[39]

As Christians we must be interested in the whole life span development with fulfillment at each level. As beings who seek to make meaning of our lives and our faith we apply our "meaning making" to the purpose of each age span. And then as ministers in the name of Jesus to others, how can we nurture meaning in the lives of others? How can we help persons to be able to say "yes" to both death and life? How can we nurture meaning in the face of significant losses as we age? How can we enable others to think and live Christianly in their process of aging?[40]

THEOLOGICAL FRAMEWORKS

The two primary structures for examination are:

1. The nature and character of God as it impacts our view of aging.
2. The view and value of humans including being created in the image of God, and being granted eternal salvation by God.

Revisioning of aging requires that we also deal with a theological view of

1. the significance of life,
2. revaluing dependence,
3. the value of time and experience,
4. change and loss,
5. the condition of temporality,
6. acceptance of mortality (ours and others'), and
7. the purpose and place of work.

The Nature of God and Implications for Our View of Aging

This theological reflection will seek to shed light on two different dimensions. One is looking at aging per se in the light of our knowledge of God, making meaning by seeking to uncover a god-centered view of this universal occurrence. As Christians we are challenged to make theological meaning of aging and to ask the question: "Does our aging have meaning for God?"[41]

A second goal is to construct a god-shaped attitude toward the subjects of aging that is congruent with our being related to God as his children.

Transcending Change

While the nature of God encompasses many facets that affect a view of aging, only certain aspects will be mentioned here. The first is paradoxical, bringing a valuing to God because he is not affected by what affects us. Because he is "greater" our identification with him is richer, as in the comfort that comes with the sovereignty of God, where God the blessed controller of all things. So with immutability, the God who has decreed for us change and growth with accompanying loss, is himself changeless and this stability lends support to us in our fluctuation. "O Thou who changes not, abide with me," is the hymn writer's plea as one needing the sense of constancy and presence. While allowing the "fathers and mothers" to pass from this early scene, God is careful to identify himself with them as the one who continues–the "I AM!" not the "I WAS!" There is confidence in a God who personally knew, but also transcends, age spans now past. Exodus targets the juxtaposition of two cardinal realities–all die, "Then Joseph died, and all his brothers, and all that generation" (1:6) while identifying himself as "I am the God of Abraham, the God of Isaac, the God of Jacob" (3:6)–transcending generations. All die but God lives on.[42]

In the New Testament James affirms that he is the Father of lights, a deity who does not change. Hebrews in the context of "remembering leaders" who spoke (past) the word of God to us, reminds us that "Jesus Christ is the same, yesterday, today and forever" (12:7-8). Facing change while linked to a faithful unchanging God can help to bind our hearts and change our perspectives on the tentativeness and instability that accompanies our own aging process and cause us to focus on him. God loves us even when we doubt our own worth and feel we have little to give back. It is his nature to be blind to the negatives of wrinkles, gray hair and trembling limbs.

Sharing and Enhancing Change

While in one sense God is enhanced by being "changeless," it is also true that in the incarnation He unveiled "what it eternally means to be God and what it temporally means to be human." Ronal Crossley exclaims, "in Christ God ages with us and for us, and in Christ we age with God and for God." And "if God ages with us and for us, then our aging to old age has meaning for us. If we age with God and for God, then our aging has meaning for God." He argues that the assumption that God is unaffected by the passing and changing of time clouds the "gospel's authentic good news for aging." In Christ, God experienced the creaturely limitations of time, change, suffering and death. God was exposed to aging through the experience of Jesus.[43] Jurgen Moltmann reasons, "God is not *unchangeable*, if to be unchangeable means that he could not in the freedom of his love open himself to the changeable history of his creation."[44] Inherent in the character of God is suffering. "In the suffering of the Son, the pain of the Father finds a voice."[45] Thus God ages *with us* and *for us* for the purpose of our salvation. This allows us to "age with God" and reshapes the meaning of our aging. "If God in Christ shares our human aging, suffering, and death, then the very process of aging itself must also be radically reinterpreted. Whatever aging means, its meaning must be sought in relationship with God. If God uses the medium of time to shape us into God's image for God's purposes, then even in the face of the relentless erosion of aging, it must be celebrated as God's good gift of life. Aging can bring us to God."[46]

Loving Unconditionally

God's unconditional love is closely tied to this faithfulness. In spite of Israel's obstinacy and frequent disobedience God loves his people. In the midst of enumerating their lacks, God assures them, "I the Lord do not change" (Malachi 3:6). Israel's changing condition does not change God's nature. His unfailing love is not limited by the worthiness of the subject nor dependent on a response. The transient field flowers and the anonymous birds are objects of this care just because he intends it.[47] Persons are loved at any age because God's nature is unconditionally loving.

Agent of Blessing and Munificence

Harris feels that emphasizing God as not only deliverer, but also as divine blesser–the one who ordains growth and provides the elements for growth–suggests clear benefits of aging. "Divine blessing in its full significance provides all generations with the power and conditions to grow vertically: to move through

childhood, maturation, and physical decline in a state of being blessed. . . . This sense of security and continuity calms fears associated with the mystery and unknowns of aging."[48] In a similar vein Steven Sapp addresses our accent on rights in place of gracious gifts, quoting John Arras and Robert Hunt's observation, "Today we expect not only to be cured of ills that were previously incurable but also to be prevented from experiencing a variety of infirmities and misfortunes that were once the common lot of humankind. *And we feel wronged if these expectations go unfulfilled.*" He then urges a return to the biblical view, "a more conscious recognition of life itself as a gift from God might make a difference in some health-care decisions in the later stages of life."[49]

Protector of Social Structures

"Biblical traditions . . . teach that the structure of society finds its origins and continuity with the will of God . . . an ordered sense of living that affirms divine providence. God both establishes a system of relationships and asserts sovereignty over it." Such legitimization and preservation reveals God's care for and intentional support through systems of the aging. "The granting of honor to otherwise vulnerable parents and aging leaders depends on the preservation of order and respect. In this way, the Lord (Yahweh) and Israel are yoked together in a 'common theology' and walking toward common goals." God's order and enforcement of it among his people demonstrates his concern and support.[50]

Weakness, decreasing production and status frequently accompanied transitions in life spans toward old age. Recognizing these factors, "the God of Israel supported an elevated status for the elderly and reinforced their claims to sustenance and respect. God by nature sought to protect the vulnerable. God did this . . . by supporting order in society and by responding to violations of its contractual ideals in angry words and actions."[51]

Proponent of Justice

God's nature as revealed in scripture suggests his championing of the weak and disenfranchised who are oppressed and exploited by the powerful and oppressive. He is deliverer who exercises justice as persons diminish in personal power, status and strength. As aging is frequently accompanied by such weakening, the aging ones may increasingly depend on God's favoring and deliverance from attitudes of slavery and uselessness even as death is faced with confidence and hope.[52] Protection for Israel's aging comes from the center of God's nature and spills over into his expectations for Israel's treatment of the vulnerable person. It was integral to their relationship with God. Respect for this God of justice motivated a sense of responsibility for the elderly. Leviticus 19:32 makes this connection. "You shall rise up before the white head, and honor the face of an old man, and (note the attachment) you will fear your God. I am the Lord."[53] Aging when seen through the nature of God has a worth often missing from our cultural perspective.

Biblical Perspectives on Human Beings That Shape Our Response to Aging Made in the Image

Creation unveils a basis for positively viewing aging. According to rabbinical teachings "an elder and child equally reflect the divine image with all its potential for growth in accordance with the extravagance of God's love."[54] The Encyclopedia Judaica quotes Rabbi Akiva as teaching, "Beloved is a person who was created in the image (Of God). (Still greater was the love in that it was made known directly that such was made in the image.) As it is said: 'In the divine image, God made humanity' " (Avoth 3:19).[55] This "imaging" does not diminish because of age. It remains constant through all spans of life and may be enhanced and increasingly unveiled by the experiences of different seasons of life.

Made to Age

Aging is neither an oddity nor a punishment. It is God's intentional plan for us as human beings. As mentioned earlier it is not the result of the fall. God determined that change and growth would be part of our existence. While life is enhanced by coming to know Christ as redeemer, the relentless process of aging and moving toward death is not changed. Our perspective toward it, however, can be radically changed by this relationship that offers Life that goes on after "aging" ceases. This is the Christian's hope–that a body once marked by the aging process and felled by the power of death–will be resurrected to new life which is ageless without the limiting factors of this one. The old order will have passed away (Revelation 21:4).

Respect for Aging Commanded by and Connected to God

In personally decreeing that parents be honored, God places value on the honor due those who accrue years of life. As the first commandment guarantees the supreme importance and role of God, the inclusion of the fifth commandment with its promised benefit indicates the prime importance of reverence in relationship between persons. The expansion of this command to treat as significant aging parents is found in Deuteronomy (5:16) and clearly states that this command issues directly from God and demonstrates his intense concern as well as close personal relationship between him and the older generation. This command along with that which decrees reverence for the Sabbath were elevated as central to Israel's credo. In Israel's Holiness Code this reverence for aging reaches its apex as the honoring of parents is equated with worship and awe as spelled out in Leviticus 19:3. "Each of you should fear (tiyra'u) mother and father and my Sabbaths you must keep. I am the Lord your God." "The term used for fear normally refers to worship of God or a sense of awe at the divine power and majesty . . . here the passage instructs children to feel awe for the most vulnerable parent first. . . . " "The verse teaches anew the theological importance of respect for parents. It places the command prior to Sabbath keeping in order and seals the passage with a divine disclosure formula. The terminology equates feels for parents with those normally expressed to God . . . (and) becomes the primary sign of a holy people."[56]

Fullness of Life at Every Life Stage Is Possible and God Enabled

Experiencing fullness of life at every stage of the aging process is a state portrayed in the teachings of Jesus without regard to age. Quality of life is found in our relationship to Him, not in life conditions. Abundance of living comes from desiring this quality of life with him that shapes inner character and causes us to reflect our being as the people of God whatever the life stage we are in. This relationship influences our perspective of aging and the aged more than any other factor as we live out in continually changing circumstances our formation in his likeness. It lends worth and sanctity to life whatever the age. "Aging does not diminish the gift of God's redemptive grace given to those who 'hunger and thirst for righteousness' (Matt. 5:6). When this truth is central, a biblical understanding of aging is possible."[57] Abundant living as Jesus revealed it is not limited by chronology or physical conditions. Believing what Jesus declares to be true is God's gift of quality of living. God views life through this lens only. "Let not the wise man boast of his wisdom or the strong man boast of his strength or the rich man boast of his riches, but let him who boasts boast about this: that he understands and knows me, that I am the Lord. . . . " (Jeremiah 9:23-24).

Salvation's Enhancement of Ageless Personhood

Awareness of the significance of God's salvific act brings to personhood irrespective of age, a sense of meaning and value as nothing else could. Add to this the value increasing realization of being called of God to be witness to the reality of this salvation in life and ministry, again without age limitation.

Browning notes, "participation of early Christians, both individually and corporately, in God's saving and redeeming work gave them a sense that their own finite efforts were caught up in the activity of God and therefore had an objective significance to them that would transcend their own suffering and eventual death."[58] To this Whitehead observes, "Through subsequent centuries this understanding of one's own life and actions as participating in God's saving plan for humankind has provided for many believing Christians a sense of ultimate personal significance. . . . Browning suggests that it might be possible to retrieve this religious image of individual significance as a means of confronting the contemporary crisis of meaning in old age. One's own limited and often apparently fruitless efforts gain potency when understood as part of God's plan for the world."[59] Thus our life experiences become valuable and enduring in the continuing life of God.

Acceptance of aging as being "of God" means looking at it as a purposeful part of God's created order and seeing persons as valuable at any age. Aging comes from a just and loving God who stands outside its boundaries but chose to place humankind under its jurisdiction, not even changing the progress of this earthly condition through salvation. However, the worth of this salvation in changing our whole outlook on this life and the next can never be overstated. Realigned with a biblical view, aging emerges from its Darth Vader image and is realized as a Creator endowed condition for our terrestrial journey toward home.

NOTES

1. J. Gordon Harris, *Biblical Perspectives on Aging,* (Philadelphia: Fortress Press, 1987).

2. Henri Nouwen and Walter J. Gaffney, *Aging,* (Garden City, NY: Doubleday & Company, Inc., 1974) 6.

3. In 1975, writing in *Pastoral Psychology,* Seward Hiltner, Professor of Theology and Personality at Princeton wrote, "I have become even more convinced in recent years that the tendency to deny, evade, or otherwise fail to take seriously the confrontation of the aging process . . . is either first or second on the list of 'repressed' but vital concerns in our present culture. Now that sexual matters can be discussed and studied seriously, and even more recently death and dying have at least begun to be confronted, the avoiding of aging becomes both more evident and more lamentable."

4. Robert L. Katz, "Jewish Values and Sociopsychological Perspectives on Aging," in Seward Hiltner, *Toward A Theology of Aging,* (New York: Human Sciences Press, 1975) 135-150.

5. Knapp in Carol LeFevre and Perry LeFevre, *Aging And The Human Spirit,* second edition (Chicago: Exploration Press, 1985) 12.

6. Katz.

7. Donald Browning, "Preface to a Practical Theology of Aging," in Hiltner, 154.

8. LeFevre, 12.

9. Nouwen.

10. William M. Clements, *Ministry With the Aging*, (San Francisco: Harper & Row, Pub. 1981).

11. Harris, 11-16.

12. Paul W. Pruyser, "Aging: Downward, Upward, or Forward?" in Hiltner, 104-105.

13. LeFevre, 4.

14. Harris in LeFevre, 117.

15. Pruyser in Hiltner, 103.

16. Ibid., 109-110.

17. Ibid., 107-111.

18. Quoted by D. F. Clingan, *Aging Persons in the Community of Faith* (Institute on Religion and Aging, 1980).

19. Rachel Zohar Dulin, *A Crown of Glory: A Biblical View Of Aging.* (New York: Paulist Press, 1988), 3.

20. Pruyser in Hiltner, 112-117.

21. Gail Sheehee, *New Passages: Mapping Your Life Across Time*, (New York: Ballantine Books, 1995).

22. Hiltner, 104.

23. Harris, x.

24. Frank Stagg, *The Bible Speaks on Aging*, (Nashville: Broadman Press, 1981), 9.

25. Clements, 23.

26. Dulin, 16.

27. Katz, 137.

28. Clements, 28.

29. Blech in LeFevre, 9.

30. Clements, 31.

31. Clements, 25.

32. Harris, 95.

33. Ibid., 96.

34. Ibid., 32, 57-58.

35. Note: For a brief but helpful summary of the attitudes toward aging and the aged in Near Eastern cultures of Old Testament times. Interestingly in light of present day conditions, he claims the breakdown in carrying out known legal codes of ethics in this area of community is attributed to hunger for power, bureaucracies, and urbanization.

36. Harris

37. Curran in LeFevre, 68.

38. Clements, 77.

39. Melvin A. Kimble, Susan H. McFadden, James W. Ellor, and James J. Seeber, eds., *Aging, Spirituality, and Religion: A Handbook*, Minneapolis: Augsburg Fortress Press, 1995), 418.

40. LeFevre, 46-47.

41. Ronald C. Crossley, "Aging With God: Old Age and New Theology" in *Church and Society*, Vol. 89, January/February 1999.

42. Stagg, 19.

43. Crossley, 11-12.

44. Jurgen Moltmann, *The Crucified God*, (Minneapolis: Fortress Press, 1993) 190. Also quoted in Crossley, 12.

45. Jurgen Moltmann, *The Way of Jesus Christ*, (Minneapolis: Fortress Press, 1993), 176.

46. Crossley, 13.

47. LeFevre, 59.

48. Harris, 3-4.

49. Stephen Sapp, *Light On A Gray Area*, (Nashville: Abingdon Press, 1992), 146-147.

50. Harris, 5.

51. Ibid., 16.

52. Ibid.

53. Harris, 60.

54. Ibid., 99.

55. Ibid.

56. Ibid., 61-64.

57. Fred Van Tatenhove, "Evangelical Perspectives," in Kimble, 420-422.

58. Hiltner, 162.

59. Whitehead in LeFevre, 61.

Chapter 8

"Always Green and Full of Sap": Facilitating Wholeness in Aging

Pamela S. Harris, MD
Karen Lampe, MA, MDiv
Brian Chaffin, MDiv

SUMMARY. Wholeness in aging is difficult to define, especially in the face of physical disability or catastrophic illness. How one meets the challenges of aging depends upon numerous physical, emotional, and spiritual factors. Rehabilitation may play an important role in restoring wholeness to those with physical disabilities. Likewise, a physical fitness program may lessen some of the effects of aging, helping the older person maintain a higher quality of life. The lived theologies of the older patients and their caregivers also interact, providing an important ground

Dr. Harris is Chief of Rehabilitation Medicine at the Veterans Administration Hospital, Kansas City, MO. She is completing a Master of Divinity degree at Saint Paul School of Theology and serves on the Pastoral staff of The Church of the Resurrection, Leadwood, KS. Karen Lampe is an active participant in local churches and the Kansas East Conference of the United Methodist Church, trained as a Rehabilitation therapist, and a Graduate of Saint Paul School of Theology. Brian Chaffin is a Pastor in Joplin, MO. He is a member of the Missouri Conference of the United Methodist Church. Brian is a graduate of Saint Paul School of Theology, Kansas City, Missouri, where he took an emphasis in gerontology.

[Haworth co-indexing entry note]: "Always Green and Full of Sap: Facilitating Wholeness in Aging." Harris, Pamela S., Karen Lampe, and Brian Chaffin. Co-published simultaneously in *Journal of Religious Gerontology* (The Haworth Pastoral Press, an imprint of The Haworth Press, Inc.) Vol. 15, No. 1/2, 2003, pp. 107-125; and: *Practical Theology for Aging* (ed: Derrel R. Watkins) The Haworth Pastoral Press, an imprint of The Haworth Press, Inc., 2003, pp. 107-125. Single or multiple copies of this article are available for a fee from The Haworth Document Delivery Service [1-800-HAWORTH, 9:00 a.m. - 5:00 p.m. (EST). E-mail address: docdelivery@haworthpress.com].

Digital Object Identifier: 10.1300/J078v15n01_09   *107* of connection in rediscovery of wholeness as well. Ultimately, our most important role as healthcare providers is to help our older patients regain and maintain this multidimensional wholeness even in times of physical challenge. *[Article copies available for a fee from The Haworth Document Delivery Service: 1-800-HAWORTH. E-mail address: <docdelivery@haworthpress.com> Website: <http://www.HaworthPress.com> © 2003 by The Haworth Press, Inc. All rights reserved.]*

KEYWORDS. Rehabilitation, normative standards, deprivation, disability, despair, wholeness, medicine as ministry, empowerment, teamwork, decision making, access, compassion, rediscovery, aerobic activity, strength training, journey, pressing, finishing

In old age they still produce fruit; they are always green and full of sap, . . .

Psalm 92:14 (NRSV)

A JOURNEY TO WHOLENESS

The psalmist's description of the righteous elder flourishing may ring strangely hollow to many elders today. Likewise, defining "successful aging" in our culture is much like trying to grasp quicksilver–it always seems to evade us. While some elders seem to remain vigorous and "young" according to the normative standards, other elders seem to face only loss and deprivation, progressive disability and despair. Aging adults may be faced with many obstacles that hinder their journey to wholeness. When the obstacle of failing physical health hinders once productive lives, either through catastrophe or the cycle of life, many are left wondering why. What good can come of the pain and suffering they are enduring? They wonder what will happen to them when they can no longer participate in society, in the community and in the church. The failing of one's health raises questions about self worth. Of great concern for many is the ever invading thought that they have lost the meaningfulness and usefulness they once had, with resultant loss of their sense of wholeness. No longer do the elders feel that they have value, rather they struggle to find their worth. They are searching for wholeness in ever changing lives. Can we truly say, therefore, that wholeness is possible in aging? Can one be whole in the face of disability or physical limitations? Our modern society looks at wholeness as completion, fullness, health, and soundness. But is such the only way to approach our life's journey, pronouncing ourselves whole only if we can attain such an unattainable standard and simultaneously guard it from the decay of time? If so, none of us should ever be whole. Perhaps, however, wholeness is more.

Wholeness is a " . . . blend of spiritual, physical, mental, emotional, and social dimensions of human growth and development."[1] For many, the dimensions of wholeness dissipate when they experience physical deficits they perceive to be the final obstacles in their lives. However, physical deficits do not have to be the determining factor in how one lives the remainder of a life. In nature, the flower must pass from the pinnacle of beauty to the next natural process of aging in order to produce seed for the future. Physical changes may thus be viewed as a change in direction in our journey to obtaining wholeness. As aging adults encounter life in a new way, it is imperative that those providing professional care, either in the physical fitness/wellness field or in the rehabilitation process, be in tune with what aging adults are experiencing. Aging adults either accept challenge as a way to start anew and redirect their gifts and talents or, on the other end of the spectrum, challenge overtakes the spiritual, physical, mental, and social dimensions of their lives and destroys wholeness in the older years.

In the journey to wholeness, people who experience physical catastrophes must rely on medical professionals to regain some sense of the physical abilities they once had. But, as the following case studies show, it requires more than physical fitness, prescription medicines, specialized surgeries, and physical rehabilitation to regain wholeness after a life-shattering experience. It requires a combination of professionalism from health care providers and determination on the part of the patient. With medical advances and wonderful post-operative rehabilitation, miraculous healing occurs. But to regain meaning and usefulness after disabling illness or injury, one's lived theology and faith become critical factors. God will not abandon us in times of trouble, but such a promise is most comforting if one is in dynamic relationship with God before tragedy strikes.

Yea, Though I Walk in the Valley of the Shadow of Death–Case Studies

Case Study 1: May 10, 1999 is a day that will never be forgotten by John and his family. On that fateful day, John was trimming a tree on his property where he had, just two years prior, built a retirement home. After nearly thirty years of being an ordained pastor in the United Methodist Church, John took early retirement to spend quality time with his wife of forty-two years, Lillian. He was retired, yet he still served two loving churches. His life had been filled with so many blessings, it seemed as though nothing could disturb the ideal lifestyle he and his wife enjoyed. They were able to visit their children and grandchildren. They would go to antique malls and bluegrass festivals or take short trips. Never did anyone think that something could happen in a split second that would change John's life forever.

One thing John always did, when any of the children drove away, was stand by the car, give each a hug, and remain there waving until they were out of sight. On May 9, 1999, the family gathered at the house to celebrate Mother's Day. As each left, John was outside, hugging and waving. The last son to leave, as he drove away, remembered looking in the rearview mirror, thinking what a loving and caring man his father was. Little did he know, that could have been the last time John said goodbye in a way that only he could. What happened the next day could have been the conclusion to what was a whole life. Yet, as he stood waving, John's blend of "spiritual, physical, mental, emotional, and social dimensions of human growth and development" were fulfilling, and he certainly felt as though his life had meaning and usefulness.

On May 10, John decided to trim a tree on the property. Trimming trees was not a big task for him, for he had always engaged in physical work, even while he served as a pastor. As he always had, he set the extension ladder in a very secure location and proceeded up to the large limb. Everything was going fine as he cut the stragglers away and then started on the large limb. The cut was perfect. When the limb hit the ground, however, it sprang upward, hitting John in the chest and knocking him away from the ladder. As he was falling the twenty feet, he threw the chainsaw and tried to grab the ladder, but the force of the limb had pushed him about six feet from the ladder. All he could do was helplessly watch it go by. When he hit the ground, John landed stiff-legged on surface roots of the tree. Upon impact, his body crippled under the massive shock.

John knew that he was seriously injured so he did not move. Lillian came to his side, saw that he was breathing and called for an ambulance. The damage was serious: John's left tibia and fibula were shattered, with a compound fracture of the left ankle and a crushed left heel. The right tibia and fibula were also shattered, and the tibial plateau was crushed as well. The bones were, as one of the orthopedic surgeons said, like crumpled foam. But the most serious injury was to John's back. The fourth lumbar vertebra was fractured and one-third of the spinal cord was compressed. John endured a thirteen-hour surgery in which the neurosurgeon created a metal cage around the spine, using plates to fuse the third, fourth, and fifth vertebrae. Fixators were fastened to both his legs to help in the reformation of bone. His hospital stay was seventeen grueling and painful weeks. On August 13, he was able finally to go home in a wheelchair, with the possibility of never walking without assistance. It was a far cry from the day he stood waving goodbye to his children.

As John and his son discussed all John had been through, issues of how to maintain wholeness despite such catastrophe arose, which they share so others facing obstacles can have hope that wholeness can be rediscovered. This man's entire life had turned upside down in seconds. No longer could he stand and work in his wood shop, no longer was he mobile enough to actively minister to his congregations, no longer was he able to enjoy his early retirement, and no longer could he participate in society, community, and church as he once did. At that moment in his life, he could have taken the attitude that he was useless and meaningless, but he did not. Rather, he trusted in God, held to his faith, and welcomed the love of his family and friends to get him through. But of all that influenced his healing, there was one point that stood out in the interview for this article. He said, "I never thought about not getting back!" What a powerful message for people who are feeling as though there is no hope to rediscover their wholeness.

As John continued with care at home for many months, all the doctors, nurses, and therapists were amazed at the progress he made in such a short time. He commented how his physical therapist inspired him to strive to improve. His caregivers took a vested interest in him as a person; he could feel the genuine love they had for him and the hope they had for his recovery. Health care providers with a positive attitude and the ability to praise the patients have an amazing effect on patients. As John said, "It's the little things that mean a lot." When John took his first step in the hospital, with the fixators still in place, the whole group of nurses and therapists gave him a standing ovation. He knew they truly cared. This should be a lesson to all who participate in the healthcare field: Love the patients as you would want to be loved.

When asked about his faith throughout the entire ordeal, John was very sure of his answers. He never questioned or blamed God, nor was he afraid of dying. Of course, he was concerned about the quality of life he would have. In fact, he was determined not to be a burden to anyone, especially his wife and family. He didn't "want to be a problem" for Lillian, so he did what was needed to heal. John never once asked God, "Why did You do this to me?" He knew what happened–a tree branch knocked him off the ladder. "I fell out of the tree. God didn't do it." Accidents and illnesses happen in life. When they do, how one perceives the experience may determine whether one recovers or not. Yet if one experiences initial wholeness, one can better deal with catastrophes when they occur.

After months of rehabilitation, numerous surgeries, and thousands of prayers, John is once again able to stand by the car, give hugs to each of his children and grandchildren, and wave goodbye while they drive away. He is not a man who is useless or meaningless. John is a man who is whole, a man who conquered the agony of the catastrophe that could have taken his life. He can walk without assistance, and although he is much weaker, he is back. "I never thought about not getting back!" John believed it, lived it, and has been able to inspire more people to do the same through sharing his story. When asked what the secret was to his rediscovery, John said, "Faith in God, maintaining health, and truly gifted and caring doctors, therapists, and nurses."

John had always stayed active throughout his ministry. The surgeon told him that he had the body of a forty-year-old, not a sixty-four-year-old. This, he said, probably saved his life. Therefore, to combat future physical obstacles, a physical fitness and wellness plan may be essential for maintaining the wholeness of life, as we shall review in subsequent sections.

Case Study 2: Compare the first case with that of another patient, also named John. The second John had been receiving therapy following a motor vehicle accident that had resulted in back and neck pain, stooped posture, poor balance, and a shuffling gait pattern. For several sessions, efforts were concentrated on resolving his physical pain. During the treatment sessions, however, John relived the accident through conversations, which revealed that he had been the driver in the accident that had resulted in his wife's long-term hospitalization and eventual death. John resented that his son had subsequently "taken the car away from me." He finally confessed to his incredible pain–not physical–but mental and spiritual. John's greatest challenge was forgiving himself, and he frequently woke at night bearing his guilt. He felt powerless to help himself.

Case Study 3: Although this particular case is about Mary, the scenario is so often repeated that the woman could have any name. Mary came to therapy because of low back pain. The first treatment session revealed that her husband had recently died. After twelve treatments, Mary's back pain resolved, but more importantly, the treatments had given her a chance to remember and retell the stories of a wedded life now ended. What had been aching was not necessarily her low back. Rehabilitation can be about restoring not only the back, but also the heart.

Case Study 4: Ethel had suffered a stroke. Her right side was severely weakened and her speech was slurred. This vital woman of seventy-eight, who loved to play bridge, entertain her grandchildren, and go for long walks, stated that she "might as well be dead." The middle-aged doctor came into her room, where she sat in her wheelchair, and he knelt beside her chair. He held her hand and listened to her garbled frustrations without offering comment, only offering eye contact that assured her of his willingness to help her bear the pain. He offered her a drink of water and a tissue, while telling her about the hope and work of rehabilitation. All this was done in a way that offered power for her recovery. His very posture did not presume dominance. He allowed her to talk, for he understood that his first job was to listen. This approach is the beginning of empowerment wherein life and hope can be restored.

MEDICINE AS MINISTRY–ROAD WORK ON THE JOURNEY

With passing years of practice, health care providers find their therapeutic techniques and communication skills challenged and fine-tuned multiple times. Most certainly, many find themselves strongly influenced by maturing Judeo-Christian belief in servanthood for the marginalized, often suffering, aging community. Restoring and healing is no longer the mechanical obligatory task of our youth, but rather a loving, dedicated affirmation of care for older adults and their families.

Rehabilitation occurs as wholeness to the individual is restored. The word "wholeness" is key for it comprises not only the mental, spiritual, and physical aspects of the patient, but also the community surrounding the individual, including family, friends, and even the medical care providers. The last group mentioned may be of surprise to some, but the wholeness of the provider is the wellspring that keeps the process of restoring and renewing effervescent within the rehabilitation process. If the caregivers provide energy, hope, power, and love to the situation, the results can be life giving. For each of these subjects, volumes could be written. However, the focus of this discussion will be on the directing of power, both to the patient and the family, as well as to specific members of the medical team when appropriate. It is within this power dynamic that a caregiver's theology comes to the forefront and can provide direction for the drama in which the characters find themselves.

Why would power be so important in the rehabilitation scenario? If power is understood as the " . . . ability to accomplish desired ends . . . "[2] and authority as power that is " . . . legitimated by the structures of society . . . ,"[3] then most aging patients will find themselves more and more powerless. They have experienced the trauma of insurance battles, over-priced prescription drugs, consequences of modern technology, non-participative decision-making,[4] loss of spouse/peers, loss of control of bodily functions, and loss of possessions, profession, and home. They have experienced this in the context of an American culture that promotes authority to dominate the weak, poor, aged person (who is, eighty percent of the time, female).[5] Additionally, the aging patient carries a fear of the unknown that can rob the elder of any shred of power that might be left. All these phenomena "strip" the elder patient, leaving the elder vulnerable to whoever crosses the threshold.[6] It is to this marginalized individual that the servant caregiver can restore power, by setting up a new paradigm of authority that works to "enrich, rather than outrank, one another."[7]

A similar method of patient/health care provider relationship was proposed in 1956 by Drs. Thomas Szasz and Marc Hollender, who assigned the language of "mutual participation" to their model.[8] Their thesis emphasized "a high degree of empathy" whereby "the satisfaction of physician and patient complement each other."[9] This model has particular advantages for a geriatric population given the incredible losses of power many elders have sustained, in contrast to other patient populations. In pediatrics, a more paternalistic attitude may be appropriate; for the general population a "consumeristic" relationship may be applicable, wherein adults exchange competent medical services for reasonable compensation.[10] With the geriatric population, however, the servant caregiver model has many advantages to commend itself.

How does this servant caregiver paradigm feel and look? Certainly, it is not a "new" paradigm at all, as it is seen over and over again in scripture. Ruth and Naomi cared for, indeed empowered, each other in a mutually dependent situation (Ruth 1:16-18). The Good Samaritan (Luke 10:29-37) took time to care for a person who had been beaten and left to die. Jesus clashed with the authorities when He healed on the Sabbath (John 5:9-15), and He cared deeply for the marginalized sick individuals who had been cast out from society (Matthew 8:1-4). At the time of the crucifixion, He reached out to ensure His mother's care (John 19:26-27). Such examples are not about domination, but are about restoring power to the powerless. Should not such caregiving be translated into our modern culture?

Within the previous cases studies, several dynamics illustrating the establishment of the servant caregiver model should be highlighted.

Timing: With the push for efficiency within healthcare systems, the idea of empowerment is extremely hard to extrapolate for any given rehabilitation situation. Yet a highly-sensitive healthcare provider begins to develop a finely-tuned approach whereby body language, listening skills, and questioning give the patient an immediate message (Case Study 4). Even as the rehabilitation advances, the patient/healthcare provider relationship is a dynamic process whereby the patient becomes more whole, regaining power, until eventually the patient achieves freedom from the rehabilitation process. Thus, it is critical that adequate time be given for explanations to patients about treatment protocols and about their rights as patients. Even if a patient chooses to be passive at times in treatment, the health care provider can continue to help that patient work toward wholeness. Such is illustrated by the case of the widow with back pain. Her grief may not have allowed her much energy to work toward her own renewal. Additionally, the loss of a long-time physical relationship can result in an unnamed, but painful, touch deprivation for the individual. Treatment therefore should include adequate time for empathetic listening, as well as helpful touch therapies, such as massage.

Teamwork: Authors Weston and Brown have differentiated between disease and illness. Disease is that which has definite diagnosable problems, whereby the focus in on the body. Illness, on the other hand, has more to do with the " . . . thoughts, feelings, and altered behavior of someone who feels sick."[11] This distinction is exemplified in Case Study 2, where the patient John feels ill secondary to his grief and guilt about his wife's death. The healthcare provider may feel totally unequipped to deal with such a difficult case, and as such, pastoral or psychiatric counseling is an appropriate recommendation. For patients to recover and for wholeness to be restored, healthcare providers must understand their own limitations and the necessity of a team of professionals serving the patients' needs.[12]

Decision Making: One of the easiest and often overlooked methods to restore power to the elder is to include the elder in the decision-making process. Even in the simplest of concerns, patients can begin to understand themselves as capable of making decisions and choices that determine their own health. Such "participative decision making" is also a dynamic process whereby patients can be involved from diagnosis to treatment alternatives and implementation,[13] including using technology such as Internet searches to explore their options. The elders can then also make long-term choices for behaviors to promote continued good health. It is important to emphasize that wholeness is not restored when individuals become dependent upon healthcare providers for decision making. This negative dynamic actually undermines wholeness of individuals. Rather, wholeness is attained when empowered patients graduate from rehabilitation with a renewed sense of life.

Access: Often, as people are less able to function as they once did, they begin to feel as though they are less valuable than they once were. Unfortunately, many businesses, churches and social facilities are not handicapped accessible, therefore shutting out many aging people. Although some of those elders are not handicapped as defined by the law, they are functionally handicapped because of physical pain or limitations in climbing stairs to places they once had no trouble accessing. The elders in the above cases experienced various changes affecting their physical abilities to participate in activities, but environmental barriers can further exacerbate the functional problems many of these older patients face. Until all facilities, public and private, make changes to accommodate those with mobility problems, however, many aging persons will feel as though they do not "fit in" any longer. It is therefore important to advocate for access to all facilities for our aging patients.

Compassion: In the Coulter lecture presented to the American Congress of Rehabilitation Medicine in October of 2000, Lauro S. Halstead, MD, discussed the power of compassion in healing. Halstead notes that these concepts involve both feeling and acting in the countless tasks healthcare professionals perform every day. "These acts and words of kindness, empathy, and understanding are part of the person-intensive, complex interaction between patient and caregiver, between someone who feels that his body is broken and invalid and someone whose job is to respond to those feelings and relieve the suffering, to mend and heal, to make whole. This is what all of us try to do, each in our own imperfect way–professional to patient, person to person, human to human."[14] Halstead goes on in the lecture to review both scientific health care and "humanistic" or complementary health care. In performing physical rehabilitation care for patients, caregivers meet the immediate needs of the elders, but they also do more. "At another level, we tend to a wounded human, a person whose feelings of self-worth are shattered. By tending to these wounds, the caregiver comes to know a sense of her own loss, her own grief, her own sorrow. . . . I would contend that the best caregivers among us experience at some level, even if only subconsciously, the other person's grief. And when this happens, there is the potential for our compassion to rise to the level of the other person's suffering."[15] In such moments, caregivers must struggle with the grief of a patient for whom the past has become a disproportionately large part of life, as if the "real" person resides only in a time now gone.[16] Empathetic caregivers may be the first to enable the elder facing catastrophic illness or injury to redefine themselves and their wholeness in present and future sense, rather than holding to past ideals.

This discussion has centered on a very subjective idea of restoring and renewing wholeness of the disempowered older patient. It is thus proposed that the mentality of the healthcare provider be one of compassionate servanthood, rather than a presumptive dominance of power so common to the American culture. Healthcare providers may be surprised, however, in the change that occurs by their adopting such a servant attitude–medicine ministers to the providers as well as the patients.

PREVENTIVE MEDICINE:
THE ROAD TO PHYSICAL REDISCOVERY

All this is not to say that every elder faces severe disability, or that acceptance of disability is the only alternative for those whom illness or injury strikes. Being physically fit helps the body combat the effects of the aging process. In catastrophes, such as in the first case study, being physically fit helps the body recover and heal at a faster rate. No matter one's current physical shape, a balanced exercise program can maintain or improve the quality of one's life. In trying to rediscover one's wholeness, proper nutrition and exercise must be part of a daily routine. Wholeness of the physical body is therefore another important step in the successful aging process.

As the body naturally ages, it does not metabolize as it once did, nor does it recover from injuries as quickly. Vascular compliance, lung capacity, lean muscle mass, bone density, and articular cartilage all decrease. This natural progression cannot be stopped, but each aging person can make positive health choices to help slow the deterioration of the body. There is an old saying, "If you're not moving forward, then you're moving backward." Human bodies are improving or they are failing. The key word to the saying is moving: the body needs to move, and exercise provides that necessary movement. If the body does not move, muscle is replaced with fat, diminishing in size and strength. The generalized deconditioning and added fat then increase the morbidity of many medical conditions. For example, added weight puts more pressure on already thinning cartilage of the joints, increasing the pain of arthritis affecting many older people. The body must therefore keep moving to press forward on the journey to wholeness.

The importance of consulting with one's personal physician prior to implementing a new exercise program cannot be stressed enough. Along with a medical professional's evaluation, a cardiac stress test will give an estimate of the amount of exercise the older person can safely handle. Each body handles exertion differently, and it is therefore imperative to seek professional evaluation so as not to increase risk of adverse events. In addition to obtaining a physician's clearance, anyone who undertakes a new exercise program should seek the advice of a licensed and certified fitness instructor.

To overcome physical limitations of an aging body, a combination of stretching, aerobic activity, and strength training should be implemented.

Stretching: Stretching should always be done before and after each aerobic and strength training session. Before walking, one should stretch the legs, back, and arms. Stretching with strength training should include all body parts to be exercised, before and after the workout. A personal physician and fitness expert can provide a list of appropriate stretches for each individual. When stretching, it is important for the older patient not to "bounce" but rather to hold the stretch for at least ten seconds.

Other options for stretching and keeping the body moveable are activities such as yoga, Tai Chi, calisthenics, and different types of dance. Classes are offered in these areas at the local gym, churches, and community centers. There are countless videos available for purchase or rent at the video store. The public library often carries exercise videos for a minimal fee or at no cost as well. These types of exercises are a great way to begin the day: the muscles are loosened up, the joints are gently stretched, the blood circulates, and the mind clears.

Aerobic Activity: All aerobic activity should be done according to an individual's target heart rate, determined by a personal physician or certified fitness expert. Aerobic activities should be done three times a week for thirty minutes to an hour each session. According to the Administration on Aging, "Walking and other aerobic exercises done at a pace which makes you breathe a little harder and work up a mild sweat for a half hour to one hour three days a week, will keep your heart, lungs, and vascular system in good working order and strengthen your bones and muscles."[17] Aerobic activities, such as walking and jogging, are excellent exercises that can be done in many places. A treadmill at home is an option for many. The local shopping mall provides a climate controlled facility year round and also serves as a place to meet people with a shared interest. Often larger cities have walking tracks through the city park or in a designated safe area. When walking outside, however, the older person should be aware of the climate and not walk in extremes of temperature. The elder should wait until the temperature and humidity are conducive to the parameters the physician or personal trainer has set prior to aerobic exercise.

Other aerobic activities that can enhance wholeness for the aging person are dancing, tennis, and riding a bicycle (either stationary or outdoors). The local fitness centers and Chamber of Commerce should have information concerning recreation leagues in particular areas. Also, many people with joint problems have found water aerobics to be beneficial without stress on the joints. The key to any aerobic activity or fitness plan is starting one and sticking to it. The older person needs to pick an activity that strikes an interest and try that activity, committing to at least three weeks to firmly establish a healthy habit.

Strength Training: Strength training, as with aerobic activity, should be done three times a week, on alternating days for about thirty minutes, depending on the program designed by an instructor. Strength training can include lifting weights with dumbbells, free weights and barbells, specially targeted gym machines, or even cans from the cupboard. If one is unable to go to a gym or does not have the necessary financial means for weights at home, produce cans of varying weight do wonders for strengthening the muscles. All major body parts need to be exercised. Target areas are the chest, back, stomach, shoulders, biceps, triceps, quadriceps, hamstrings, and calves. A good rule of thumb for the quantity of exercise is 3 sets for each body part with 8-12 repetitions per set. In doing the exercises, the older person should never jerk the weights with a fast motion, as this could damage the ligaments around joints and tear muscle the person is trying to build. Each repetition should be done with a slow controlled rhythm and with proper form.

Through strength training, the muscles become stronger and endurance increases. Strength training provides a way to regain function lost in sedentary lifestyles and the aging process. Such training is not limited to the able-bodied; exercise programs have been developed for patients to perform at a bed or wheelchair level. Becoming stronger helps persons who use wheelchairs or walkers to be more mobile. By increasing strength in the arms, shoulders, chest, and back, one is better able to propel a wheelchair or help elevate the body. Strengthening the legs improves elevation from chairs as well as walking speed and safety. Lifting weights stimulates the body and the mind, and thus staying active will enhance one's physical and mental prowess. By building stronger muscles, elders may again be able to participate in some of the activities they once did, and in that rediscovery, to find wholeness.

As evidenced in the first case study, being physically fit helps the body recover when catastrophes occur. While many older people are not initially in good physical shape, a personal fitness program can help them in reconditioning. To achieve and maintain wholeness, one must move forward so as not to move backward. No matter the older person's condition, there is no time like the present to begin to rediscover the physically fit whole body.

TO EVERYTHING, THERE IS A SEASON–OUR WINTER JOURNEY

> Remember your creator in the days of your youth, before the days of trouble come, and the years draw near when you will say, 'I have no pleasure in them'; before the sun and the light and the moon and the stars are darkened and the clouds return with the rain; in the day when the guards of the house tremble, and the strong men are bent, and the women who grind cease working because they are few, and those who look through the windows see dimly; when the doors on the street are shut, and the sound of the grinding is low, and one rises up at the sound of a bird, and all the daughters of song are brought low; when one is afraid of heights, and terrors are in the road; the almond tree blossoms, the grasshopper drags itself along and desire fails; because all must go to their eternal home, and the mourners will go about the streets; before the silver cord is snapped, and the golden bowl is broken, and the pitcher is broken at the fountain, and the wheel broken at the cistern, and the dust returns to the earth as it was, and the breath returns to God who gave it. Vanity of vanities, says the Teacher; all is vanity. Ecclesiastes 12:1-8 (New Revised Standard Version)

While the physical and physiological changes of normal aging are well known, "The Teacher" gives a most eloquent allegory for aging in the passage above. Even in those days, recognition was given dimming cognition, vision, hearing, and strength as part of the aging process. Yet while it is true there is no universal fountain of youth to spare us from all physical changes, it is also true that we need not succumb to aging as totally passive participants, as we have seen in the previous discussion. Also, even in the face of illness or injury, we need not accept disability as robbing us of wholeness. Change may herald renewal as we find strengths and talents we never knew in the midst of challenge. Aging need not limit our potential nor does it absolve us from our responsibility for answering God's call in our lives.

Scripture is full of examples of those called to immense work of God in later life. God's call may come at unexpected times, in unexpected ways, even in our old age. Though scholars may disagree about the system of dating for ages given in scripture, the absolute ages of the people called are not important. What is clear is that many of those called by God were called in their older days. Genesis 5 tells us that Adam and Seth were each in their older years before becoming fathers. Genesis 7 relates that Noah was "six hundred years old" when the flood came, yet he became the mechanism of salvation for humankind.

Not all elders see the completion of their work, but they faithfully begin the journey to which God calls them. Abram was seventy-five years old when he was called by God to leave his country and go to an unknown land. In his faithfulness, God blessed Abram, giving him the name Abraham and entering into a covenant with him when Abraham was ninety-nine. It was even later that God granted Abraham and Sarah the son of the covenant "in his old age," through which all nations were subsequently blessed. Though Abraham did not see most of the promises of God actually come to fruition, he is credited as one of the most faithful people of the scriptures, being satisfied to trust God. "All of these died in faith without having received the promises, but from a distance they saw and greeted them" (Hebrews 11:13, New Revised Standard Version). Moses was similarly called after he had married and established a new life in the desert. Yet leaving all to follow what the Lord commanded, he liberated the Israelites from captivity, led and sustained them through a prolonged journey in the desert, codified the laws of the group, established a system of judges, and organized the first tabernacle of worship. He prepared the Israelites for subsequent conquest of the land God had promised, although he died at a reported one hundred and twenty years of age without seeing that conquest completed. While Moses did not himself enter the promised land, Deuteronomy 34: 7 notes, however, that God gave Moses the needed strength to complete his portion of God's plan, saying: " . . . his sight was unimpaired and his vigor had not abated" (New Revised Standard Version). Rulers, prophets, and sages of the Israelites continued in the work of God into their final days, not retiring from work God had called them to do. Even after death, many of the Israelite leaders continued to inspire and inform the children of God through the rituals of the religion and stories told commemorating the mighty deeds of those called by God. For example, King David's estate contributed a significant part of the materials for the magnificent temple of the Lord built by David's son, Solomon. David himself did not see the house of the Lord built, but he was instrumental in providing the resources for its completion.

Another example of God's special calling to elders is that of Simeon and Anna in Luke 2. Simeon and Anna, despite their advanced years, were the ones to recognize the promised Messiah, blessing Him and proclaiming Him to those in the temple. Noted for their character, piety, and faithfulness of religious practice, the two elders were infused with God's Holy Spirit and led to be the heralds of His salvation. Such wisdom and discernment is indeed a special gift from God, cultivated through the experiences of a long life. As Kathleen Fischer says in her book, *Winter Grace: Spirituality and Aging,* "Wisdom comes from contact with God. The fruits of this communion are the wonder and gratitude found in living each moment fully, the love and freedom learned in solitude and prayer. The sharing of this wisdom is not primarily in terms of what we say or do for the young, but through the persons we have become. At bottom, winter grace is the entry of God into our lives, a coming that gives us a heart of wisdom."[18] Simeon and Anna demonstrated such wisdom in the winter of their lives that allowed God to use them in a tremendous way when many would think them "useless."

OUR JOURNEY TO SPIRITUAL REDISCOVERY

Sociologists, psychologists, and students of virtually all sciences have described the essential tasks of aging. Erikson identified the chief task of the old as achieving integrity of the ego despite internal and external assaults. But while physical and social aspects of life may be disrupted by disease or disability, religious beliefs may provide a stable context for life, helping the elder maintain personal continuity through life's transitions.[19] People are not helpless in the face of challenge: "How people assess and deal with situations–in short, how they cope–has very important implications for their well being . . . religion is often a central part of this process for the elderly."[20] Such coping may be seen as maintenance of internal continuity. "Internal continuity is the persistence of a structure of ideas and memories. The inner structure is formed by the values, beliefs, knowledge, worldview, philosophy of life, and moral framework that are the core of the personality. It also includes the preferences, capacities, coping skills, and abilities that influence how the person interacts with the world. Included here are ontological beliefs, religious beliefs, values, norms, memories of religious experience, religious worldview, and the place of religion and spirituality in the self and identity. Spiritual ideas, identity, and skills are often also an important part of coping. Faith, contemplation, prayer, and trust in God can all be important coping mechanisms."[21] More than simply cognitive processes, however, " . . . when people of greatest maturity meet situations of greatest challenge . . . people move from the abstractions of a religion in theory to the concreteness of a religion in action."[22]

The effect of the spiritual life in what has become scientific health care cannot be underestimated. What is now considered "humanistic" care was the predominant model of medical care until the scientific model began taking over in the latter 19th century.[23] The recognition of the spiritual dimension on the physical body is once again experiencing increased attention, however. In the Coulter lecture, Halstead reviewed seven studies, each representing a scientific look at interventions of "humanistic" health care for several different illnesses. One study showed mean survival of breast cancer patients who participated in a support group for a year to be twice that of those who did not at ten years. Another study found increased exercise tolerance, maximum workload and cardiac function in patients with coronary artery disease who participated in meditation twenty minutes a day. In a third study, pastors participated in a double-blind randomized trial of distant healing (prayer) for patients with acquired immune deficiency syndrome (AIDS). The distant healing was conducted without the knowledge of the patients with AIDS. Over a six-month period, the treatment group showed fewer and less severe AIDS complications, had less fever, and had fewer doctor visits and hospitalizations, all without any appreciable change in blood counts. Similarly, a strict scientific review of 23 other studies on distant healing showed a 57% positive treatment effect.[24] Halstead notes, "Whatever one may think about these studies and distant healing, my own view is that we all have a spiritual self and a spiritual life, regardless of our affiliation with organized religion, and that we do not pay enough attention to this aspect of our patients when they are going through the worst crisis of their lives."[25] In touching on such spiritual issues with patients, caregivers are themselves challenged in their own spiritual beliefs. Such introspection ultimately refines the caregiver's lived theology, firming the place in which the caregiver's own faith is anchored. From that anchor, the caregiver is able to help others rediscover spiritual wholeness in challenge. While good health habits, personal fitness, and rehabilitation for injury and illness are important elements in cultivating wholeness, a personal relationship between God and the elder is ultimately the heart of the wholeness the elder seeks.

PRESSING ON TOWARD THE GOAL–FINISHING THE RACE

"Successful aging is to feel satisfied and fulfilled, to be loved and loving, to have hope and a sense of future. It is to be excited about life, to find meaning and purpose in everyday existence, freely to pursue one's goals until that last moment. An ideal, yes. Achievable, perhaps. A goal worth pursuing, absolutely."[26] Even in the face of physical illness or disability, one may find wholeness. "Through sharing experience with others in the healing arts, many of us who are paying attention have been learning that there is more to being well than just the removal of symptoms. We are learning that to be healthy does not mean to be symptom-free. We are learning that health is not just the opposite of illness: health is the consciousness of one's wholeness–and that means accepting one's limitations as well as one's strengths. We are also learning that we can become aware of our wholeness and still die. We can experience 'health' and well-being even though our bodies might have conditions labeled 'terminal illness.' This understanding of wholeness accepts death as a part of life."[27] All persons have the potential to grow toward wholeness in later life. "Wholeness has to do with 'setting one's heart' (a literal translation of *credo* popularly interpreted to mean 'I believe') in ways that foster both commitment and connectedness as persons seek to know and live the Truth in relation to themselves, others, creation, and One-Who-Transcends (Little, 1983). Wholeness leads to generative love and an increasing openness to the power of stories, rituals, and symbols of one's faith tradition as means of both transforming and being transformed (see McFadden, 1985)."[28] Such love and connectedness takes shape in the ministry of the church, in activities such as rituals and sacraments; prayer, fellowship, and support groups; educational programs; calling on those in institutions or shut-in at home; counseling; and outreach.[29] Rather than relying upon strictly medical treatment, "wholistic" health care recognizes the need for persons to experience "inner healing." Such healing recognizes the inseparable nature of body, mind and spirit. "Inner healing means healing of the intellectual, volitional, and affective makeup of a person–healing past memories and emotional hurts . . . Healing may mean comforting and supporting persons experiencing an incurable disease. Even though cure is not possible, an inner peace and acceptance may result from the presence and love of others."[30]

One who mediated such care to countless others was John Wesley. Not only was Wesley instrumental in revival within his own Church of England and in the founding of American Methodism, but he also demonstrated servant care for his neighbor. Through promotion of the "means of grace" such as visiting the sick, feeding and clothing the poor, and combating social ills of his day, he demonstrated care for marginalized and disenfranchised in the community. He promoted the best medical science of his day, providing his circuit-riding preachers with his *Primitive Physic*–often the preacher was the most learned man of the parts and the book Wesley authored the only source of medical care in the frontier world. In addition to cures for various ailments, Wesley included in the work general rules for health: keeping those of weak constitution isolated from the ill, cleaning houses, eating plain foods in moderation, and drinking sufficient water. "One grand preventive of pain and sickness of various kinds, seems intimated by the great Author of nature in the very sentence that intails death upon us: 'In the sweat of thy face shalt though eat bread, till thou return to the ground.' The power of exercise, both to preserve and restore health, is greater than can well be conceived; especially in those who add temperance thereto; who . . . steadily observe both that kind and measure of food, which experience shews to be most friendly to health and strength."[31] Wesley encouraged his followers to be as regimented in their physical care as they were in their spiritual practices. "Observe all the time the greatest exactness in your regimen or manner of living. Abstain from all mixed, all highly seasoned food. Use plain diet, easy of digestion; and this as sparingly as you can, consistent with ease and strength. Drink only water. Use as much exercise daily in the open air, as you can without weariness. Sup at six or seven on the lightest food; go to bed early, and rise betimes. To persevere with steadiness in this course is often more than half the cure. Above all, add to the rest, (for it is not labor lost) that old unfashionable medicine, prayer."[32] In his later years, after he was unable to meet the rigorous travel demands of a preaching circuit, Wesley continued to work, collecting door-to-door for the poor of London into his last years. For his work, John Wesley is often credited with the Protestant concern for the development of health ministry as well as general advancement of the practice of medicine.[33] His life serves as an example of integration of "spiritual, physical, mental, emotional, and social dimensions" of wholeness.

One of our main tasks in caregiving professions is to be tangible evidence that the Creator God of the universe always guides us and walks with us in our journey to wholeness. In God, every elder can truly be "always green and full of sap."

NOTES

1. Melvin A. Kimble, "Pastoral Care," *Aging, Spirituality, and Religion: A Handbook*, eds. Melvin A. Kimble, Susan H. McFadden, James W. Ellor, and James J. Seeber, (Minneapolis: Fortress Press, 1995), 134.

2. Letty M. Russell, *Household of Freedom: Authority in Feminist Theology*, (Philadelphia: The Westminster Press, 1987), 21.

3. Ibid.

4. Deborah S. Ballard-Reisch, "A Model of Participative Decision Making for Physician-Patient Interaction," *Health Communications* 2:2 (1990), 91-104.

5. Mary M. Knutsen, "A Feminist Theology of Aging," *Aging, Spirituality, and Religion*, 463.

6. Ballard-Reisch, 103.

7. Russell, *Household*, 33.

8. Thomas S. Szasz, MD, and March H. Hollender, MD, "A Contribution to the Philosophy of Medicine," *Archives of Internal Medicine*, 97 (1956): 585-592.

9. Ibid.

10. Annalee E. Beisecker and Thomas D. Beisecker, "Using Metaphors to Characterize Doctor-Patient Relationships: Paternalism Versus Consumerism," *Health Communications* 5:1 (1993): 41-58.

11. W. Wayne West and Judith Belle Brown, "The Importance of Patient Beliefs," *Communicating with Medical Patients*, eds. Moira Stewart and Debra Roter, (London: Sage Publications, 1989), 79.

12. Harold G. Koenig and Andrew J. Weaver, *Counseling Troubled Older Adults: A Handbook for Pastors and Religious Caregivers*, (Nashville: Abingdon Press, 1997). This text illustrates the importance of a teamwork approach: if you don't know how to handle the problem, help the client find someone able to help them. See pages 78, 83, 90, 93, 105, 114, 168, 174, 206.

13. Ballard-Reisch, "Model of Participative Decision Making," 94.

14. Lauro S. Halstead, MD, "The Power of Compassion and Caring in Rehabilitation Healing," *Archives of Physical Medicine and Rehabilitation* 82 (February 2001):149.

15. Ibid., 150-151.

16. Ibid.

17. Saadia Greenberg, "Fitness Facts for Older Americans," pub. Administration on Aging; available from http://www.aoa.dhhs.gov/aoa/eldractn/fitfact.html; Internet; accessed 5 February 2001.

18. Kathleen Fischer, *Winter Grace*, (Nashville: Upper Room Books, 1998), 40.

19. Kenneth I. Pargament, Kimberly S. Van Haitsma, David S. Ensing, "Religion and Coping," *Aging, Spirituality, and Religion*, 57.

20. Ibid., 62.

21. Robert C. Atchley, "The Continuity of the Spiritual Self," *Aging, Spirituality, and Religion*, 70.

22. Pargament, Van Haitsma, Ensing, "Religion and Coping," *Aging, Spirituality, and Religion*, 47.

23. Halstead, "Power of Compassion," 150.

24. Ibid., 153.

25. Ibid.

26. Harold G. Koenig, "Religion and Health in Later Life," *Aging, Spirituality, and Religion*, 9.

27. Margaret Kornfeld, *Cultivating Wholeness: A Guide to Care and Counseling in Faith Communities*, (New York: Continuum, 1998), 8.

28. Linda Vogel, "Spiritual Development in Later Life," *Aging, Spirituality, and Religion*, 74.

29. Kornfeld, 39.

30. Abigail Rian Evans, *The Healing Church: Practical Programs for Health Ministries*, (Cleveland: United Church Press, 1999), 125.

31. John Wesley, MA, *Primitive Physic: Or an Easy and Natural Method of Curing Most Diseases, Twenty-second Edition*, (Nashville: The United Methodist Publishing House, 1992), v.

32. Ibid., vii-viii.

33. Evans, *Healing Church*, 24.

Chapter 9

A Christian Education
for the Spiritual Growth
of Senior Adults

Martha S. Bergen, PhD

SUMMARY. Spiritual maturity among older adults is not automatic. The achievement of this most significant and worthy goal is, in part, an individual's choice. However, it is assisted by the deliberate efforts of Christian education, as a church seeks to meet the needs of seniors by appealing to their life concerns. How this is done may vary, but the needs and interests of senior adults dictate that it must be done. This article provides an overview of older adults' needs as they relate to spiritual development, and then offers some general suggestions a church might consider for guiding them toward spiritual maturity. *[Article copies available for a fee from The Haworth Document Delivery Service: 1-800-HAWORTH. E-mail address: <docdelivery@haworthpress.com> Website: <http://www.HaworthPress.com> © 2003 by The Haworth Press, Inc. All rights reserved.]*

KEYWORDS. Ageism, particular needs, physiological needs, self-esteem, spiritual needs, well-being, spiritual-maturity, spiritual-growth,

Martha S. Bergen is Associate Professor of Christian Education, Hannibal-LaGrange College, Hannibal, MO. Martha completed several courses in adult education and in gerontology on her masters and doctoral degree plans. She teaches a course on ministry with senior adults at Hannibal-LaGrange College.

[Haworth co-indexing entry note]: "A Christian Education for the Spiritual Growth of Senior Adults." Bergen, Martha S. Co-published simultaneously in *Journal of Religious Gerontology* (The Haworth Pastoral Press, an imprint of The Haworth Press, Inc.) Vol. 15, No. 1/2, 2003, pp. 127-141; and: *Practical Theology for Aging* (ed: Derrel R. Watkins) The Haworth Pastoral Press, an imprint of The Haworth Press, Inc., 2003, pp. 127-141. Single or multiple copies of this article are available for a fee from The Haworth Document Delivery Service [1-800-HAWORTH, 9:00 a.m. - 5:00 p.m. (EST). E-mail address: docdelivery@haworthpress.com].

http://www.haworthpress.com/store/product.asp?sku=J078
© 2003 by The Haworth Press, Inc. All rights reserved.
Digital Object Identifier: 10.1300/J078v15n01_10

worship, evangelism, discipleship, mission, learning, fellowship, purpose

The period of senior adulthood, like any other stage within the human life span, deserves attention within the realm of spiritual growth and development. Spiritual maturity, contrary to what some may think, does not naturally occur simply as a byproduct of aging. Studies refute the myth that older adults become more religious as they grow older. In fact, evidence suggests the contrary.[1] Generally, one's interests during the senior years tend to reflect one's inclinations during earlier years. Furthermore, religiosity and spiritual maturity are not necessarily equated. Therefore, if older adults are to achieve spiritual maturity, it must be assisted by the deliberate and purposeful attention of the church, as older adults "tend to explore God in institutional churches."[2]

A close examination of American society reveals that ageism, prejudice toward the aged, exists. Moreover, the church proves to be no exception when it comes to the practice of ageism. "One can note," say Arn and Arn, "an absence of effective congregational ministries that focus on the life experiences and spiritual needs of persons over 55 . . . [and] few opportunities . . . [for] service to others through the church."[3] One reason for this may be the insensitivity or ignorance of church leaders regarding the needs of seniors; unfortunately, however, even within the church one's worth is often diminished simply because he or she grows "old." As a result, spiritual growth is likely hindered. If the church is going to be the example of Christ in the world as He commanded her to be, she should set the pace for eliminating ageism and elevating and restoring older adulthood to its proper biblical perspective that of dignity, worth, and honor.[4] Churches that are serious about senior adult ministry will reflect such an attitude, for it is this attitude that provides a basis for ministry. Therefore, within the proper context and framework of a church's Christian education program, the spiritual needs of older adults may be addressed, and opportunities for Christian service and fellowship provided.

CHARACTERISTICS OF SENIOR ADULTS

Before examining some of the ways Christian education might assist older adults in their spiritual growth, it is important to consider a brief profile of senior adults and some of the characteristics they possess. Americans aged sixty-five years or older have tripled since 1900. Making up about 4.1% of the American population at that time, they currently make up approximately 12.8% of the population today. That means one in every eight persons is a senior adult.[5] Not only are senior adults comprising more and more of the American population, the older population itself continues to grow older. Life expectancy at the time of birth reached a record high by 1995 of 75.8 years. By the year 2050 it is anticipated that life expectancy will increase to eighty-two years.[6] Research from the American Association of Retired Persons (AARP) shows that in 1996 those persons between the ages of sixty-five and seventy-four years had increased eight times (18.7 million) over what it was in 1900. In the seventy-five to eighty-four year age group, there was an increase of sixteen times more (11.4 million), and those who were eighty-five years of age or above grew thirty-one fold (3.8 million).[7] Consequently, more and more references are made to the "young old" and the "old-old" to differentiate variations within this growing spectrum of Americans characterized as older adults.

Arn and Arn speak of today's older adults as "new seniors."[8] Having little to do with chronological age, this, rather, depicts a mindset. New seniors do not see themselves as deteriorating and old. They have goals and aspirations. They are active and work, despite vocational retirement, giving of their time in volunteer capacities. They utilize opportunities for learning and growth, as well as for play.[9] They are financially more secure than their counterparts of previous generations. Many, rather than being cared for by their families, have become caregivers for their own children, now adults, and grandchildren.[10] To be sure, there are also those with crucial, specialized needs, i.e., failing health, institutionalization, memory loss, loss of a loved one, and even imminent death. As noted by Simmons, the way in which older adults are viewed will shape how Christian education is done for them.[11] Thus, to understand Christian education in relationship to older adults necessitates an awareness of "an evolving understanding of aging."[12] Nevertheless, whatever one's need or circumstance, the role of Christian education is that of moving persons toward the ultimate goal of spiritual maturity. Needs and circumstances will change, but the ultimate goal never does. The church must first acknowledge needs, then seek to meet them where appropriate as part of spiritual maturation.

SOME PARTICULAR NEEDS OF OLDER ADULTS

To be human is to have needs. While some needs are the same for all persons, other needs vary throughout the life span. Maslow's hierarchy of needs, for example, points to the fact that all persons need such things as food, clothing, security, affection, achievement, and meaning in life.[13] And even among these needs, there are differences in degree across the various ages of the life span. Hence, older adults possess their own set of needs. Christian education should speak to the needs of older adults, as to all persons, modeling the exam-

ple of Christ who did everything from feed the hungry to provide significance
and purpose for the aimless.

PHYSIOLOGICAL NEEDS

Perhaps the first things some think of regarding older adults are the physical
decrements and losses that become evident with aging. These include everything from decrements in the senses to slower response time, as well as certain
health problems. In short, the body simply wears out. Particular manifestations
of this vary from individual to individual. Churches show their concern for
older adults when they provide such things as audio assistance, wheelchair
ramps, and elevators so as to make experiences at the church facility meaningful and significant for those who attend.

Some older adults, because of physical limitations, will be homebound or
institutionalized. Representatives from the church who assist with Bible study
or scriptural thoughts, administer communion, or offer a gesture of care and
concern give evidence that these all-too-often-forgotten ones matter within the
Kingdom of God.

SOCIAL NEEDS

For older adults, losses within the social arena can be among the most devastating. The network of family and friends provides stability, comfort, and
support like no other human relationships. Although one's status may change
with retirement, usually one still has family and friends. But when these relationships are severed, life becomes more difficult and challenging. With aging
comes the loss of significant others. And because opportunities for additional
contacts become fewer in number, there is usually little hope of finding new
friends to fill the void one experiences to the degree he or she had known earlier. The church, however, becomes a beacon of hope and a more significant
network of community in light of this. Thus, the term "family of God" takes on
a more important connotation.

PSYCHOLOGICAL NEEDS

Closely related to social needs are psychological needs. Irrespective of a
particular personality type or degree of mental health, persons desire a sense of
meaning and purpose. They need to get along well with others, be respected
and accepted, and enjoy a sense of self-esteem. Some older adults do not pos-

sess a mature view of the world in general, much less a healthy view of themselves. As is true physiologically and socially, earlier choices will profoundly
affect one's later condition. Making good choices and receiving affirmation
for them earlier in life facilitate psychological health and well-being later in
life. Erik Erikson's psychosocial stages attest to this. These stages present crises that depict the tensions of psychological development across the life span.
The crisis, or turning point, for older adults is "ego integrity vs. despair."[14] Entering the last phase of life, one either despairs, having a sense of hopelessness,
and, thus, believing there is no further chance for wholeness and meaning; or
one accepts his life as it is, thereby achieving integrity and maturity.[15]

As one chooses the path of integrity, life is viewed as meaningful and special, even with its ups and downs. For older adults, life becomes increasingly
more difficult. Yet, the choice toward integrity allows one to keep things together . . . [and] make sense out of self and life.[16] Perhaps the best way the
church can help one achieve integrity is by loving, respecting, serving, and
sustaining people of every age, so that as one approaches older adulthood, that
person is better equipped and motivated to choose integrity over despair. Older
adults are more likely to do this when the church has cared enough to move
them toward spiritual maturity throughout every stage of their lives.

SPIRITUAL NEEDS

Spiritual needs, because the human personality is so intricate, are interwo-
ven with various other categories of needs. This multifaceted complexity
makes difficult the task of specifying what falls neatly into certain areas. However, the most basic and yet cogent of spiritual needs for older adults, as with
any age group, is that of a right relationship with holy God. The writer of the
Book of Ecclesiastes reveals a profound truth. While "God has made everything beautiful for its own time, [so also] He has planted eternity in the human
heart" (Eccles. 3:11, NLT). Every person, whether willing to accept it or not
and whether fully cognizant of it or not, perceives, or at least hopes, that this
earthly existence is not all there is. Because God has placed eternity within the
human heart, there is the need (or underlying desire) to know Him and, therefore, attain the purpose for which humanity was created. To know God is to
know His character and emulate it demonstrating such intangibles as love, sac-
rificial service, righteousness, justice, and mercy. Spiritual maturity will never
take place aside from this basic truth. And since the church primarily deals
with the spiritual dimension of life, it is the church's responsibility to help persons realize this profound truth and grow them in it.

The second of spiritual needs is "like unto the first," and that is a right relationship with other people. A part of spiritual wholeness and well-being demands love, acceptance, and forgiveness toward others. For James Fowler, A universalizing faith is the highest level of faith development, the culminating image of mature faith.[17] It is at this stage that one will act upon what he or she believes, have no need to conform, have an unselfish passion for changing the world, and act out of love and justice.[18] Knowing God and loving Him supremely will express itself in a right relationship with others.[19]

Additionally, there is the need spiritually to be connected with those of the community of faith. A healthy spirituality demands linkage to the family of believers, each drawing upon one another's strengths and giftedness for the good of the whole.[20] Being a part of the Body of Christ gives one a sense of connectedness and roots, as persons desire to belong to and be a part of something more lasting than self.[21] Relatedly, there is the need to fulfill a purpose in life. People need to know that their lives matter and make some positive difference in the world. This is especially true of seniors, some of whom may doubt their worth, value, and contribution.

Perhaps the most challenging of spiritual needs is that of coming to terms with life's mortality, particularly one's own. The acceptance of death as a natural part of life gives evidence of spiritual maturity. Becker points out, older persons, when asked what they fear most about death, frequently express that it is dying, not death, they fear.[22] Questions about the hour of helplessness and pain associated with death cause trepidation, as the reluctance to give up strength, health, and vitality brings about a struggle. The Christian copes with this struggle by looking to Christ, the One who *suffered and died* for sinners. Because of His death, and thereby His resurrection, one's own death is an entrance into God's eternal presence . . . In this hope we can learn the art of dying gracefully.[23]

THE MEANING OF SPIRITUAL MATURITY

Defining the term spiritual maturity is a rather complex task. As stated earlier, it is not necessarily equated with religiosity. An examination of Scripture reveals this poignant truth. The prophets, as well as Jesus Himself, condemned many for their sacrifices and rituals when their hearts were not right and these were done out of improper motives.[24] While one who is spiritually mature may express it in religious actions, religious actions in and of themselves cannot be accurate gauges of one's spiritual development.

One can have spiritual wellness without *spiritual maturity*, just as an infant can be physically well when far from mature. SWB [spiritual well-being] is a status; maturity is the result of a process of growth. Yet maturity cannot be fully attained without having SWB. Thus in traditional Protestantism and contemporary evangelicalism, one cannot have spiritual life without trusting Jesus Christ as Savior; without life, there can be no growth.[25]

Jesus, in His Sermon on the Mount, spoke many teachings describing what constitutes a life of maturity and right living. Among them was the command: "But you are to be perfect, even as your Father in heaven is perfect" (Matt. 5:48, NLT). While in the flesh one always struggles to do what is right, it should always be one's aim and ambition from pure motives to strive toward this standard. To be perfect is to be mature.

According to Christian ethicist T. B. Maston, spiritual maturity expresses itself in the following ways:[26] (1) the increasing ability to adjust to life's inevitabilities, (2) acting less from outside pressures and more from principles of inner convictions, (3) faith based upon life's essentials, not nonessentials, (4) religion (one's own as well as others) measured more by vitalities rather than formalities, (5) motivation out of love rather than fear, (6) a consistent cognizance of Christ's presence and the Holy Spirit's leadership in life, and (7) a life that is dependable and predictable.

In the Gospel of Luke Jesus is recorded as saying, "A student is not above his teacher, but everyone who is fully trained will be like his teacher" (Luke 6:40, NIV). It is true that one becomes like those to whom he listens. Teachers with integrity will lead one toward truth. Jesus Himself was a masterful teacher who pointed all who would accept it to truth. Choosing to follow His teachings makes one mature.

Additionally, the Apostle Paul in speaking about Christian leaders states, "Their responsibility is to equip God's people . . . that we will be mature and full grown in the Lord, measuring up to the full stature of Christ" (Eph. 4:12-13, NLT). From this may be concluded the ultimate goal and, hence, the definition of spiritual maturity *BEING LIKE CHRIST!* This is the church's greatest and most noble challenge. Though Christlikeness is a lifelong task, Christian education has the potential for helping older adults attain this most important goal.

MINISTRIES FUNDAMENTAL FOR SPIRITUAL GROWTH

In a typical church congregation today, those above the age of fifty-five make up one-third to one-half of the church according to Arn and Arn.[27]

Churches which are committed to helping older adults cultivate their spiritual development must recognize who older adults are, acknowledge their various needs, value them as persons made in God's image, and be willing to provide time, monies, and leadership for their overall well-being. With this in mind, some areas of concern for Christian education are considered.

Horace Kerr categorizes the church's ministry with senior adults into five basic areas:[28] (1) spiritual enrichment; (2) learning opportunities; (3) socialization; (4) service opportunities; and (5) services needed. These might also be seen as needs senior adults have in relationship to the church. Each is necessary for a balanced ministry. While the crux of this article relates more specifically to what is done for spiritual enrichment, Kerr's other areas cannot be divorced from the emphasis of Christian education. Since humans are holistic, each of these relates to one another. And because humans are indeed made in the image of God, all of the categories have something of a religious dimension and, therefore, must be addressed by the church for a comprehensive ministry with older adults.

The church functions in a variety of ways to assist persons in their spiritual development. For older adults this may take the form of anything from worship to Bible study, music to missions, or social events to special interest classes. In light of the "age wave," the surge of seniors within American society, traditional ministries will no longer be sufficient to meet most needs. Thus, ministries and church programming should be "broad-based . . . reflecting diversity in ages, lifestyles, and needs."[29] Given below are a few Christian education ministry suggestions for the purpose of helping one on the journey to spiritual maturity and wholeness.

WORSHIP

Worship is the foremost task of the church, be it corporate or individual. Without worship, there would be no foundation for spiritual growth. While some seek to define worship by the various styles which exist, the most fundamental definition is "a response to who God is."[30] Persons must be given the opportunity to respond to God if worship is to occur. Although the church primarily deals with corporate worship, it should also encourage worship on the individual level. A church's senior pastor will be the leader of worship, but there are several things that might be done to aid older adults in their corporate worship experience. In addition to church plant facilities which are geared to the needs of older adults, i.e., audio assistance, comfortable seating, adequate lighting and ventilation, ramps, and handicap accessible restrooms and walkways, older adults are more likely to worship when they themselves have input into worship. Involving older adults in worship planning and leadership will increase their chances for participation and enhance the possibility of meaningful worship. Senior adults should be allowed opportunities for the leadership of public Scripture readings, litanies, prayers, and testimonials. Illustrations used in homilies and sermons should include examples and experiences of those across the life span. At least one denomination[31] includes a day within the church year to highlight senior adults, giving them leadership and recognition in most, if not all, parts of worship.

Worship involves the core of life and should address persons at their points of need. Jesus said, "God is spirit; and those who worship Him must worship in spirit and truth" (John 4:24, NASV). Sometimes "the most significant worship ... may ... well come from a valley of death or through a fountain of tears."[32] The difficult questions of life often summon one to worship, as life's trials tend to sharpen the focus on what truly matters. Kathleen Fischer speaks of "winter grace" in her book by that title. She describes winter grace in part as "the capacity to affirm life in the face of death."[33] It is understood best when older adults embody it.[34] Thus, old age is redeemed when there is "a passionate commitment to living as fully as possible, whatever the restrictions."[35] This level of maturity helps rather than hinders worship and can serve as an inspiration to others.

EVANGELISM

Christian education must also seek to evangelize. As Jesus sought to bring persons into the Kingdom of God, so the church is charged with this task. Before His crucifixion and resurrection Jesus prayed to the Father on behalf of those who followed Him, "As you sent me into the world, I am sending them into the world" (John 17:18, NLT). Even in churches where evangelism efforts are most ardent, they have often been unsuccessful in reaching the older adult population. Among reasons for this include the following:[36] (1) traditionally, evangelistic emphases have been placed upon youth and young adults, (2) older adults are "seasoned consumers," knowing the fake from the real, (3) inappropriate paradigms are used, and (4) a lack of organizational structure for evangelism among older adults exists. The first order of business regarding evangelism is for the church to acknowledge that senior adults need evangelization, just as other age groups. Moreover, seniors should also be among those who help the church to evangelize. Older adults are more likely to respond positively when those of their own age group are involved in evangelism. When this is done, organizational efforts and paradigms will likely shift to include older adults and give them opportunity to become partakers of God's Kingdom.

Although methods of evangelism may vary from church to church as well as across denominational lines, one thing is certain: The Christian community must reach out to others, sharing with them the good news of Jesus Christ. The most effective means of evangelism for older adults will revolve around relationships with them and the fulfillment of needs in association with their life changes.

DISCIPLESHIP

As persons make the choice to engage in a personal relationship with Christ, that relationship must be nurtured in order to grow and flourish. This is best done in a small-group setting as opposed to the church at large. Jesus, though He spoke and occasionally taught the masses, actually worked giving greater amounts of time on a more intimate level to the twelve apostles. And it was His efforts with these few that turned the world upside down for Christendom.

The most significant small-group setting within the church historically has centered on Bible study. Whether traditionally referred to by such terms as Sunday school or church school, the common purpose of studying God's word brings together, usually by age, persons in virtually every church. Typically, Sunday school among some has been perceived as an organization only for children. Though this was true at its inception, the Bible is not just a book for children. Senior adults also need, and many want to study, the scriptures. Some are quite familiar with them, having loved and read the Bible throughout their lives. To these, the Bible is especially significant for the challenges they face during the latter years. Others have little or no knowledge of the scriptures, may not see the need for studying them, or simply lack the desire or motivation to study.

The writer of the Book of Hebrews refers to the written word of God as "full of living power" (Heb. 4:12, NLT). The psalmist speaks of God's word as giving direction: "Thy word is a lamp to my feet, and a light to my path" (Ps. 119:105, NASV). Because God's word is truth, it is life changing. As such, the church should help seniors revere the Bible, study it, and apply it. However, this will be a challenge given the current ambience of today's senior adults.

> Because of the active lifestyle of today's seniors, Bible study competes for their attention just as it does for the attention of younger generations. Older seniors grew up in a culture where the Bible was read at home, studied as literature in schools, and quoted in public addresses. Today seniors rarely see or hear the Bible referenced in daily life. Unless they have cultivated the personal discipline of regular Bible study, they will find other activities to fill their days.[37]

While age and gender have been the usual means of grouping persons for Bible study, seniors may be more likely to engage in meaningful study of the Bible when they are grouped by homogeneity according to such things as (1) "lifestyle"– in relationship to work/retirement, marital status, age of children/grandchildren; (2) "location"–homes, businesses, community centers; (3) "time/day"–options other than Sunday mornings; (4) "teaching approach"–lecture, discussion, independent study; (5) "language/culture"–in areas where immigrants are numerous; (6) "affinity"–those sharing similar interests; and (7) "intergenerational groupings"–a combination of ages across the life span.[38]

The homebound and those living in nursing homes should also be given opportunity for Bible study to the extent they are able to participate. Though the degree, time, and level of study will likely differ from that for healthier senior adults, comprehensive Christian education programs and ministries do not neglect these who are frailer in body. Such efforts help keep older adults connected not only with God, but also with their church.

Some churches provide a "telephone class" for those who are homebound, operating somewhat like a conference call. A designated teacher highlights the week's lesson, and participants have opportunity for input and discussion just as if they were at the church. In other cases churches might send capable representatives on a regular basis, either to an individual's home or a nursing home facility, to provide Bible study for those who are unable to attend their church. Representatives should be those who relate well to these senior adults and are familiar with their needs and limitations. They must also have a command of the scriptures and possess the ability to teach them. The provision of devotional literature for those who are able to read may help foster regular Bible readings for older adults. Audio recordings are also an option.

Much of discipleship will hinge upon the effectiveness of Bible study, as the Bible provides the foundation for Christian living. However, discipleship also encompasses other aspects of the Christian life. Opportunities for older adults to participate in classes or seminars on topics such as Christian ethics, church history, distinctive of the Christian faith (e.g., prayer, grace), or special topics (e.g., the Holy Spirit, sin, heaven) assist Christian living and foster spiritual maturity.

SERVICE

As a whole seniors adults are a gracious and giving group of people. They desire to serve others, expecting little or nothing in return. They joy in the reward of the experience itself. Consequently, it is not unusual to find them as volunteers for a host of noble causes. Among these are areas within the church itself. When given the opportunity, senior adults serve as teachers, ushers, greeters, committee members, deacons, elders, and choir members to name a few. They are loyal and dependable, setting an example of service for their younger counterparts. Senior adults are also likely to volunteer for benevolent ministries, e.g., food pantry, clothes closet; specialized ministries, e.g., church prayer chain, outreach events; or more commonplace tasks, e.g., kitchen duties, organizing and overseeing them. This gives seniors a sense of self-worth, as they make significant contributions to the warp and woof of church life.

Spiritual growth may also be broadened as senior adults have opportunity for short-term mission endeavors, some of which occur overseas. Seniors are less likely to be hindered by time and money constraints and, thus, are the most feasible prospects for many mission tasks. Their level of maturity and commitment and breadth of life experience give them advantages over other age groups. Whether older adults have experienced overseas travel or not, the chance to serve outside one's familiar territory opens a new dimension for ministry service. This often changes one's perspective on the world. Christian senior adults, wherever they serve, want to be used by God to help others. As churches provide service opportunities for them, spiritual maturity is potentially enhanced.

LEARNING OPPORTUNITIES

Learning is a lifelong task, despite the popular adage "you can't teach an old dog new tricks." To cease to learn is to cease to live. Older adults, like others, take pride and gain confidence in themselves when new information or skills are learned. For this reason, they ought to be provided those opportunities. Christian education programs that see the development of the whole person as enhancing spiritual growth, will likely provide learning experiences for seniors, as well as encourage them in their quest to expand their knowledge and skills in areas beyond what the church itself may offer. However, whether these are sponsored directly by the church or some other entity, a range of relevant topics should be offered. The needs and interests of the seniors who support them will determine the extent of topics, length, and intensity. Some schools and universities provide courses designed specifically for older adults. These may range from more concentrated, short-term studies such as elderhostels to accredited degree programs tailored with the senior adult in mind. The church itself might host a particular workshop for the duration of a weekend or offer classes over an extended period of weeks, rotating various topics.

Nursing homes usually provide older adults some opportunity for special interests and crafts. Most older adults enjoy reading even if they are limited physically. Books and magazines potentially open a new world to seniors, especially if they are unable to participate in other kinds of learning experiences.

FELLOWSHIP

One of the greatest dynamics of the human experience is that of communicating with and relating to others. The church as a community of believers necessitates that its members work together toward a common purpose for the good of the whole. This shared experience of working toward a common goal promotes unity and goes beyond a mere sense of duty. The mystery of Christian fellowship is that it cannot be contrived; it occurs as a natural byproduct of the Christian experience when persons are willing to be vulnerable and choose to accept and love each other, in spite of their differences. Older adults are at a point in their lives when they potentially possess the maturity required to accept persons unconditionally. The tie that binds in Christian fellowship is the love of Christ demonstrated in everyday living. John, in his first epistle states, "If we are living in the light of God's presence, just as Christ is, then we have fellowship with each other . . . " (1 John 1:7, NLT).

Christian education promotes fellowship among older adults as it encourages and enables the expression of Christian love. Whether done over a shared meal, within a Bible study group, around a sickbed, or through a ministry event, genuine Christian fellowship is a necessary part of the Christian experience. Furthermore, it provides a vital component for the success of Christian ministry in general. One who gives evidence of spiritual maturity will share comradeship with those of the Christian community.

REACHING THE ULTIMATE GOAL OF SPIRITUAL MATURITY

The senior years seemingly possess the greatest potential for one's spiritual growth and maturity. Having encountered a lifetime of diverse experiences, one has a greater capacity for understanding God, self, and others. Furthermore, recollecting these experiences permits one to see that God's hand has been at work over a lifetime and, therefore, offers hope and reassurance for the future.[39] Likewise, one is free to embrace "a larger love and compassion, . . . [and] good will and thoughtfulness toward others."[40] Christian education directs one toward this realization, helping to shape and mold a proper biblical perspective of life and aging.

When we begin to see the process of growing older as an ascending rather than a descending journey, new horizons begin to open. With such a view we do not yearn for what used to be. Instead, we seek ways of harvesting the experiences of a lifetime so that the flowering of that life might bring forth new beauty. . . . Because spiritual maturity helps us discover our true purpose in life, it allows us to welcome aging as a natural progression of changes by which we attain the highest level of human experience.[41]

True purpose is linked to the incarnate Christ; He is the hope of all senior adults! Simeon knew this truth. That is why he could embrace life for as long as God had a purpose for him, and why he could accept the end of life when that purpose was accomplished. God revealed to Simeon that he would not die until he had seen the Messiah. And when he was an old man, this eagerly anticipated event occurred. Having seen God's salvation, Simeon was then ready to die. "Simeon took him [the Christ child] in his arms and praised God, saying: Sovereign Lord, as you have promised, . . . now dismiss your servant in peace. For my eyes have seen your salvation . . . " (Luke 2:28-30, NIV). Like Simeon, older adults are ready for the next step when Christian education has faithfully led them toward spiritual maturity; hence, they are able to declare, "whether we live or die, we are the Lord's" (Rom. 14:8, NKJV). With this perspective, older adulthood can indeed be the most spiritually enriching and rewarding time of life.

NOTES

1. Note, for example, Sheila C. McKenzie, *Aging and Old Age* (Scott, Foresman and Company: Glenview, IL), 1980, 15-16. See also Mark A. Lamport's "Adolescent Spirituality: Age of Conversion and Factors of Development," in *Christian Education Journal*, 10 (Spring 1990): 17-30.

2. Cassidy S. Dale as cited in Senior Adults and A.D. 2000, *Mature Living*, January 2000, 13.

3. Win Arn, and Charles Arn, *Catch the Age Wave: A Handbook for Effective Ministry with Senior Adults* (Kansas City, MO: Beacon Hill Press), 1999, 26-27.

4. See, for example, Lev. 19:32; Prov. 16:31; and Prov. 20:29.

5. AA Profile of Older Americans 1997, @ AARP Research. Web site: <http://research.aarp.org/general/profile97.html> .

6. D. W. E. Smith, *Human Longevity* (New York: Oxford University Press), 1993, n.p. and the U.S. Bureau of the Census, 1997; cited in Richard Schulz and Timothy Salthouse, *Adult Development and Aging*, 3d ed. (Upper Saddle River, NJ: Prentice Hall), 1999, 5.

7. "A Profile of Older Americans 1997.

8. Arn and Arn, 27.

9. Ibid., 27-28.

10. John G. "Jay" Johnston, *Forward Together: A New Vision for Senior Adult Ministry* (Nashville: LifeWay Press, 1998), 8.

11. Melvin A. Kimble, Susan H. McFadden, James W. Ellor, and James Seeber, eds. *Aging, Spirituality, and Religion: A Handbook* (Minneapolis: Fortress Press, 1995), 220.

12. Ibid.

13. Horace Kerr, *How to Minister to Senior Adults in Your Church* (Nashville: Broadman Press, 1980), 21.

14. Erik H. Erikson, *Childhood and Society*, 2d ed. (New York: W.W. Norton & Company, Inc., 1963), 268.

15. Ibid., 268-69; see also discussion from Harold G. Koenig, *Aging and God: Spiritual Pathways to Mental Health in Midlife and Later Years* (New York: The Haworth Pastoral Press, 1994), 75-76.

16. Charles M. Sell, *Transitions through Adult Life* (Grand Rapids: Zondervan Publishing House, 1991), 213.

17. James W. Fowler, *Stages of Faith: The Psychology of Human Development and the Quest for Meaning* (San Francisco: Harper & Row, 1981), 199.

18. Lucien Coleman, *Understanding Today's Adults* (Nashville: Convention Press, 1982), 71-72.

19. See 1 John 4:20-21.

20. Note Eph. 4:16.

21. William L. Hendricks, *A Theology for Aging* (Nashville: Broadman Press, 1986), 82-83.

22. Arthur H. Becker, *Ministry with Older Persons: A Guide for Clergy and Congregations* (Minneapolis: Augsburg Publishing House, 1986), 90.

23. Ibid., 90-92.

24. Note, for example, Isa. 1:10-20; Joel 2:12-13; Hos. 6:6; and Mark. 7:6-23.

25. James J. Seeber, ed., *Spiritual Maturity in the Later Years* (New York: The Haworth Press, 1990), 9.

26. Jack Gulledge, *The Senior Years: Getting There Being There* (Nashville: Convention Press, 1983), 69.

27. Arn and Arn, 32.

28. Kerr, 89-111.

29. Johnston, 20-21.

30. Ron Owens, *Return to Worship: A God-centered Approach* (Nashville: Broadman & Holman, 1999), 41.

31. Southern Baptists designate the first Sunday in May as "Senior Adult Day."

32. Owens, 40.

33. Kathleen Fischer, *Winter Grace: Spirituality for the Later Years* (New York: Paulist Press, 1985), 7.

34. Ibid., 6.

35. Andrew J. Weaver, Harold G. Koenig, and Phyllis C. Roe, eds., *Reflections on Aging and Spiritual Growth* (Nashville: Abingdon Press, 1998), 49.

36. Arn and Arn, 74-77.

37. Johnston, 31.

38. Ibid., 45-47.

39. Kerr, 20.

40. Fischer, 5.

41. Arn and Arn, 119.

Chapter 10

Preaching to Senior Citizens

Al Fasol, ThD

SUMMARY. This article addresses two questions: How is preaching to a congregation of senior citizens the same as preaching to younger persons; and how is it different? It includes some practical suggestions for sermon preparation and delivery by ministers whose congregations contain a number of older persons with specific needs. *[Article copies available for a fee from The Haworth Document Delivery Service: 1-800-HAWORTH. E-mail address: <docdelivery@haworthpress.com> Website: <http://www.HaworthPress.com> © 2003 by The Haworth Press, Inc. All rights reserved.]*

KEYWORDS. Senior, homiletics, guidance, retirement, hermeneutics, sermon, text, particularize, authority, rhetoric, source credibility, integrity, expertise, dynamism, adaptation, encoding, decode, frame of reference, predictability, application

"When I was a little girl," Lynn reflected, "I thought, ministers always think they have to be condescending when they speak to the youth. They seemed to assume several things about youths without ever talking to youths. They assumed we were not interested in what they had to say.

Al Fasol is Distinguished Professor of Preaching, E. Hermond Westmoreland Professor of Preaching, Southwestern Baptist Theological Seminary, Fort Worth, TX. Dr. Fasol is the author of books and articles on preaching and public communication.

[Haworth co-indexing entry note]: "Preaching to Senior Citizens." Fasol, Al. Co-published simultaneously in *Journal of Religious Gerontology* (The Haworth Pastoral Press, an imprint of The Haworth Press, Inc.) Vol. 15, No. 1/2, 2003, pp. 143-152; and: *Practical Theology for Aging* (ed: Derrel R. Watkins) The Haworth Pastoral Press, an imprint of The Haworth Press, Inc., 2003, pp. 143-152. Single or multiple copies of this article are available for a fee from The Haworth Document Delivery Service [1-800-HAWORTH, 9:00 a.m. - 5:00 p.m. (EST). E-mail address: docdelivery@haworthpress.com].

Digital Object Identifier: 10.1300/J078v15n01_11   *143*

They assumed we could not handle any concepts deeper than 'Run Spot run. See Spot run.' They assumed we found God boring and it was their responsibility to 'brighten' God up for us a bit. They assumed we were not interested in learning, especially not learning anything about God and the Bible. I guess they assumed we were preoccupied with our bodies and had no time to dwell on our souls." Lynn paused twenty seconds or so before concluding: "And now that I am old, I find ministers making the same assumptions. And, again, they make their assumptions without talking to us! It is as if when we were young and now that we are old, they think our minds cannot function nearly as well as theirs and so they speak condescendingly to us, and frankly I am tired of it!"

PREACHING TO SENIOR ADULTS–DIFFERENT OR SAME

Lynn had much more to say and she said it all emphatically! Is Lynn an exception? Is she isolated in her concerns? No to both questions. In ministering to and being ministered unto by many Christians sixty-five years of age and above, I have found Lynn verbalizes these concerns in the same way many of them would. My ministry experience with senior citizens has been primarily through pastorates and interim pastorates in Texas, New Mexico, New Jersey, Arkansas, Illinois, and Missouri. If Lynn is an exceptional senior citizen, the exceptions are numerous and their number is growing steadily.

A recent issue of the AARP Bulletin indicated many people in their seventies prefer to refer to themselves as 'older middle age.' We all know some people are 'old' when they are chronologically young and some people are 'young' when they are chronologically old. Some senior citizens indeed do suffer from mental debilitations at a higher rate than younger people do. To assume that mental capacities have drastically diminished for all 'older' people is an egregious mistake too many ministers make.

When does a person attain senior citizen status? The AARP recruits members when they celebrate their fiftieth birthday. Some restaurants offer 'senior' discounts beginning at age fifty-five. Some movie theaters offer discount prices to those sixty-two and above. An airline sends applications for senior citizen discounts for those sixty-three and above. For many years, retirement was required to begin at age sixty-five. Some companies claim they do not have a forced retirement age, but do require an annual review for employees age seventy and over. An ongoing joke in the ministry refers to pastor search committees seeking pastors "no older than thirty-five with at least thirty years of pastoral experience." Presumably, a pastor older than thirty-five will not "appeal to the younger adults." Is age thirty-five too old to be considered young? Is age seventy too young to be considered old?

We leave these virtually unanswerable questions with all of their variables to other writers. Our concern is, do we need to do anything different in preaching–whether it be in sermon preparation or in sermon delivery–when speaking to senior citizens? The answer is: no and yes.

THE "NO" PART OF THE ANSWER
RELATES TO BASIC HOMILETICS

1. Seek the guidance of the Holy Spirit in determining the biblical text for your sermon. As you pray about the text, do not pray with a semi-closed mind. That is, do not think to yourself, "Many passages of the Bible no longer pertain to older people." Be open to the entire counsel of God whenever you preach, and do not presume to know more about your congregation than the Holy Spirit does.

2. Continue to exercise sound hermeneutics as you exegete the text. The temptation to read our personal biases *into* the text is strong these days. In many ways, so-called "postmodern" thinking dictates we be *receptor oriented* in our hermeneutics, and *source oriented* in our preaching. This is exactly the opposite of good hermeneutics and good homiletics. We must acknowledge God as the author of all truth. The Bible is God's Holy Word and must be regarded as such. Thus, we must be source oriented as we read and study Scripture. God is the source, not our personal, transient feelings about what we want the Bible to say at the moment. Then, as we preach, we must be receptor oriented. We must work hard to be sure the congregation understands the message and understands the message is from the Bible, and not just the passing feelings we have on the passage at the moment.

3. We must continue to balance the appeals in the sermon. Some in the congregation are auditory learners, they like explanation of the text. This is good, because explanation of the text is where feeding from the Word takes place. Whether it be by sharing the context of the text, by making some theological assertions derived from your exegetical studies, by word pictures, or by some other means, the congregation will be gratified to learn something about the Bible. Others are visuals. They need an analogy, an illustration–either a figure of speech or an anecdote–to enable them to "see" what we are saying to them. Some people are kinesthetic in their approach to receiving messages. They need application of the text. They appreciate information, and they benefit from illustrations, but they need for someone to tell them how, when, where, why the message has direct bearing in their lives. All of us receive messages in all three ways, but each of us has a primary way of receiving a message. As you

prepare a sermon, seek some balance in explanation, illustration, and application.

4. Analyze the relationship between the text and the sermon. This is often done under the rubric of biblical authority. The direct biblical sermon is just that–what the text teaches, the sermon preaches. (Direct biblical preaching is often used synonymously with the term *expository preaching*. They are not necessarily one and the same.)

A sermon might also have secondary biblical authority, in which the sermon could complete an implication of the text, or the sermon could particularize a general truth of the text. The commandment "thou shalt not kill," for example, is often interpreted in its implications. Some preachers infer the commandment to be a prohibition against the death penalty, others would apply it to abortion, and some apply it to pacifism. Particularizing a general truth can be illustrated from Romans 12:9b "Abhor that which is evil." Under that broad admonition a large number of applications could be made. Some preachers have used it to speak against drug abuse, child pornography, or participating in a lottery. Casual biblical authority is a popular category among preachers. The casual biblical sermon selects some suggestion from the text, or focuses on some incidental item in the text.

A beautiful sermon, with causal biblical authority has been preached from Philippians 4:22 "All the saints salute you, chiefly those in Caesar's household." The direct idea of the text is simply that Christians send their greetings. The suggestion, though, that these greetings included people working in the very household where decrees against Christianity were authored, leads to a wonderful sermon. Harry Emerson Fosdick and J. D. Gray have both developed sermons from this text dealing with being a Christian in a difficult place. Frequently, preachers will focus on an incidental item in the text. This just about as frequently leads to a poor sermon. Recently, a speaker at a seminary chapel developed a sermon from Luke 5:1-11. Jesus had taught the people from a boat. When he finished his teaching, he told Peter to row to the deeper part of the water. He then told them to cast their nets. Peter explained they had toiled the night through and caught nothing, but at Jesus' word they would try again. They ended up with more fish than two boats could carry. As a result, Peter worshiped Jesus and followed him. The sermon at the seminary chapel from this text was developed in the most casual way possible. The points were: We must weave our nets, we must wash our nets, and we must work our net. The nets, obviously, are incidental in the text, yet the sermon focused on them.

Combination biblical authority is also possible, and that is simply any combination within the sermon of the various types of biblical authority.

5. Continue to employ good rules of rhetoric in your preparation. A thought clearly expressed is always worth much more than a thought unclearly but passionately expressed. As a fun exercise, read the sayings of Jesus in the gospels. Note how Jesus said so many profound things in simple language: "A sower went out to sow," "A certain man had two sons. The younger said unto his father, 'Give me mine inheritance,'" "sell all that you have and follow me," or "Who then do you think was a neighbor to this man?" Jesus knew how to get the most out of simple, everyday words. Many congregations wish their pastor would go and do likewise.

6. *Source credibility* does not change. This may be the most important item in this survey of significant communication techniques. Congregations measure us from the first moments they lay eyes on us. They are trying to determine what they are in for when we preach. Most congregants would agree they presume we are honorable persons (integrity) who know what we are talking about (expertise). They are trying to determine whether we are bombastic preachers or not (dynamism). Lets take a look at each of these items since each is vital to our credibility with a congregation.

Integrity is first because it is vital. People need to know they can believe in us. The history of Christianity is replete with charlatans. Even Paul had to defend his integrity, especially with the Corinthians (cf. 2 Corinthians, especially 5:10-15). If people cannot believe in us as servants of God eagerly desiring to be servants of the Word, they cannot believe the message we preach. We need to live up to 2 Cor. 4:5 "For we preach not ourselves, but Christ Jesus and ourselves your servants for Jesus' sake."

Expertise is important because people need for us to know how to rightly explain the word of truth. Most in our congregations will forgive, overlook, or tease us about some mental error. (If you quote John 3:16, for example, and assign it to Acts 3:16, you can be certain you will hear about it from several people, and most them will tease you about it.) We must be students of the Bible. The congregation is counting on us to diligent in our study.

Dynamism is an interesting study. Most communication studies show the higher the dynamism, the more quickly persuasive the speaker. That is why the classic 'shout, stomp, and sweat' preacher draws an immediate response, whether it be a favorable response, or not. The high dynamism speaker has a major problem. Many people relate to the speaker rather than the Lord. The high dynamism speaker, such as Billy Graham does, must constantly point beyond the speaker to the Lord.

Like a sliding scale, the lower dynamism, the longer it takes for a speaker to persuade a congregation. Many preachers who have a mid-level dynamism are accustomed to hearing people say, "You are growing on me." Either way, the most important thing you as a preacher can do is be true to your unique gifts and personality. Whether you be a high or mid-level dynamism speaker, be true to yourself.

THE YES PART OF THE ANSWER
REFERS TO YOUR CONGREGATION

Yes, some adaptations must be made when preaching to senior citizens. We make adaptations for every sermon and every congregation. We will look at these adaptations in general then we will look at some specific instances when preaching to senior citizens.

1. The first general adaptation is one we preachers make every time we prepare a sermon. As we think about the wording of the sermon, we are doing what communication professionals tell us is *encoding*. Encoding is the process by which we select the words that we think will enable the congregation to understand what we are saying. When the congregation hears these words, they will *decode*. Decoding, we hope, will allow them to understand the sermon. Communication is fascinating at this very point. So many variables enter into the process, it is almost amazing communication can be accomplished at all. Every word has both a denotative (definition) meaning, and a connotative (essentially what we feel about the word) meaning. Some of these feeling about words are positive and some are negative, and that differs with each person. Fortunately, we have enough common understanding of most words that the communication process can continue, and sermons can be preached.
2. Closely related to encoding and decoding is couching our words in a *frame of reference* familiar to the congregation. When Jesus said, "A sower went out to sow," he spoke in a frame of reference for all his listeners. Each of them could picture the sower and the seeds and the rocky ground, etc., because Jesus spoke within their frames of reference. Each congregation will have frames of reference much in common with other congregations. Each congregation will have individual frames of reference. Learn as much as you can about your congregation and honor their collective and individual frames of reference.
3. Remember, predictability is deadening. Predictability can be deadening in either content or delivery or both. Predictability in content means the congregation knows what you are going to say before you say it. When this occurs on a regular basis, the congregation will mentally abandon the preacher. Preachers in America's "Bible Belt" joke of not being able to preach on John 3, for good reason. Most congregations will tell you every preacher has a sermon on John 3, and they can tell you what the preacher is going to say about Jesus, Nicodemus, and being born again before the preacher says it. Communications experts warn us when we

are predictable, we have deadened the *impact* of our message. Most communication studies on impact have been done in the sales realm and in the political world. Conclusions from those studies are applicable to preaching.

Predictability can also occur in sermon delivery. In the middle part of the twentieth century, many preachers spoke in what was formally called a ministerial tone, but often facetiously called a ministerial whine. The ministerial tone was built on an exaggerated use of inflections with the higher inflections at the beginning of the sentence, and then sliding down the scale to a lower pitch inflection at the end of the sentence. Listeners used to ride the "waves" of this ministerial tone, listening to the ups and downs of the voice and had little reason to concentrate on the content much less make a favorable response. If there are ministerial tones today, they are found more often than not in volume, rather than inflection, patterns. Preachers today tend to be loud until they become tired, then they retreat to something close to a dramatic whisper, and then when they recover some strength, get loud again. All of these cause the congregation to pay more attention to how the message is said rather than to the content of the message. Whenever preachers do this, they cause congregations to maximize the *messenger* rather than the *message*. As a result, impact is diminished.

4. Closely related to impact is the fact that the *emotional* message we send travels much faster than the *intellectual* message we are sending. By emotional we refer to delivery of the sermon, and by intellectual we refer to the content of the message. People will see and feel what we are saying much more quickly than they hear what we are saying. Listeners see our body language, especially our facial expressions, and make a quick determination of how they are expected to feel about what we are saying. Then they hear the words, but by that time, new body language signal are registering with them. Our body language travels to the listeners with the speed of light. Our words plod along behind at the speed of sound. That is why so many charlatans have fooled many congregations. That is why so many gifted speakers have built communities of "faith" centered on the speaker's personality rather than upon the Lord. Our emotional messages, therefore, must always be in support of our content. That way we can magnify the message and minimize the messenger.

APPLICATION TO SENIOR CITIZENS

Of these various communications principles, the encoding/decoding, and frame of reference require the most adaptation when preaching to senior citizens.

When encoding the sermon, remember senior citizens place value on the words spoken as well as on how they are spoken. That is why the senior citizen is less impressed when the preachers says, for instance, "Like, Jesus is, you know, like Wow, man!" The senior citizen agrees with the sentiment, but wonders why you don't, won't, or worse, can't find the words to express your emotions. The senior citizen had the good fortune to be exposed to speakers and writers who did express in words what they felt. The senior citizen, on those occasions, was transported both mentally and emotionally. They liked that experience and want more of it. They marvel that anyone could be content riding the crests of emotional experiences at the expense of intellectual experiences. For the senior citizen, the real high comes when we communicate both the intellectual and the emotional messages. The senior citizen wants both to know and to feel the message.

Compare two excerpts from recent sermons preached on Sunday mornings in a church worship service. The subject was the holiness of God.

> Excerpt #1. "God is different, people. I mean, He is different, totally, awesomely different. I mean, we got to understand God is different. Do you hear me, people? God is so different, there is no way to tell you except that He is different than us."

> Excerpt #2. "The holiness of God means God is set apart from us. Because God is holy, God commands our deepest respect, our profound dedication. God calls from us our best in everything we say and do. Why is God justified in making this demand of us? Because, despite being set apart, God took the form of a man, but not just any kind of man, a servant kind of man. But not just any kind of servant, but an obedient servant. Not just any kind of obedience, but obedience unto death. God chose this humility, died so we may have life, and arose from the dead. As a result every knee shall bow and every tongue confess that Jesus Christ is Lord!"

One of these excerpts has much more appeal, much more meaning, and provides a much deeper experience of worship not only for the senior citizen, but especially for senior citizens.

Frames of reference are always important. The senior citizen has a large frame of reference. The senior citizen lived through much of the twentieth century and is not experiencing the twenty-first century. The expanse of human knowledge has grown exponentially in that time. A few senior citizens will remember a time when there were no cars, trucks, or buses. Almost all senior citizens can remember the arrival of television. They were children or young adults during the "Great Depression" and World War II. These events shaped their lives and their ways of perceiving reality. Their generation popularized Rock and Roll music. (Their generation did not invent it, they will tell you. Rock and Roll was invented centuries before in primitive societies.) They survived summers without air conditioning, and they found information they needed in books in places called libraries. They also provided the expertise which led to today's computers, and the communications revolution, and they love communicating by e-mail rather than snail-mail.

They also grieved at the news from Littleton, Colorado and from other school shootings. A contemporary preacher, using the self pity approach, said his generation has it much worse than any generation previous to his. Why? Because they have to survive things such as Littleton, Colorado, the Oklahoma City bombing, and the destruction of the World Trade Center on September 11, 2001. Senior citizens must survive those things too. It is always a drastic mistake to think senior citizens live in the past only, and are not affected by recent tragedies.

The frames of reference for senior citizens is indeed a large one. However, that is a great advantage for the preacher. It opens a larger realm of experiences from which illustrative material may be drawn. The preacher may refer to the Great Depression in reference to the biblical teaching about perseverance; or to World War II, and perhaps specifically to D-Day in reference to commitment; or to Marilyn Monroe as an example of the loneliness of being the subject of idol worship; or to Billy Graham as a prophetic voice. In addition references may be made to a wide spectrum of literature. Senior citizens, as a matter of routine learned something of societal values and good citizenship from reading Jane Eyre, Charles Dickens, Daniel Defoe, Bret Harte, Samuel Butler. You can refer to a multitude of life experiences. Senior citizens, for instance, drove their cars into an actual "Service Station" where their gasoline tanks would be filled while their oil was being checked and their windows cleaned. They never had to leave their cars to have them serviced!

Senior citizens love humor. Not only contrived jokes, but they understand satire and dry humor. They will give you a wry smile, for example, when you compare the service station of yesterday with the self serve stations of today. They will reward you with gales of laughter when you share with them your experience trying to cook with one of Mom's recipes and searching in vain for instructions as to how to set the microwave oven.

Senior citizens are a loyal people. In general, senior citizens cannot do enough for anyone they like, and would prefer to have little to do with any one they do not like. They like preachers who see them as viable and vital people who have worlds of wisdom to share. They like preachers who take time to know something of who they are and from whence they have come. They like preachers who speak to them as people who still have contributions to make. They like preachers who do not speak condescendingly to them.

Have you ever preached to a senior citizen group in your church? It is a wonderful experience. To paraphrase from an old movie titled *State Fair* (starring Jean Crain and Dana Andrews), "Don't miss it if you can!"

SOME SUGGESTED READING ABOUT PREACHING

Carl, William J., ed. *Graying Gracefully: Preaching to Older Adults.* Louisville: Louisville: Westminster John Knox, 1997.

Claypool, John R. *The Preaching Event.* San Francisco: HarperSanFrancisco, 1989.

Fasol, Al. *A Complete Guide to Sermon Delivery.* Nashville: Broadman & Holman Publishers, 1996.

Hightower, James E. and Martin Thielen, compilers. *Preaching That Heals: Pastoral Preaching For Hurting People.* Nashville: Convention Press, 1991.

Lowry, Eugene L. *The Sermon: Dancing the Edge of Mystery.* Nashville: Abingdon Press, 1997.

Wagley, Laurence A. *Preaching With The Small Congregation.* Nashville: Abingdon Press, 1989.

Chapter 11

A Practical Theological Model for Worship with Alzheimer's Patients: Using the Validation Technique

DeeAnn Klapp, DMin

SUMMARY. This article forwards a model of ministry specifically designed to include persons with Alzheimer's Disease in worship at care facilities. Validation techniques, which are compatible with Biblical teaching and principles, are found to be a viable means of engaging residents in meaningful worship. *[Article copies available for a fee from The Haworth Document Delivery Service: 1-800-HAWORTH. E-mail address: <docdelivery@haworthpress.com> Website: <http://www.HaworthPress.com> © 2003 by The Haworth Press, Inc. All rights reserved.]*

KEYWORDS. Model, Alzheimer's, validation, worship, individuation, integration, boundaries, differentiation, marginality, harmonious, transfiguration, conformity, affirmation, God's memory, sacrament, Holy

Dr. Klapp is a United Methodist Pastor in Iowa. She works with nursing homes in her region to provide worship services for residents, especially those suffering from Alzheimer's Disease. She is a Graduate of Garrett Theological Seminary (MDiv) and Saint Paul School of Theology (DMin).

[Haworth co-indexing entry note]: "A Practical Theological Model for Worship with Alzheimer's Patients: Using the Validation Technique." Klapp, DeeAnn. Co-published simultaneously in *Journal of Religious Gerontology* (The Haworth Pastoral Press, an imprint of The Haworth Press, Inc.) Vol. 15, No. 1/2, 2003, pp. 153-170 and: *Practical Theology for Aging* (ed: Derrel R. Watkins) The Haworth Pastoral Press, an imprint of The Haworth Press, Inc., 2003, pp. 153-170. Single or multiple copies of this article are available for a fee from The Haworth Document Delivery Service [1-800-HAWORTH, 9:00 a.m. - 5:00 p.m. (EST). E-mail address: docdelivery@haworthpress.com].

http://www.haworthpress.com/store/product.asp?sku=J078
© 2003 by The Haworth Press, Inc. All rights reserved.
Digital Object Identifier: 10.1300/J078v15n01_12

153

Communion, manifestation, disoriented, therapy, developmental, method, assessment, maloriented, validator, compatibility

Even to your old age, I shall be the same. (Is. 46:4)

A THEOLOGICAL MODEL FOR THE PRACTICE OF MINISTRY

Reflection on both Scripture and experience of the Christian mystics, I have designed a model for illustrating a foundational theology for ministry among the institutionalized elderly. Through prayerful study and research, I perceive two essential movements grounded in the nature of God and Person of Christ revealed by the Spirit.

The first is Worship (Adoration), characterized by an alternating rhythm of inward devotion and outward deed, which is entirely subject to the bidding of God. Worship is equally dependent upon our faithful response: loving and trusting obedience.

The second movement is directed by a principle of Individuation and Integration, which I perceive as being inherent in God's activity and in humanity as created in God's image. This principle is operative in the correlation of the redemption of the world with individual salvation, which theories of atonement must address. It is also evident in the "tension" between personal devotion and corporate worship.

Both movements, Worship as devotion and deed (Adoration), and the principle of Individuation and Integration, are manifest in the Person of Jesus and the work of the Holy Spirit. To illustrate these movements, their independence and their implications, I have designed the matrix in Figure 1.

This model begins with God's initiative expressed as Grace. Grace is communicated through the Word and the eternal Word made incarnate in Jesus Christ to humanity. Christ comes to us from God as the Son of Man and Servant. All of creation is the field of the work of God by the power of the Holy Spirit. The grace of God is experienced, lived, and broadly communicated through individuals, and through the Church as the body, in individual and corporate worship that weds prayer with service (Adoration). Finally, that grace, united with human adoration, returns through the salvific and perfect work of Christ as glory to God who first gave it.

The boundaries between the individual/community and devotion/deed are orderly, yet fluid. Prayer and action eventually become one continuous act of adoration. Likewise, the individuals and community are encompassed by the larger context of relationship with God through Jesus Christ. The Holy Spirit is

FIGURE 1

God's Initiative and Action

Our Response and Action

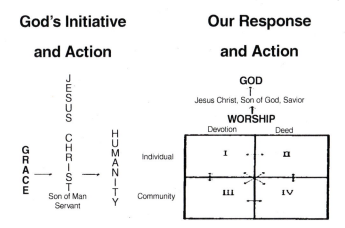

the agent, which elicits and empowers the adoration of the individual and the community by revealing the Son.

The principle of individuation and integration is similar to Jung Young Lee's emphasis on the concept of differentiation as a process of God's gift of creation. "Creation then is a process of separating what is united. Just as cells separate and create new cells in organisms, by dividing light from darkness or dry land from water, the world was born. Creation makes things different. In chaos things are indifferent, but in creation, they change. The repetition 'of every kind' suggests the importance of variety in the creative process."[1]

Lee creatively pulls things apart to find harmonious unity within the margin of marginality. However, at some semi-conscious level, the process of Integration is imbedded and espoused in his own oriental culture: "In Asia, and particularly in Korea, 'I' and 'we' are synonymous. For example, my parents are our parents, my home is our home . . . I-am is pluralistic because it is relational . . . in other words, I-am is defined in terms of we-are, because we-are is considered to be more fundamental than I-am."[1]

Lee's theological insights and concept of marginality are instructional in the conceptualization of the spiritual plight of Alzheimer's patients who are socially isolated and psychologically marginalized. Positing Jesus as the margin of the marginalized, theologically includes even these souls, deemed helpless and hopeless by the world, within in the margins of God's creative trace. In such a state of degeneration, the Alzheimer's patient has very little resource to cooperate. Although Lee might affirm that Christ is present to the marginalized, that is but a thin theological thread tossed out gingerly where a strong hauling chain, a spiritual lifeline, is desperately needed. My theological model launches that lifeline.

The alternating rhythm of devotion and deed, personal and corporate relationship with God, is present in all aspects of Jesus' life through the process of individuation and integration. He sought the solitude of the hillside for prayer, and then returned to save the disciples at sea (Mark 6:47-51). He descended from the mount of His transfiguration to be met by the multitude and a father desperate for the deliverance of his possessed son (Matt. 17:14). This suggests that prayer is the power pack for action in conformity with God's will. Through his life, Jesus closely blends prayer, proclamation and action into one continuous act of Adoration; a pageant of glory to the Father. When imposed upon the matrix previously discussed, the drama of Christ's passion vividly illustrates the fluid interplay of all four quadrants (see Figure 2).

The Holy Spirit is the energy of God, which reveals the Son (John 16:14), convicts the sinner (John 16:9), empowers believers (Acts 1:8), edifies the community (Eph. 4:11-13), and escorts the soul homeward to God by way of Jesus Christ (John 14:3). It is the presence of God's love with and within the yielded heart that enables one in human finitude to see, receive, reflect and respond to the Almighty. By the Holy Spirit, God has made it possible that "we all with unveiled face, beholding the glory of the Lord are being changed into His likeness" (2Cor. 3:18) This transforming power is instructive, curative, redemptive, and communicative as illustrated dramatically by the variety of gifts listed in 1 Corinthians 12. The principle of Individuation and Integration is operative in the Spirit as human spirit is joined with the divine in the individual and with the community of believers, the Church. This Spirit, which calls each soul and binds all in love as one body, is the lifeline of lives darkened and paralyzed by Alzheimer's disease.

THEOLOGY MODEL AND THE CHURCH

My theological model also serves to illustrate the position and nature of the Church within the context of a mystical spirituality and practical service. Jurgen Moltmann's concept of the Church in terms of glory speaks to the totality of adoration previously discussed. Humanity enters into this pageant of praise through the hospitality of the Trinity. Once again we see the principle of *individuation and integration*:

> . . . the glorifying of the Father and Son through the Holy Spirit . . . the Trinity in the glorification's from its eschatological goal, open for the gathering and uniting of me and the whole creation with God and in

God . . . the Holy Spirit glorifies Christ in the world and the world in Christ to the glory of the Father. By effecting this he unites creation with the Son and the Father as he unites the Son himself with the Father.[2]

As the force that glorifies, the Holy Spirit is also the power of unification: "The unity of the triune God is the goal of uniting man and creation with the Father and the Son in the Spirit. The history of the Kingdom of God on earth is nothing other than the history of the uniting of what has been separated, and freeing of what has been broken, in this being the history of the glorification of God."[3]

Christ is in every way a unity of both head and body. The body, the Church does not and cannot exist without Christ, the head. Together, the Church and the Spirit of Christ are Christ. "Christ is therefore only Christ in the full sense together with the Church."[4] How does the Church figure on the matrix (see Figure 3)?

By this revision of the original model, the Church (shaded area) is firmly embedded in the matrix centered upon and directed toward Christ, which by no means, prevents the revelation of Christ within the freedom of God to arenas outside the Church's immediate range. The white area within the square is the range of mission yet unrealized by the Church. Herein are the marginalized, the poor, the unchurched, the non-Christian, the agonistic, and the atheist. All are well within prevenient grace and mission of the Church yet unclaimed, unliberated, and/or non-confessional. As Moltmann states:

> It (the Church) then has no need to look sideways in suspicion or jealousy at the saving efficacies of the Spirit outside the church; instead it can recognize them thankfully as signs that the Spirit is greater than the Church and that God's purpose of salvation reaches beyond the Church.[5]

Moltmann cites three assurances of Christ's presence from the New Testament:

1. Christ is present in the apostolate, the sacraments, and in fellowship.
2. Christ is present in the "least of these."
3. Christ is present in the coming Parousia.[6]

The Alzheimer's resident qualifies as one among "the least of these."

WORSHIP

My theological model depicts worship as Adoration, an all-inclusive singularly directed response to God. Shawn Madigan, author of *Spirituality Rooted in Liturgy,* would agree. She quotes Origen:

The one who links together prayer with deeds of duty and first seemly actions with that prayer is the one who prays without ceasing; for the virtuous deeds are taken up as part of prayer. . .The whole life of the saint is one might, integrated prayer."[7]

I believe worship, thus defined, is the most important thing Christians do. It is, therefore, the most important aspect of faith to make accessible to the "least of these." It is also the "primary mode of remembering and expressing Christian faith."[8] Essential to the expression of worship are singing, reading, and the proclamation of the Word in the midst of the gathered community.[9] A worship experience for the resident with Alzheimer's disease may be the only opportunity for long forgotten memories of childhood songs, fragments of Scripture, and religious acts to be stimulated and remembered. Worship that includes corporate prayer gives opportunity for the person to spiritually link with others in fellowship with God through the power of the Holy Spirit.

Saliers cites four basic features:

1. Gestures of gratitude such as praise and thanksgiving to God for God's Self even more than the blessings given.
2. Acts that remember and retell the story of who God is and what God has done through singing, reading, and proclaiming the Word of God in fellowship.
3. Acts that recall who we are, and acknowledge our humanity, our creatureliness, and our deep need for God. Praise reveals the soul contrasted against God's holiness . . .
4. Communal prayer directs the heart to the need of others and opens the spirit to the touch of the Holy Spirit.[10]

Through the Word, our words and actions of praise, thanksgiving, confession, intercession, and our participation in the Sacraments, the soul remembers God. In his paper "Worship and Sanctification," Dr. Henry H. Knight III affirms that remembrance is not in essence a recalling of past events or persons. "Rather, *anamnesis* is remembrance in which the event or person becomes present to us–it is something like experiencing that event or person anew, as a present reality."[11]

Moreover, through worship comes the affirmation that God remember the soul. In his article "Memory, the Community Looks Backward," Stephen Sapp writes: "Whether the individual remembers, or even whether the community remembers for the individual, the Western religious tradition certainly affirms that *God* remembers. Some comfort, therefore, can be found in the fact that

God's memory is unfailing, even if that of any given human being is defective or even totally lost. God never forgets."[12]

The affirmation given by God to Israel in the midst of loss and forsakenness is a word for the Alzheimer's patient in the midst of confusion and memory loss. "But Zion said, 'The Lord has forsaken me, and the Lord has forgotten me.' 'Can a woman forget her nursing child, and have no compassion on the son of her womb? Even these may forget, but I will not forget you" (Is. 49:14-15).

Certainly the conviction of the author of Psalm 139 that the Spirit of God, who is knowledgeable even of our unformed words, scattered thoughts, comings and goings, our sitting and rising, from the edge of the sea to the depths of *sheol*, and as high as the heights of heaven, is that one whom God remembers. The conviction of Apostle Paul that nothing can separate us from the love of God in Jesus (Rom. 8:36) is that of one whom God remembers. God's memory is more than mere recognition. It implies providential and salvific action. God remembers with divine Presence. The prophet cries out, "Thou who knowest, O Lord, remember me, take notice of me" (Jer. 15:15).

David Keck focuses on Memory; not that of the patient whose memory is deteriorating, but God's memory, which is infinite, eternal, and flawless. He asserts that: "God's very presence, grace and mercy are expressed through the

FIGURE 2. Christ's Passion

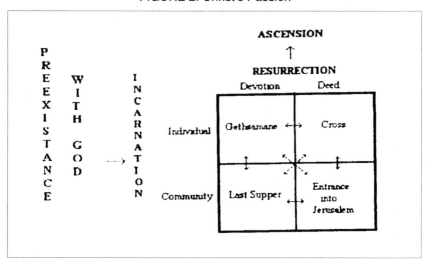

FIGURE 3. The Church

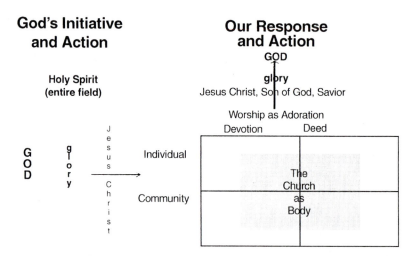

divine memory. The blinded Samson's strength is reborn when God answers his prayer to be remembered (Judges 17:28), and Rachel is able to conceive because 'God remembered Rachel'"[13] (Gen. 30:20).

Keck further cites that the prophets, psalmists, apostles, and even Jesus invoked God's memory. He equates God's memory with God's fidelity. Because God remembers, the resident who cannot has hope. It is ultimately God's memory, not one's own, through which Alzheimer's resident has communion with God in the power and realm of the Spirit. The divine presence and care, to the depth of the soul, beyond all consciousness, is indeed the mystical experience. Keck observes that in *Dark Night of the Soul*, St. John of the Cross "suggests perhaps that dementia-like states and a seeming isolation from God are not alien to the purgation trials of mysticism."[14]

Given that the prophets, psalmist, apostles, and especially Jesus called forth God's memory, it is appropriate and critical for the person with Alzheimer's disease to also rely upon God's remembrance. To Salier's list of worship essentials, I add a fifth element: Invocation of the Memory of God.

Calling forth our remembrance of God, the celebration of the Sacrament of Holy Communion is integral to Worship. By its very nature, features of this Sacrament embrace the helplessness characteristic of the Alzheimer patient. This sacred encounter may be assisted by, but is not dependent upon, cognitive receptivity of information about God.

"I am not saying that worship does not provide information about God which we cognitively appropriate and then will to emulate. Rather, I am suggesting that in worship we encounter the God revealed in Jesus Christ, who is present by way of the Holy Spirit and made known to us through faith, which is the gift of the Holy Spirit."[15] The power of Christ's act initiates recognition in the person's spirit. In the Emmaus road episode, it was at table our risen Lord was recognized (Luke 24:30-31).

"Don't you find it interesting that they recognized him only when he was at table with them? They did not see him, even when he interpreted the scriptures for them. It was only when Jesus repeated those familiar four-fold table actions of taking, blessing, breaking, and giving of bread that they were given the recognition. It was only at the table that the scripture made sense, that their eyes were opened and they at last began to understand what was happening among them."[16] The reality of Christ's constancy over all time overarches the temporally time-confused and disoriented resident. Here, at the table of our Lord, the person is enveloped in the true and greater Reality.

"Proclaiming the death of the Lord until he comes points to the future that is known. Whenever Christians gather in memory of Jesus Christ, the past, the present, and the future come together."[17]

The celebration of the Sacrament spiritually reaffirms the identity of the person who no longer remembers his or her own name. St. Augustine believed that through the sharing of the bread and cup of Christ's life, death, and resurrection, we receive our identity.[18] Don Saliers states that, " . . . gathering for the Word and the prayers and the Lord's Supper was an identity-conferring activity. It was a manifestation of who they were and who they were yet to become."[19]

Finally, it is at the table of our Lord that the person with Alzheimer's disease, isolated from society, loved ones and self, through loss, has communion with God and all the saints.

"Life in accordance with the teaching of the apostles and in the continuing practice of the breaking of the bread, referred to in Acts 2:4ff, sustains the living memory of Jesus. What is said and done by the community gathered is embodied in the community scattered in word and deed.[20] Given these parameters of Worship, how might persons with Alzheimer's disease be led in authentic worship?"

VALIDATION AS A MEANS OF MINISTRY

"And when did we see You sick, or in prison, and come to You?" And the King will say to them. Truly I say to you, to the extent that you did it to

one of these brothers of mine, even the least of them, you did it to unto Me
(Matt. 25:39-40).

A major barrier for ministry to institutionalized persons with Alzheimer's disease is difficulty in communication. For instance, during a visitation, a person may relate to the pastor as their child, or be distracted by a desperate search for a "lost" item or deceased loved one. The pastor may be erroneously accused of stealing some possession, or attempting to do harm. Disoriented residents may sway back and forth, pound their fists, curse and act out. Some have retreated so completely that they relate to no one.

Formerly, a kindly voice, short familiar Scripture passage, a brief prayer and maybe a gentle touch has been the extent of spiritual nurturing for these folks so close to the Kingdom, yet psychologically light years distant from those who would minister to their needs. Any theory which contributes to the practice of ministry without contradiction against sound theological and biblical teaching would be a boon to the spiritual needs of "the least of these." Validation (formerly Validation Therapy) holds such promise.

WHAT IS VALIDATION?

In her book, *Validation Breakthrough,* Noami Feil defines Validation as a "therapy for communicating with the old-old people who are diagnosed as having Alzheimer's disease and related dementias."[21] At a Validation workshop held in Topeka, Kansas on December 4, 1996, Feil further elaborated by saying Validation was basically three things:

1. It is a developmental theory of late life which posits that when people get very old it is appropriate for them to express feelings they have locked up inside. Analogous to muscles that weaken with age and effect physical control, emotional controls are slipping.
2. It is a method using fifteen basic simple verbal and non-verbal techniques and interventions. Feil has identified four stages of deterioration. Verbal techniques are used for stages I and II; nonverbal methods, for lower functioning levels III and IV.
3. It is a unique way of working with groups that is not reality orientation, remotivation, reminiscing, or cognitive therapy, although all of these may partly contribute to the interaction of group members. The function of the group is to help members work on resolution of life issues and emotions that have erupted in old age in the forms of disorientation, confusion, unintelligible jargon, raw emotion, repetitive movement, and total withdrawal.[22]

The following are the basic principles of Validation:

1. All people are unique and must be treated as individuals.
2. All people are valuable, no matter how disoriented they are.
3. There is a reason behind the behavior of disoriented people.
4. Behavior of old-old age is not merely a function of anatomic changes in the brain, but reflects a combination of physical, social, and psychological changes that take place over the lifespan.
5. Old-old people cannot be forced to change their behaviors. Behaviors can change only if the person wants to change them.
6. Old-old people must be accepted without judgment.
7. Particular life tasks are associated with each stage of life. Failure to complete a task at the appropriate stage of life may lead to psychological problems.
8. When more recent memory fails, older adults try to restore balance to their lives by retrieving earlier memories. When eyesight fails, they use the mind's eye to see. When hearing goes, they listen to sounds from the past.
9. Painful feelings that are expressed, acknowledged, and validated by a trusted listener will diminish. Painful feelings that are ignored or suppressed will gain strength.
10. Empathy builds trust, reduces anxiety, and restores dignity.[23]

Feil has also established criteria to determine candidates who are most likely to benefit from Validation. It is not for everyone. It is designed for persons with early onset of Alzheimer's disease, and not the very old with significant history of mental illness, or those who have suffered organic trauma, or oriented, well-elderly. Those who qualify would also be the most difficult persons for pastors to visit.

Critical to Validation is the assessment of the person's level of functioning. Feil cites four stages of resolution. Although a resident might vacillate in several or all levels at different times of the day, one stage is most predominant. Validation methods correspond with each level of functioning. Essential to the therapy at all levels is the therapist's ability to "center" by a means of breathing techniques.[24] This enables the therapist to step aside of self in order to be fully present to the person receiving Validation.

The first stage of final resolution Feil terms "Maloriented." This person functions fairly well with the exception of saying things that are untrue. For example, a woman with short-term memory loss may have mislaid her ring and insist that it was stolen. She does not want to deal with her emotions, is in denial about physical losses, and is working very hard to rationalize her disability and maintain all appearance of normality. She resists touch. She displays harsh intolerance for people who cannot (will not) exercise self-control. There are six verbal strategies of therapy for persons in this stage.

The second progressive stage is "Time Confusion." Burdened by too many losses and emotional exhaustion, these people have given up on the present and relive the past. They are not oriented to clock time. As Feil describes them:

Instead of tracking minutes, they track memories. They lose track of present time and trace their lifetime. One feeling triggers another. A person or an object is the present the symbol–the ticket to yesterday.[25]

Speech is slow. The ability to write is gone, but reading may yet be possible. Muscles are loose and movement is graceful. Rational thinking deteriorates along with eyesight and hearing. Facts are not correctly remembered. Feelings can be verbalized. There is recall of past events, but little short-term memory. The person readily senses who is genuine and who is not. Feelings are often symbolized: for example, "a person is hungry for love. Love = food. They demand food right after lunch."[26]

Although it might be awkward for a visitor to see the resident rocking a doll like a preschooler, it is helpful to realize that the resident is not reverting back to childhood, but reliving her own adulthood by remembering her feelings of usefulness, purpose, and satisfaction.[27] A visitor may serve as symbol for parent, or sibling, with whom the person is longing to resolve unfinished business.

At this stage, emotional controls have begun to weaken. The person reverts back to the most basic, universal feelings: love, fear, anger, and sadness. He/she is unable to categorize and is likely to think in images rather than words.[28] Attention span is short. Controls learned and practiced as an adult fade so that basic instincts such as sex, love and food demand immediate gratification.[29]

In addition to the techniques of fact questions, rephrasing, the use of preferred sense and polarity, touch is critical at the level of Time confusion. There are nine other techniques useful in engaging the person at level II.[30]

If the person is not consistently validated at level II, the deterioration will progress to level III, which Feil terms as the Repetitive Movement stage. Verbal skills are lost and are substituted with sounds and "pre-language movement" as a means to express emotion, process unresolved conflict, and sustain self-nurture.[31] Movement is not random or meaningless, but linked with the conflict or loss itself. For example, a man pounding his fist on his leg may be physically expressing his need for the sense of self-worth and purpose he once had as a worker in construction. The woman rocking back and forth muttering "ma, ma, ma, ma," may be remembering when she was mothered and felt safe and loved.[32]

In addition to eleven characteristics that accompany Repetitive Movement stage, Feil theorizes that the person has resigned to isolation and self-stimulation. Movements, vocalizations, lack of focus, inability to think, are all signs of turning inward to find solace in early memories and reassurance. This is a continual attempt to resolve and express feelings.[33] The outside world is being shut out so that the inside world can do resolution work with diminishing resources.

Methods of communicating with a person at stage III include tactile and audile stimulations. Touch is associated with earliest memories that are embedded as imprints in the mind.[34] Feil describes seven types of touch that are most effective and the emotion/response they are likely to elicit.[35] As with the Time Confused, music also is an important means of communication with persons at Stage III. Although they speak incoherently, they may sing clearly. Familiar songs, simple prayers, even nursery rhymes may be used to stimulate response. At this stage, mirroring behavior and affect is essential. The man pounding his fist, the woman soulfully rocking might relate with the validator who likewise mirrors their actions and validates their feelings.

The person at level II who has not been validated eventually slides into the last level: Vegetation. These are the people most difficult to reach and the most frequently overlooked. Their inner and outer world is almost entirely shut down. Eyes are unfocused, bland, but more often closed. Movement is almost imperceptible. There is no recognition of loved ones. Feelings are no longer expressed. It is critical for the validator to know the history of the person in the Vegetation stage because there are no other personal clues. They are the "living dead people."[36] They require person-to-person attention, touch and nurturing for the duration of their lives. Any response, such as eye contact, facial expression, faint singing, tears or crying, the slightest movement of hands or fee, is one small step from Vegetation.

THE VALIDATION GROUP

Validation Group is designed to help enable persons at Stage II and Stage III to interact, express feelings, work on common issues, retrieve social roles, and regain their sense of self-worth. The goals of the group are to stimulate energy (response), a renewed sense of identity, verbal interchange, the establishment of social controls, and to generate a greater sense of well-being.[37]

Roles are assigned that are suited to the past history of specific members of the group. For example, a person who had been active in organizations may be assigned the role of Group Leader. Some one who likes to sing becomes the Song Leader. A former housewife takes the role of Hostess and serves light refreshments. Included might be poetry readers, secretary, chair arranger, and decorations chairperson. Roles are devised to engage each of the members of the group as much as possible.

Group meetings are simply structured. The appointed leader opens the meeting by welcoming the participants. Music follows. Conversation revolves around specific topics such as the need to belong, friendship, boredom, and helping each other. The following activity involves movement such as a game of catch with a large soft ball. As members' names are called, they "catch the ball." Simple arts and crafts projects like crayon drawing, kneading and creating with dough can also be shared as part of the group experience. These are ways through which persons can express feelings that will generate a deeper sense of self-worth.

THE VALIDATOR

The validator does not mistake the child-like behavior of the disoriented old-old for childishness. Punishing or parental words and patronizing or condescending demeanor are avoided in deference to the feelings, privacy and personhood of the very aged. The validator translates expressed feelings in words, which supports, "validates" the person's sense of dignity and self-worth and accepts the person behind the behavior.[38] Without "playing into" the person's disorientation, which would be manipulative, or "feeding the fantasy" which would be dishonest, the validator is an attentive, empathetic listener providing a safe place for the person to diffuse feelings denied or buried for a lifetime.

VALIDATION AS A MEANS OF PASTORAL CARE

I have outlined the tenets of Validation in considerable detail to demonstrate its inherent compatibility with the work of ministry. Although Validation was conceived and developed within nonreligious disciplines, all of the materials I have studied clearly involve a profound spiritual dimension. Validation holds no contempt for religious conviction. It incorporates memories of religious training as part of the general pool of potential stimulants to retard further emotional deterioration. It allows the therapeutic value of faith.

The profile of a validator's work is consistent with the biblical texts I have reviewed: reverence for the worth of the individual, unconditional acceptance of the person beyond the behavior, the concern to preserve the inner life of the person, and self-denial to meet the person's greater need. As participant in a

Validation group I observed that the roles, activities, and overall characteristics of the meeting provide an excellent structure for a weekly worship service. Given the theological considerations afore mentioned, the person with Alzheimer's disease is not beyond the sight, presence or reach of God's Spirit. When awareness of movement and body are lost, God's awareness of position and motion remain. The person whose language cannot be deciphered, or is silent, is completely understood by God. Even those who have slipped in the night of Vegetation have not slid beneath God's consciousness. These convictions are a bay window of hope for pastoral intervention and have provided the impetus for my Praxis Project.

CONCLUSION: VALIDATION IN MINISTRY

Blessed are the poor in spirit, for theirs is the Kingdom of Heaven. (Matt. 5:33)

After seeing a stage production of *The Miracle Worker*, Validation therapist Scott Averill observed that the condition of a resident with Alzheimer's disease is a little like that of Helen Keller as a deaf and blind child. She was a person submerged beneath disability who was little understood, thrashed out desperately to communicate, and was unable to meaningfully interact with the world outside her inner life. The skill, faith, and perseverance of Ann Sullivan, repeatedly tested by failed trials, at last broke through silent darkness to touch the mind, heart, and spirit of her challenging pupil.

The resident with Alzheimer's disease is a person submerged beneath depths of progressive disability who is little understood, frustrated in attempts to communicate, and is unable to meaningfully interact with the world outside inner life. The scope of this writing is my search to find the signs that will touch the heart, mind, and soul of my most challenging parishioner.

A review of biblical texts confirms that Alzheimer's patients are persons of inestimable worth before God. They are hardly beyond the reach of God! Theological reflection affirms that by virtue of their losses, utter helplessness and impoverished life, a resident with Alzheimer's disease may be a particular concern of the protection, guardianship and care of God. They may, in fact, be far closer to the Kingdom than those self-reliant, non-impaired persons who decidedly have no need of God. Intellect, or lack of it, does not determine or preclude the touch of the Holy Spirit upon the heart. Even though the person may forget, God remembers.

Validation rationale and methods, which are compatible with the attributes of the Gospel, are applicable to ministry and pastoral care. The Validation group model can be adapted to include all of the elements of authentic worship as *adoration*, which is the principal expression of faith for fellowship with God in Christ and His Church.

In context of the model described, the ministry of worship among residents with Alzheimer's disease utilizing Validation techniques of communication can be plotted on the matrix in Figure 4.

This ministry is represented by the spray of dots within the shaded area (the Church), at and beyond its borders. This array portrays the variations of individual involvement in church, varieties of personal faith, and faith expressed as acts of devotion and deed. Some persons having little or no connection with the Body of Christ are encompassed by the Church's outreach: in this case, the Ministry of the Least of These. The primary means of that outreach is the Worship service which employs Validation as to communicate the reality of the presence of God and invite the person's reception of that Grace through Word, Praise, Prayer, Community and Sacrament. In the Sacrament of Holy Communion, the Church as the Body of Christ, spiritually present to those who cannot physically attend church, forms a new, connected community of faith. This newly formed, spiritually connected community is evident by residents sharing, helping, praying with and for one another, and communing together.

FIGURE 4

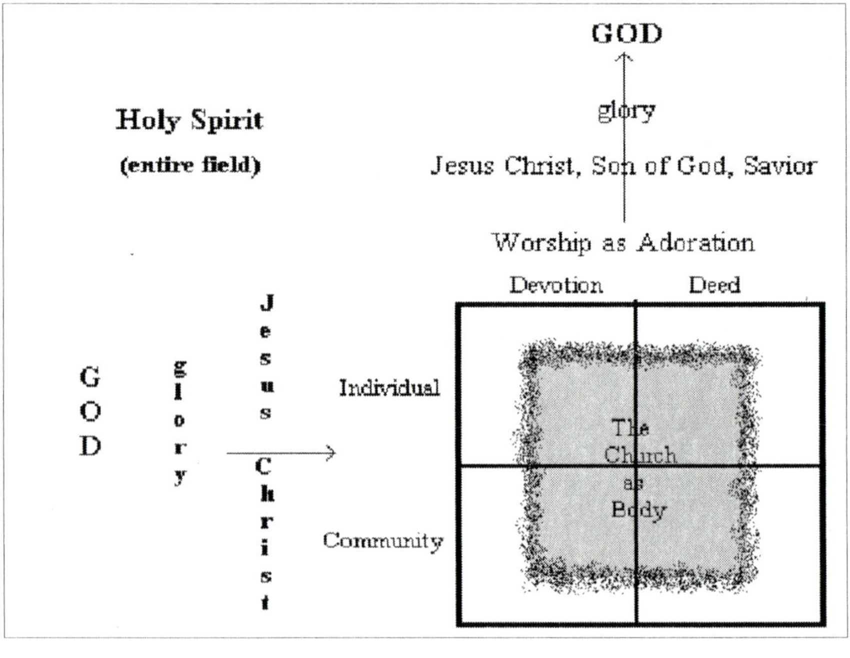

NOTES

1. Jung Young Lee, *Marginality–The Key to Multicultural Theology* (Minneapolis: Fortress Press, 1995). 104.
2. Jurgen Moltmann, *The church in the Power of the Spirit.* (Minneapolis, Minnesota: Fortress Press, 1993), 199, 60.
3. Ibid., 62.
4. Ibid., 72.3
5. Ibid., 65.
6. Ibid., 125.
7. Shawn Madigan, *Spirituality Rooted in Liturgy* (Washington: The Pastoral Press, 1983), 8-9.
8. Don E. Saliers, *Worship and Spirituality* (Philadelphia,: Westminster Press, 1984), 36.
9. Ibid., 36.
10. Ibid., 38-39.
11. Dr. Henry Knight, "Worship and Sanctification," 2, class handout, used with permission, Saint Paul School of Theology, Kansas City.
12. Sapp, 1997, 54.
13. Jane Marie Thibault, *A Deepening Love Affair: The Gift of God in Later Life.* (Nashville: The Upper Room Press, 1993), 10.
14. Ibid., 104.
15. Knight, 8.
16. William H. Willimon, *With God and Generous Hearts* (Nashville: The UpperRoom Press, 1986), 141.
17. Madigan, 1988, 69.
18. Saliers, 1984, 75.
19. Ibid., 77.
20. Ibid., 77.
21. Naomi Feil, *The Validation Breakthrough; Simple Techniques for Communicating with People With "Alzheimer's-Type Dementia"* (Baltimore: Health Professionals Press, 1992), 27.
22. Feil, Audial recorded notes from Validation Workshop Seminar conducted by Naomi Feil at Topeka Kansas, Dec. 4th, 1996.
23. Feil, 1993, 29.
24. Naomi Feil, *Validation, The Feil Method* (Cleveland: Edward Feil Productions, 1992), 50.
25. Ibid., 51.
26. Ibid., 53.
27. Ibid., 86.
28. Ibid., 53.
29. Ibid., 53.
30. Ibid., 69-71.
31. Ibid., 53.
32. Ibid., 34.
33. Ibid., 56.
34. Ibid., 73.
35. Ibid., 27.

36. Audial recorded notes. Naomi Feil used this expression several times to connote the totally withdrawn old-old person during the Validation Workshop in Topeka, Kansas, December 4, 1996.

37. Feil, 1992, 81.

38. Ibid., 35.

Chapter 12

New Significance and Identity:
A Practical Theological Perspective

Julie A. Gorman, DMin

SUMMARY. This article looks at personal worth and identity, dependence, time and experience, change and loss, death, work and leisure from a distinctively Christian point of view that frees us from the distortions and dread of aging. We are called to embrace life as new creations through the years. *[Article copies available for a fee from The Haworth Document Delivery Service: 1-800-HAWORTH. E-mail address: <docdelivery@haworthpress.com> Website: <http://www.HaworthPress.com> © 2003 by The Haworth Press, Inc. All rights reserved.]*

KEYWORDS. Identities, memories, reframing, dependence, self-examination, lifestyle, dependence, interdependence, interconnection, *kairos*, hope, death, mortality, reformation, vocation

---

Julie A. Gorman teaches Christian Formation and Discipleship at Fuller Theological Seminary, Pasadena, CA. Dr. Gorman served fifteen years as Pastor of Adults and Families in a number of churches in the Los Angeles area. She has authored a number of books and served as editor of Baker Books, *The Dictionary of Christian Education.*

[Haworth co-indexing entry note]: "New Significance and Identity: A Practical Theological Perspective." Gorman, Julie A. Co-published simultaneously in *Journal of Religious Gerontology* (The Haworth Pastoral Press, an imprint of The Haworth Press, Inc.) Vol. 15, No. 1/2, 2003, pp. 171-186; and: *Practical Theology for Aging* (ed: Derrel R. Watkins) The Haworth Pastoral Press, an imprint of The Haworth Press, Inc., 2003, pp. 171-186. Single or multiple copies of this article are available for a fee from The Haworth Document Delivery Service [1-800-HAWORTH, 9:00 a.m. - 5:00 p.m. (EST). E-mail address: docdelivery@haworthpress.com].

http://www.haworthpress.com/store/product.asp?sku=J078
© 2003 by The Haworth Press, Inc. All rights reserved.
Digital Object Identifier: 10.1300/J078v15n01_13

EXPERIENCING A DIFFERENT KIND OF WORTH

The worth of one's experiences may become more evident or more integrated into a whole with the process of aging. Over a period of years the sought after elements of reputation, influence, beauty, wealth or accomplishment seem to be never fully achieved in a secure and lasting way. (See the film Mr. Holland's Opus.) This often establishes a new basis for self-worth that is built on greater maturity of insight. What a person has become takes precedence over the ever tarnishing what they have done. Life and thus the person become valuable not because of production or usefulness, but more because of portraying an account of God's care and saving action.[1]

CHANGING IDENTITIES

"You can't teach an old dog new tricks," suggests that aging causes a hardening of traditional ways of operating. In actuality the transient but dynamic nature of aging can cause adjustment so as to cope with new circumstances. The twenty-one-year-old, entering a new realm of life, may be jarred into changing because of that aging. Likewise the transitions that come with mid-life awareness often stirs persons into action. Nouwen summarizes the "invitation" that goes with the circumstances of aging. "Every time life asks us to give up a desire, to change our direction, or redefine our goals; every time we lose a friend, break a relationship, or start a new plan, we are invited to widen our perspectives and to touch, under the superficial waves of our daily wishes, the deeper currents of hope. Every time we are jolted by life, we are 'faced with the need to make new departures.' "[2]

In aging, persons often find themselves breaking free from previously binding conventional expectations. Whereas earlier versions have marched to someone else's drumbeat age may enable persons to transcend conformities that hinder their integrity. Reversal of career patterns, reexamination of inhibitions, reevaluating what is of importance to a person and realization of who they really are may come with passing years. Eighty-five year old Florida Scott-Maxwell captures it in, "A long life makes me feel nearer truth . . . I want to tell people approaching and perhaps fearing age that it is a time of discovery. If they say–'Of what?' I can only answer, 'We must each find out for ourselves, otherwise it won't be discovery.'"[3]

One of the most exciting arenas of newness that has implications for theological structures is that of seeing new significance to the experiences of life. God frequently called individuals and Israel as a whole to remember their histories with him, to "remember the way I have led you in the past" (see 2 Sam.

7:8-9). Having a past (a product of aging) can bring to a person the opportunity for meaning formation as that person grows older. Why does God gift us with memories? "Is there anything about the accumulation of experience which provides an opportunity for growth in spirit?" Ross Snyder calls the first stage of this meaning formation process "Life Saga,"–what has given a person's life direction, meaning and substance. It is a "membering" or joining together of experiences that will reveal a unifying construction of the self. And in so doing, the meaning of the past changes. He invites persons to discover the song they have been singing with their life. What elements have enabled the person to persevere, to "make it through" the difficult times? This identification of values and ideas and purposes that have been interiorized leads persons to what is called an "awakened eye." Such awakening allows seeing in a new way who we are and how we live. It can uncover an inherent theology and cause us to enter a new mode of existence. The recent popularity of the book, "Tuesdays With Morrie," accents this fullness of being that comes with being a person who brings purposive unification to life's experiences over time. His reflections become pure gold to the younger reporter who hears the wise summations of his mentor. Developing this self awareness through such "re-membering" may become a theological instrument which provides an opening that the Spirit requires, a recentering which provides a path into new freedom and enablement. In the same disposition (aptitude) as the Prodigal Son, this re-membering of the past can create the conditions for "coming to oneself" and the subsequent embracing of a new beginning. In dialogue with God and with self, the meaning of the past is transformed and the Spirit is set free to recontextualize previous experiences and grant new hope and creative energy to the person in the present and the future.[4]

If we are to restructure our view of aging to reflect what we say we believe, we must include the reframing of many of our "traditionally acceptable ways of thinking." Each of the following topics represent "sacred cows" or "unquestioned assumptions" which shape our lives, our society and ultimately distort our beliefs so they are out of sync with a biblical theology of aging. The first of these that need to be revisited is

1. Recognition and Acceptance of One's Dependence

Dependence is un-American. From founding fathers we learned to proudly "declare our independence," to be needy of no one. We boast of "making it on our own," of "doing our own thing," "of being our own person." Children are the only subjects for whom dependency is assumed to be appropriate. Their helplessness and neediness create strong bonds with those who feel needed. But fear and pressure of our social system soon prompt us to inculcate in our children the exclusive preeminence of individualism, autonomy and freedom of each to pursue his or her own desires. As one author suggests, "The genius of the American self-image–individualism, self-reliance, progress, and prosperity–predisposes us to an ethical individualism and makes us forgetful of our interdependence and social connectedness."[5] One of the most powerful sources of this avoidance of dependence is the drive to earn money. Having one's own source of income greatly reduces dependence on others. Children are taught to "do things for money" which in turn gives them greater freedom to "spend their own money on what they want." We seldom expect children to make contribution to the family treasury. "Making it on your own" is a detrimental value that contributes to a negative view of aging. Sapp observes, "Not only are Americans taught from the beginning of life to cherish for their own sakes their independence, privacy, freedom from authority, and sense of self-worth based on economic productivity; their sense of commitment, responsibility, and obligation to other family members, especially perhaps to those who are older, is also undermined by these very values and the strong emphasis on peer-group orientation and 'social adjustment.'" This attitude is not easily shed. We detest giving up control. Our finitude has a way of bringing out this dread of recognizing our ultimate dependence after we've fooled everyone into believing we are masters of our own destiny. "The recognition of finitude may on the other hand liberate us to a new kind of freedom, a freedom which is more realistically based and which is related to our dependence. We may be released from that distortion of freedom which arises from a sense of being master of our destiny and open to unlimited possibilities. The recognition of finitude and dependency . . . may cause us to examine our life style, our values, our goals. Such self-examination may be the point of break-through for Spirit, for being drawn toward a life style which does not depend on physical power and independence."[6] It is therefore not surprising that "what the American elderly seem to fear most is 'demeaning dependence' on their children and other kin. Rather, the ideal is to remain 'one's own person.'"[7] Tragedy can strip us of the separation of independence but we end up feeling guilty for needing others and search for ways to "pay them back" so we can regain our sense of autonomy. There is no denial of the fact that increasing age leads to a state of increasing dependence.

Paradoxically, the essence of the Christian faith is that of being aware of and embracing one's fundamental dependence on God. This inverse principle joins others of radical opposites to our assumed modus operandi (the way up is down, to be poor is rich, giving is preferred to receiving, etc.) that distinguish biblical lifestyle as marching to a different drumbeat. There is ample evidence in scripture that God values complete dependence on him (the acknowledgement of his being in control) and at times removes all hope that the situation is still under our control (e.g., heating the furnace seven times hotter in Daniel). This dependency motif is contrary to the better known paradigm which most persons ascribe to the Bible, "God helps those who help themselves."

Dependence on God says we don't have to BE God. This theological struggle of self-sufficiency has been a human problem from the beginning. "The problem with aging in late twentieth-century America may well be only another in the long run of reprises of that drama played out at the dawn of time, in the mythical garden of Genesis 3, namely, the unwillingness of humankind to be satisfied with merely being 'in the image of God' and the desire instead to 'be like God,' i.e., independent, not beholden to anyone, self-sufficient."[8]

This attitude of acknowledging our insufficiency and of facing up to the fact that none of us lives by or for oneself at any stage of life is what our faith is about. Such attitudes promote a discipleship that is grounded in the theology of the cross. This means a willingness to sacrifice for each other, to give up "rights," to assume care for one another, to cease demanding our own way, to receive what life brings including hardships as realistic but unable to separate us from the love of God.[9]

"Being dependent" is re-envisioned as an essential ingredient that prompts deeper ties as the insufficient one casts self on God in faith. This in turn expands knowing the reality of the unmerited, freely offered grace of God. Richard Halvorsen goes so far as to identify dependence as a vital distinguishing mark of maturing.[10] "One of the clearest evidences of Christian maturity is an increasing awareness of one's need–an increasing lack of self-confidence and an increasing sense of one's dependence upon the Holy Spirit. . . . Christian growth is accompanied by an increasing sense of the futility of human effort and its utter inadequacy at its very best. But this sense of need is always more than balanced by a growing realization that Christ has made ample provision and the need is the door to spiritual fulfillment."[11] As the old hymn states, "Nothing in my hand I bring, simply to Thy cross I cling." "Clinging," having to depend on God to pull it off, being totally dependent on his ability "without our help" is not a comfortable experience for most persons in this culture.

Being dependent often reveals profound truth heretofore unknown. Henri Nouwen's life was transformed through his experience with a severely handicapped young man called Adam. Again, paradoxically, "the dependent aging or the retarded give in their receiving. . . . Theirs is the gift of being open to caring love, of being able to receive such love." This condition is a profound symbol reflecting the condition of us all before God. "Even those of us who seem to have the fullest command of our faculties and who are in the best of health are finally dependent. . . . In this ultimate sense what appears to be our capacity to give is grounded in our being in some more ultimate sense receivers. Our capacity to care, even as our need to be cared for, rests on another." . . . In this "we have a clue to discerning the theological meaning in the aging process across the whole life span and especially in those years we call the aging years."[12] For an excellent reflection on the value of being dependent see Nouwen's work on the Passion of Jesus, where he points out that after spending three years of "doing," Jesus' greatest "work" was his passion experience where he was "done to" for the remainder of his life.

But such a concept is counter to deep-seated drives that propel us in opposite ways. If we do succumb to that "amazing grace" for our salvation, we then move right back into our "self-help" syndrome when it comes to "growing in Christ." Struggle feels so much more significant than "letting God remold us from within." This does not rule out our involvement in the "working out of our salvation" but even the resulting victories of that "working" are dependent on the Spirit's framing of God's image within us.

Things get even trickier when we realize that God designed this same interconnected dependency for members of the body to experience together with one another. As all are dependent on their common God, so each is interdependent with the other. This "submitting to," "giving up of so-called 'rights,' seeking the common good, seems quite foreign to persons who join groups for "what they can get out of them." "Community" and intimacy, while sought after in emotional fantasies, are avoided as reality. The myths, deeply ingrained, bring fear of accepting what God says as true. "If all of us could recapture a lively sense of our ultimate and absolute dependence, a large step would be taken toward a renewed recognition of our need for one another and thus our necessary *inter*dependence. . . . This shift in attitude might make the increased dependence upon other people that accompanies growing older easier to accept."[13]

This myth fosters others such as rights over gratitude. "If we refuse to admit dependence, . . . we cannot express gratitude to God or to fellow human beings, and we tend to concentrate on rights as a way of escaping the acknowledgment of our dependence: If what I am receiving from you is my *right*, then I am not really dependent on you for it."[14]

The recent awareness and denunciation of "co-dependency" has raised our defenses even more. We must cultivate a balanced treatment of this subject and enable persons to think in critical and theologically centered ways about this traditional anathema can be viewed apart from cultural baggage. In a book called *Homeless Mind* there is this statement: "Modernity has accomplished many far-reaching transformations, but it has not fundamentally changed the finitude, fragility and mortality of the human condition. What it has accomplished is to seriously weaken those definitions of reality that previously made that human condition easier to bear."[15]

2. A Revised View of Time and Experience

"Time marches on," sounds fatalistic. Is there any distinction in how a Christian looks at time differently? Of course there is the hope of life after time–a hope that is composed of something other than "just more of the same." The process of aging makes us extremely conscious of time and reminds us in the words of the old gospel song, "I'm just a passing through" this temporal existence of physical life. This realization should in the words of Psalm 90:12 "Teach us to count our days." The passing of time, if it does nothing else, should sober us into making the best use of what we have.[16]

Bouwsma sees connectedness between the biblical idea of time and the worth of the individual personality. "The biblical God has underscored the positive significance of time, process, and change through His continuing presence and intervention within the unique and unrepeatable evens of human history. Thus, the pattern of the life experience of each individual is unique.[17]

The individual's past, as a history of his or her personal encounter with life– and with God–is holy as well.[18] With a theological perspective we are able to interpret positively our time past in terms that are more than life's "doings." As Bouwsma writes, "The past demonstrates God's care and will for men and therefore cannot be ignored or repudiated. The significance of the past also points to the indelible importance of all human experience. It gives meaning to the particular temporal experiences that have shaped each individual during the whole course of his life."[19] Thus we are frequently called to "remember" our past times so as to view all time as sacred. In other words, because time, in theological framing, provides a record of God's faithful caring and saving acts, life is not just production or usefulness. Life's time, like the "heavens" and the "firmament" declares the glory and shows the handiwork of God. History becomes a holy platform for knowing God. This concept, again when viewed from a God-centered perspective, means that the present and the future also bear the marks of his presence and his intrusion. Such resetting causes a Christian to look at the experiences and events of life in a new way–asking what they reveal about God, a query that sees these temporal moments as holy. Challenges and growth with all their required change, are to be embraced.

This interconnection of past, present and future imply continuity with change being absorbed and integrated into what has gone before and what is yet to be. Interestingly God presents himself as a God of continuity, frequently referring to his past actions as reason for accepting present and future truth. For example in the return from exile he reminds the struggling temple constructors that he is the same covenant keeping God of ages past. Jesuit theologian William Lynch writes "that hope is born of imagination and imagination requires a continuity with the past."[20] Thus the process of "re-membering," enabling persons to look back over time and experience and see patterns and values can construct a theological structure for seeing time differently and for redeeming experiences unique to the person. Likewise as mentioned earlier, Jesus' call to participate in the future realization of God's plan, by taking part in his saving and redeeming work in the present brought a sense of significance that transcended time and the hardships of the moment.[21]

Though considered timeless, God presents himself as the Alpha and the Omega, adapting to our time-framed perspective. And in the process of raising Jesus from the dead as demonstration of his love and goodness, God shows that he "has chosen to accept temporal sequence as definitive of God's own eternal life; thus God ages with creation and the creature who, by aging, reflects the image of that temporal God."[22]

Finally, aging over time can prompt valuable insights and practices. Claudel, writing in his Journal at eighty observes: "Some sigh for yesterday! Some for tomorrow! But you must reach old age before you can understand the meaning, the splendid, absolute, unchallengeable, irreplaceable meaning of the word today!"[23] The mystic, deCaussade would bring the spiritual into this realization calling it "the sanctity of the present moment."

Others would define time as *kairos*–moments of significance–rather than *chronos*–clock time that is running out. A *kairos* moment can take place at any point in time, not being limited by lateness or age. It is an opportune moment that transforms our life. Both Jesus and John referred to this as "the fullness of time" or "the right time." To see time in this way is to live with creation being an ongoing phenomenon rather than a past event. It is to "seize the day" and realize that any moment could become a transforming one because of God's presence and power in that moment. Time is thus approached with anticipation to learn "how God will yet work out creation's purpose through us." Thomas Robb offers this illustration emphasizing the value of our continuing readiness to receive over valuation determined by clock time. "A painting is not a masterpiece because of the number of hours or days required to complete it, but because of the interaction that occurs between the viewer, the canvas and oils, and the artist. A concerto is not a masterpiece because of the age of its composer, but because of the interaction that takes place between the listener, the musician and the composer. Because they occur in *kairos* time rather than *chronos* time, such encounters are not limited to the lifetime of the composer or the painter. Their works are timeless."[24]

3. Looking at Change and Loss Differently

The aging process is most often linked with continual change and the pain of loss of what once was. In young adulthood we begin the adaptation. Levi

Strauss provides jeans with "a scoch more room." Millions of Americans work out daily to try to regain the figure and endurance they once had as a gift of nature. In middle age the alterations become more serious–loss of hair, energy, idealism, time left to live. But it is the later years where loss becomes a dreaded "label" of the "end times." Such losses include health, friends, time, job, physical beauty, economic stability, independence, status. While millions of persons move into these years with well stocked larders, the inevitability of coming changes is anticipated with fear and depression. It is then we are forced to live more realistically.

A Christian response to these circumstances is a critical test of our maturity. Evelyn Whitehead in summarizing an article on adulthood by Bouwsma suggests, "The essential note of the Christian biblical understanding of human maturity . . . is its emphasis on the dynamic processes of continuing change and growth. This focus on continual development distinguishes the biblical view from a more classical notion of adult maturity as a state which–once achieved–is to be sustained without deviation."[25] Looking at this "process" of growing into the likeness of Christ, the circumstances that accompany aging become opportunities to increase in growing toward the full stature of Christ. In other words, what appears as "loss" on one side may also be reinterpreted as "gain" in another dimension. The Apostle Paul expresses this new valuing experience in his life–what he once valued as "it" now is devalued while the "real it" is the sought after treasure. Evelyn Christensen wrote a classic exposition of this premise in a book called "Gaining Through Losing." From a wider, wiser perspective we can actually come to desire something we previously were unaware even existed. In a wonderful way aging allows this. All persons are aware of things they formerly thought were the height of their desire (e.g., staying up late, proving they could push their bodies beyond limits, participating in habits detrimental to health without seemingly facing the effect, etc.) which now seem pointless and foolish in light of presently cherished values. Some of the most significant works of insight into spirituality have come from those who looked reality in the face and when on to mine the glory of God that was uncovered in seeming losses. The stripping away of what we think we value often leads to awareness of greatest treasure. The "wisdom" of the elderly does not come without a price. But persons who thought they "couldn't live" without something and spent years dreading that loss, found that the more "Spartan" lifestyle that loss impelled, led them to know greater fulfillment. Nothing we experience this side of heaven totally fulfills. Even with the elation of success, completion, reaching out goal–there is always the angst of more. God has placed this "hunger" in us that we might realize we will never be totally satisfied with anything but himself. This drives us onward. It refines our evaluation of loss and change if we place focus of trust in the goodness of God.

The centrality of this commitment causes us to respond differently. Thus Bouwsma admonishes, "The Christian is not to evade the challenges, the struggles, the difficulties and dangers of life, but to accept, make his way through, and grow in them."[26] The "journey" is the thing! We as pilgrims are not "there" yet. And in the weaning away from what we think we value, we actually move closer to the heart of God and what he values. Growth, brought on by life stages, is a wonderful unveiling of more satisfying, more complete, more enduring, more God-centered truth. Aging with its changing allows that. Hauerwas suggests the value to the corporate body of life stories shared. "Illness is not something that must be overcome, not simply chaos, but rather an occasion for the discovery that we are on a journey, a quest, through which we learn 'who I always have been' but did not know. . . . Ill people, not caregivers, need to regard themselves as the heroes of their own stories. This requires that we understand that heroism is not to be identified with those that can 'do something' but rather is to be found in those who persevere through suffering. . . . Our healing is not the overcoming of our illnesses but rather our ability to share our going on with one another through the community our stories create."[27]

Who would want to go through teenage years again? Who would want to remain forever at any one year of life? We cannot stand still. " . . . The Christian conception of immaturity–is the refusal to grow, the inability to cope with an open and indeterminate future (that is, the future itself), in effect the rejection of life as a process."[28] The "experience of *change* in aging can be interpreted as an invitation from God to continue the process of growth toward full human maturity."[29] "Suffering produces endurance, and endurance produces character, and character produces hope" (Romans 4:3-4).

The "emptying" of losses allows for the refilling with greater, more lasting and satisfying gains. This is not embracing pain for itself–but seeing God through the pain–not rejoicing in having lost–but in discovering deeper awarenesses and experiences of connectedness through the circumstance of loss. Out of death (its horrors not minimized) comes resurrection with its heretofore unrealized pluses. The losses, while vivid reminders of our finitude, allow us to see things as they are with God as our unchanging Hope. Chrysostom focuses on advances possible: "For he that runneth this bodily race, when gray hairs have overtaken him, probably is not able to run as he did before; for the whole contest depends on the body; but thou–wherefore doest thou lessen thy speed? For in this race there is need of a soul, a soul thoroughly awakened: and the soul is rather strengthened in old age; then it is in its full vigor, then it is in its pride."[30]

As Pearl Buck reasoned upon the question, "Would I wish to be 'young' again? No, for I have learned too much to wish to lose it. . . . I am a far more valuable person today that I was 50 years ago, or 40 years ago, or 30, 20, or even 10. I HAVE LEARNED SO MUCH SINCE I WAS 70!"[31]

4. A Different Outlook on Death (our own and others')

God has made possible death as well as life. "A time to be born, and a time to die" (Ecclesiastes 3:1-2). Why do we seek the one and run from the other? What distortions do we encounter in looking at this phenomenon Christianly? Although medical science has been able to almost double the life span of the previous century, it's still not enough. Stephen Sapp identifies us as a "death-denying" society, even label death as the "new pornography." He quotes one author as declaring, "Death is an imposition on the human race, and no longer acceptable." And another as asserting that death "is simply un-American. Its inevitability is an affront to our inalienable rights of 'life, liberty, and the pursuit of happiness.'"[32] He then observes, "This attitude toward death, reflecting as it does an inability to accept our finitude and mortality, contributes greatly to the problem we have acknowledging and dealing with aging."[33]

We find it difficult, if not impossible, to find meaning in our society for suffering and death, recognizing them only as "enemies to be fought."[34] Using the metaphor of a torn cloth Callahan compares the valiant attempts of medical science to rescue us from death saying that no matter how much is done we are always left with a "ragged edge," limitations and situations as bad as those cured (health care issues, life support dilemmas). In trying to overcome our mortality we will never win "the struggle with the ragged edge. We can only move the edge somewhere else, where it will once again tear roughly, and again and again."[35]

So why mortality? What has taken us down the path of rejection of death? Loss through physical death must never be denied. There is pain in separation. Jesus did not abolish physical death for others nor for himself. Life is not the same for those left behind. God serves as "comforter" to those who mourn. And God brings hope in wiping out spiritual death.

While calling death "the last, great enemy" Paul never denies its necessity or actuality. In dying there is Life (I Cor. 15). "To die is gain"(Philippians 1:21). "Whether we live or whether we die, we are the Lord's" (Rom. 14:8). In the Old Testament death was an accepted phenomenon. Abraham "died in a good old age, an old man and full of years" (Genesis 25:8). "To die 'full of years' seems to suggest that one has reached one's 'capacity for years of life,' just as a cup can hold only so much water before it becomes 'full of water.' Most people readily recognize the folly of continuing to pour water into a cup already filled to capacity. . . . From a biblical point of view the goal should be not merely *more* life but *better* life, even if the absolute length is shortened."[36]

The whole creation may "groan for redemption" (Romans 8:22) but with a limited view human kind resists escaping from all that causes our "groaning."

The acceptance of our own death (and thus that of others) as the end of aging is "the ultimate example of recognizing our dependence upon a gracious, merciful, and loving God."[37] "Today we expect not only to be cured of ills that were previously incurable but also to be prevented from experiencing a variety of infirmities and misfortunes that were once the common lot of humankind. *And we feel wronged if these expectations go unfulfilled.*"[38]

It is common to focus on death as "leaving" rather than "coming." When one frames this movement in the motif of the Prodigal Son, "leaving" is in the context of the hardship of "the far country" while homecoming is the celebration of a party with family and friends. Nobody is enjoined to seek death, but the "sting" has been removed and the "presence" is there "in the valley of the shadow." "Endings" because they are a part of this life are always mixed joy and shadow side of pain. Every ecstasy is twinged with some agony and every "agony" knows a secret "ecstasy." Even great pain holds a richness in the realization of having known it, having experienced a deeper need and acknowledgement of grace that ever before. This is a mark of our incompleteness in this existence. Speaking of his own death, Paul laments, "I have a great desire to depart and be with Christ, which is better by far; but it is more necessary that I remain in the body" (Philippians 1:23). Our condition of knowing "resurrection" only by faith is often overshadowed by the sighted version of experiencing the circumstance of ceasing to live rather than beginning to LIVE. Were we to have a choice over staying in the womb or facing birth and life in an unknown environment, most of us would probably choose womb. Again, the "center" for a theological perspective on mortality must move from us and our limitations to God and his abundance.

A Christian perspective on mortality causes life itself to be more precious, a gift from God. As already mentioned, each moment is seen as sacred, each experience as unrepeatable and thus treasured, each person unique, each day an opportunity to discover God in its web and our having to depend upon Him for our existence and fulfillment.

Chaim Potok, in *My Name Is Asher Lev*, recounts a conversation with his father concerning a bird lying on its side by a curb.

"Is it dead, Papa?" I was six and could not bring myself to look at it.
"Yes," I heard him say in a sad and distant way.
"Why did it die?"
"Everything that lives must die."
"Everything?"
"Yes."

"You too Papa? And Mama?"

"Yes."

"And me?"

"Yes," he said. Then added in Yiddish, "But may it be only after you live a long and good life, my Asher."

I could not grasp it. I forced myself to look at the bird. Everything alive would one day be as still as that bird?

"Why?" I asked.

"That's the way the Ribbono Shel Olom made His world, Asher."

"Why?"

"So life would be precious, Asher. Something that is yours forever is never precious!"[39]

Human *life* is precious. And, "Precious in the sight of the Lord is the *death* of his saints." (Psalm 116:15) Precious also is *our hope.* "His divine power has given us everything we need for life and godliness through our knowledge of him who called us by his own glory and goodness. Through these he has given us his very great and precious promises, so that through them you may participate in the divine nature and escape the corruption in the world. . . . " (2 Peter 1:3-4) "Now this is eternal life: that they may know you, the only true God, and Jesus Christ, whom you have sent" (John 17:3).

5. A New Perspective on Work and Leisure

If the present paradigm of aging is to be changed, reformation of traditional thinking about work will certainly play a part. The two major foci the lend impact to our view of aging are the role of work through the age spans and the defining of individual worth by this medium.

PERSPECTIVE OF JUDAISM

Rabbi Katz distinguishes the Jewish meaning of work and rest from work as fulfilling a different purpose and moral obligation from that found in other traditions. "Work, in the ethos of the Western, middle-class culture, amounts to no less than the primary source of an individual's self-image, his identity, and his self-esteem. A person is valued because he produces."[40] Not being a part of the work force, is a traumatic experience that signals loss of all the above and surrounds the person with an aura of unproductive impotence. However, in Jewish thought work was given by God for creation and nurture of what God had provided. And leisure at the end of work, is the time of refreshing. As the

Sabbath was "the climax of creation, so the time of maturity represents the highest point of man's development. . . . Ceasing to work does not mean becoming idle or aimless. With leisure comes the opportunity for another kind of activity, the goal of which is the cultivation of one's soul and its potentialities . . . . We find in Judaism . . . a magnificent defense of leisure. In the language of the rabbis, Judaism sanctifies time. . . . You fulfill yourself . . . without feeling inner guilt and without experiencing rejection by the community."[41] "The Sages and the Prophets did not hope for the coming of the Messiah in order that they might rule over the world, or have dominion over the other nations, or that they might be glorified by other peoples, or in order to eat and drink–but that they be free to engage in the study of Torah and its wisdom, without anyone to oppress them or distract them, so that they might thereby deserve the life of eternity. In that time (of Messiah), . . . goodness will be available in great abundance, precious things as commonplace as dust. *And the business of the entire world will be only to know God. . . .*"[42]

REFORMATION EMPHASIS

The Protestant Reformation refined the nature and value of work. In response to the valuation scale assigned to different types of work, Luther emphasized the repositioning of any kind of work as "vocation" or "calling" when done to the glory of God. The mundane reveals an obedience that is as God-pleasing as the ecclesiastical duties. In a more contemporary emphasis Roman Catholic Joe Holland declares: "All work is profoundly religious, even if we are not conscious of that fact. Work is nothing less than human participation in the divine creativity expressed in the creativity of the universe. Work is a fundamental cultural way by which we reveal God's actively creative love. Work is a fundamental cultural place where we express our dynamic rootedness in the rest of our natural world, and ultimately in the Creator."[43]

RETIREMENT

If the above "vocational calling" perspective were embraced perhaps some persons might continue working with greater fulfillment and satisfaction. And others might choose to pursue their "calling" through a different purposeful activity after moving our of their lifetime employment. Bonhoeffer claims, "Vocation [is] . . . where your deep gladness and the world's deep hunger meet." As Seniors transition into Sabbath refreshment, they may find authenticity and congruence in their true vocation, following a call to (in Blackabee's words) recognize what Christ is doing in this world and then joining him in this creative "work." Such emphasis on fulfillment for seniors being seen as significantly carrying out their calling suggests that churches not only focus on "ministering to and for our senior citizens, but also to make way for a continuing ministry by them."[44] What a contrast this is to the apprehensions arising as more and more persons become involved in long retirements, a critical "situation . . . that leads to what we call a 'new class' without function, or a generation *inutile*, struggling to find a purpose or use in modern society."[45]

The central focus is on living out our calling by doing what we do as honoring God through the vocational expression that "brings deep gladness while meeting the world's deep hunger" and "working" with our Creator there.

Work must be seen for what it is in its limited frame. It is not the basis for our worth. We are not what we do. God made us to be more. "Christian theology affirms strongly that one's value does not rest in what one does or has but merely in the fact that one is." Sapp quoting Whitehead in article 11: And this value in what one is has been determined by the one who is without equal and without end. And He declares his commitment to us through all ages, "To your old age I am the one (who will look after you); to gray hair I will carry (you). I myself have created (you) and will lift you up; I myself will carry and deliver (you)" (Isaiah 46:4).

NOTES

1. Carol LeFevre and Perry LeFevre, *Aging and The Human Spirit: Second edition* (Chicago: Exploration Press, 1985), 58-60.

2. Nouwen quoted in Paul Tournier, *Learn To Grow Old,* (New York: Harper & Row, 1972), 67.

3. Scott-Maxwell. "The Measure of My Days" in Henry J. Nouwen, *Adam: God's Beloved.* (Maryknoll, NY: Orbis, 1977), 75.

4. LeFevre and LeFevre, 50-53.

5. Churchill in Stephen Sapp, *Light on a Gray Area.* (Nashville: Abingdon Press, 1992). 166.

6. LeFevre and LeFevre, 49.

7. Ken Dychtwald and Joe Flower, *Age Wave* (New York: Bantam Books, 1990), 167.

8. Stephen Sapp, "An Alternative Christian View of Aging," in *Journal of Religion & Aging,* Vol. 4 (1), 1987. 1-13.

9. Ibid., 8-9.

10. CF. Bouwsma who defines maturing as accepting the continual process of changing.

11. Richard C. Halverson, *Christian Maturity,* (Los Angeles: Cowman Publications, 1956), 21-22.

12. LeFevre and LeFevre, 55.

13. Ibid., 58-60.

14. Stephen Sapp, *Light On A Gray Area.* (Nashville: Abingdon Press, 1992), 140-141.

15. Ibid.

16. Melvin A. Kimble, in Melvin A. Kimble, Susan H. McFadden, James W. Ellor, and James J. Seeber, eds, *Aging, Spirituality, and Religion,* (Minneapolis: Augsburg Fortress Press, 1995), 424.

17. William J. Bouwsma. "Christian Adulthood," in *Adulthood,* Vol. 105. No. 2, Spring 1976, 77-92.

18. Whitehead in LeFevre, 60.

19. Bouwsma in LeFevre, 60.

20. William M. Clements, ed. *Ministry With The Aging.* (San Francisco, CA: Harper & Row Publishers, 1981), 96.

21. LeFevre and LeFevre, 61.

22. Ronald C. Crossley, "Aging With God: Old Age and New Theology," in *Church and Society,* Vol. 89, January-February, 1999, 14.

23. In Seward Hiltner, *Toward A Theology of Aging.* (New York: Human Sciences Press, 1975), 146.

24. Thomas B. Robb, *Growing Up: Pastoral Nurture For The Later Years.* (New York: The Haworth Press, Inc.,1991), 22.

25. LeFevre and LeFevre, 62.

26. Bouwsma in LeFevre and LeFevre, 63.

27. Stanley Hauerwas, "Embodied Holiness," 32-33.

28. Bouwsma in LeFevre and LeFevre, 63.

29. Ibid., 63.

30. Chrysostom in Brynolf K. Lyon, *Toward A Practical Theology of Aging,* (Philadelphia: Fortress Press, 1985), 45.

31. Buck in Dulin, 3.

32. David Hendin, *Death As a Fact of Life.* (New York: Warner Books, 1973), 85.

33. Sapp, *Light in. . . ,* 142.

34. Callahan, "Setting Limits," 32 in Sapp, Ibid., 141.

35. Callahan, "What Kind of Life?" in Sapp, *Light In . . . ,* 142.

36. Ibid., 144-145.

37. Ibid., 141.

38. Ibid., 146-147.

39. Potok in Nouwen, 137-138.

40. Hiltner, 148.

41. Katz in Hiltner, 149.

42. Maimonides, Mishnah Torah, Hilchot, Melachim, in Hiltner, 149.

43. Holland in Sapp, 148.

44. Earl C. Dahlstrom, "Toward a Theology of Aging" in *Covenant Quarterly,* Vol. 37, February 1979, 11.

45. Morris and Bass in Sapp, 147.

Chapter 13

Live a Little Before You Die a Lot: Creative Living in the Later Years

Lucien Coleman, EdD
Derrel R. Watkins, PhD, ACSW

SUMMARY. Calling for a radical new paradigm for living the latter third of life, this article suggests that persons can continue to grow, improve, create, and experience a quality of life never known by previous generations of older persons. Issues such as freedom, courage, adaptability, and expansiveness, along with an openness to God's transforming power, are suggested as a means of accomplishing this goal. *[Article copies available for a fee from The Haworth Document Delivery Service: 1-800-HAWORTH. E-mail address: <docdelivery@haworthpress.com> Website: <http://www.HaworthPress.com> © 2003 by The Haworth Press, Inc. All rights reserved.]*

Lucien Coleman is Professor of Adult Education, Retired, Southwestern Baptist Theological Seminary, Fort Worth, TX. Formerly Professor of Christian Education, The Southern Baptist Theological Seminary, Louisville, KY, Dr. Coleman is the author of over 12 books in the field of Christian Education. Derrel R. Watkins is Adjunct Faculty, The Institute for Gerontological Studies, School of Social Work, Baylor University, Waco, TX; Professor of Social Work Emeritus, Southwestern Baptist Theological Seminary, Fort Worth, TX; and Oubri A. Poppele Chair (Gerontology) in Health and Welfare Ministries (retired), Saint Paul School of Theology, Kansas City, MO.

[Haworth co-indexing entry note]: "Live a Little Before You Die a Lot: Creative Living in the Later Years." Coleman, Lucien and Derrel R. Watkins. Co-published simultaneously in *Journal of Religious Gerontology* (The Haworth Pastoral Press, an imprint of The Haworth Press, Inc.) Vol. 15, No. 1/2, 2003, pp. 187-200; and: *Practical Theology for Aging* (ed: Derrel R. Watkins) The Haworth Pastoral Press, an imprint of The Haworth Press, Inc., 2003, pp. 187-200. Single or multiple copies of this article are available for a fee from The Haworth Document Delivery Service [1-800-HAWORTH, 9:00 a.m. - 5:00 p.m. (EST). E-mail address: docdelivery@haworthpress.com].

http://www.haworthpress.com/store/product.asp?sku=J078
© 2003 by The Haworth Press, Inc. All rights reserved.
Digital Object Identifier: 10.1300/J078v15n01_14

KEYWORDS. Generation, attitudes, experience, creative aging, senescence, freedom, courage, adaptability, expansiveness, transforming power, disengagement, continuity, modernization, conformity, happiness, lateral thinking, vertical thinking

OLDER PERSONS AND NEW WAYS OF THINKING

One of the prevailing unfounded myths about older persons is that they are afraid of change. They resist learning anything new. This is indeed an unfounded assumption for many senior adults. Of course, there are some who fit the stereotype, but probably no more than the number of persons of all generations who also resist change.

Think, if you will, about who these senior citizens are and what they have experienced in their lifetime. They have experienced the proliferation of automobiles. Many of the oldest old can remember a time when there were no automobiles in their hometowns. They were there when the telephone became a household appliance for the first time. Radio, television, airplanes, talking movies, cylinder records, wire recording, plastic recording platters, tape recording, computers, compact disc recording, DVD, are only a small portion of the accomplishments of this older generations.

The generation we perceive as older are the ones who invented most of these common technologies. They invented the "miracle" drugs that have made most life threatening diseases things of the past. They invented home and automobile air conditioning and central heating. These were not common in their childhood. Airplane travel was developed during their formative years. Rocket ships that could carry persons to the moon came into being during their lifetime. We could go on and on but suffice it to say that the older generations of today have experienced more dramatic paradigm shifting changes than all other generations in history combined. While change is common for younger generations, the older generations were forced out of a life of sameness to deal with "future shock," "the third wave," and dramatic economic "power shifts."[1]

All generations, including older ones, struggle to deal with rapid changes in their lives. Some of these changes may be caused by societal and/or economic shifts. Some are caused by catastrophes. Others may come simply as a result of life course transitions. Derrel likes to shock younger college students by telling them that they are all "senior citizens" to someone. When young persons pass through the "rite of passage" of getting their driver's license and purchasing their own automobile, they are no longer totally dependent on others for transportation. They are now, within the parameters established by their parents, making their own decisions about when, where, and how they will go. To the preadolescent, those 16 year olds are now "old."

Church leaders have discovered that the young old (60-70) do not enjoy being grouped with persons who are seventy-five plus. When a group of young or median adults are asked the question, "How many of you would like to live to be 100?" very few will express such a desire. There are prevailing stereotypes that continue to feed an ever-present form of ageism in our society. Very few congregations of over 100 members will even consider accepting a pastor who is over 60. The assumption seems to be that older persons have no vision or they are unwilling to change worship styles in order to reach the youth, etc. Many of the older members of the congregation will express the same attitude. They will relinquish or refuse to accept leadership positions in the church in favor of letting younger persons have those positions. This might be acceptable except in the case where the older person's wisdom and experience is needed.

OLDER PERSONS' ATTITUDES

As we think about the patchwork quilt of experiences and attitudes among older persons in America today, recall the familiar words with which Charles Dickens began *The Tale of Two Cities:*

> *It was the best of times, it was the worst of times,*
> *it was the age of wisdom, it was the age of foolishness,*
> ....
> *it was the season of Light, it was the season of Darkness,*
> *it was the spring of hope, it was the winter of despair.*

Within our aging population, one can find individuals who personify every phrase of that classic passage.

Old age is the "winter of despair," if viewed through the eyes of a 79-year-old widow who said to her pastor, "Sometimes I can't understand why God has not taken me. My heart isn't going to get any better. I just sit in my chair and watch the days go by. I can't read anymore. My eyes are bad. I've suffered many years, and there is no reason for me to stay on this earth."

On the other hand, old age sounds like the "spring of hope" when a 78-year-old retired educator talks about it:

> I can now do the many things I've wanted to do but couldn't find time to while working. . . . I can fish, hunt, go canoeing, boating, hiking, bird watching, do a lot of photography work, catch up on my stamp and coin collection, find time to do some carving and lathe work, and read the things I've saved up for 25 years. We can visit our children in Texas and

New Mexico when we choose, go camping anytime we like, sleep late if we desire (but we never do–there are too many things to do)!

The *fact* of old age is a reality that will come to most of us; but the *experience* of old age varies to a remarkable degree. What makes the difference? Why do some experience the later years as "the worst of times," and some as the "best of times?" Obviously, certain external circumstances have a lot to do with the quality of life in later years. Probably the most significant of these is the status of one's health. David Oliver, the Kellogg Lecturer for 1991, reminded us that getting "old" was the result of a disabling accident or illness, rather than a matter of chronological age.

And, certainly, economic stability is an important factor. Numerous studies have shown that financial security correlates highly with life-satisfaction among elderly people. Yet, while such factors are obviously influential, they neither *guarantee* nor *preclude* joyful and productive participation in the later years of life.

On one hand, there are elders who, despite economic security and relatively good health, spend their last years in a state of melancholy hopelessness. On the other hand, many older adults manage to transcend the dismal stereotypes of aging prescribed by prevalent social myths. They are characterized by the optimism of that 76-year-old woman who insisted, "I intend to live a little before I die a lot." This quality of transcendence in older persons is not easily defined. But, for our present purposes, we will call it "creative aging."

"Creativity" implies vitality, growth, movement, productivity, discovery and openness to new horizons of experience. It is the quality exemplified by Lucien's cherished friend, Helen Parker, who, blind from birth, launched a prolific career as a writer and inspirational speaker in her retirement years.

It is the adventuresome spirit of W. O. Taylor, who at the age of 105 was Southwestern Baptist Theological Seminary's oldest alumnus, and who took his grandson hitchhiking and bicycling across Europe when he was in his 70s.[2]

Creative aging is the gutsy determination of the 67-year-old widower who, despite a leg operation that made it painful to kneel, continued his gardening while still mourning the death of his wife. "I'd rather die on my feet than live on my knees," he said, "and I do not intend to go gentle into that good night."[3]

Creative aging, to paraphrase something a friend once said, is "where the spirit of song is kept; where the feet want to dance, even if they can't." Creativity is not necessarily finding something new and extremely different to do. It is a continuation of who and what you have always been. It reaches back into your past and brings out your dreams. It takes what you presently are and challenges you to be what you have already thought you could be. It looks to the future and realistically opens doors you thought had already been closed.

You cannot ignore senescence. Your body will not perform all of the athletic feats it could at age 20 or 30. You can, however, find ways of achieving your hopes and aspirations and dream new dreams and make them come true as well. George Bernard Shaw, in "Back to Methuselah" said, "Some see things as they are and ask why? I dream of things that never were and ask why not?"[4] On the day of the first Christian Pentecost the Apostle Peter delivered a sermon in which he quoted a passage from the Prophet Joel,

> In the last days, God says, I will pour out my spirit on all people. Your sons and daughters will prophesy, your young men will see visions, *your old men will dream dreams* [emphasis ours].[5]

What is the secret to creative aging? What special qualities contribute to that spirit of song in the later years? The subject must be approached with modesty, since the literature on creativity is vast and wide-ranging; and so is the literature on the experience of aging.

But, let us venture to suggest four variables that seem to characterize those older men and women whose feet want to keep dancing: Freedom, courage, adaptability, and expansiveness, along with an openness to God's transforming power.

FREEDOM

One of the hallmarks of the creative life, at any age, is freedom. Those who negotiate the later years of life creatively seem to have the inner strength to break the shackles of our society's stereotypic attitudes toward old age.

Despite overwhelming evidence to the contrary, the dominant paradigm of elderhood in our society implies incompetence, frailty, senility, loneliness, mental rigidity, uselessness and dependency. Tragically, many older people acquiesce to these expectations. The stereotypes become their self-fulfilling prophecy. They voluntarily surrender their license to live creatively and joyfully by accepting the yoke of ageism laid upon them by family members, social institutions, the mass media, and, in many cases, even their churches. University of Chicago psychologist, Mihaly Csikszentmihalyi observes that retirement or leisure " . . . provides a relaxing respite from work, but it generally consists of passively absorbing information, without using any skills or exploring new opportunities for action. As a result life passes in a sequence of boring and anxious experiences over which a person has little control."[6]

Since this stereotype of retirement and aging is so pervasive in our churches, how can we change it? Perhaps a lesson from scientific philosophy could help. In his influential essay, *The Structure of Scientific Revolutions,* Thomas Kuhn argues that unswerving commitment to established theories can be a powerful deterrent to innovation in scientific communities.[7] For example, before Copernicus could formulate his radically different heliocentric concept of the universe, he had to break away from the Ptolemaic assumptions that had dominated the thinking of astronomers for more 18 centuries.

The key to creative living in old age is analogous to Kuhn's description of scientific discovery. To live openly, expectantly and courageously in old age, one must manage to transcend the crippling expectations of a youth-centered culture. Most of us older persons grew up thinking that the world had to revolve around children, youth, and young adults. The "Disengagement Theory" of aging reinforced that paradigm by declaring that withdrawing from active involvement in most of the normal aspects of society was beneficial to both youth and older persons. New paradigms have arisen, such as the "Continuity Theory" and the "Modernization Theory,"[8] that focus our attention on continuing to improve ourselves and engage in as much of the "market place" as our health and stamina will allow. Old age isn't what it used to be and it is not what it will be in the very near future.

Kuhn, reflecting on the construction of new paradigms in science, makes some important observations that might help us to understand why there is so much general resistance of change with regard to aging in societies around the world. Like science, societies tend to suppress novelties that undermine long-held assumptions. This is true of persons of all ages. Scientific research is based upon a strong set of preconceptions and most researchers will work hard in an attempt to keep nature in conceptual boxes. New paradigms require the reconstruction of those preconceptions and the freedom to re-evaluate "prior facts." There is often a lag in responding to new facts by scientists and by society in general. Kuhn says, "Once a paradigm is entrenched theoretical alternatives are strongly resisted."[9]

The presence in almost every society around the world of a rapidly increasing number of older persons is creating an anomaly that calls for a radical rethinking of our attitudes and policies regarding older persons. Kuhn suggests that paradigm changes most often develop as a result of encounters with such an anomaly.[10]

Those of us who are involved in Christian churches face constant resistance from church leaders and congregants alike. In addition, we must fight personal battles regarding our own bias regarding our own aging. We have been conditioned to think that it is time to sit down and enjoy our retirement. Somehow we assimilated the attitude that we are to disengage from work and leadership and simply enjoy the leisure that our years of work have earned.

While the Bible recognizes the limitations of some forms of frailty that may accompany old age, it does not recognize a time of cessation of labor and responsibility. Retirement for Christians should mean a time of freedom to pursue dreams and opportunities for service that were limited when we were bound by the restrictions of employment. In Romans 12:2, Paul admittedly was speaking, without reference to age, of the transformation of personal values and standards of morality. But his challenge, "Do not conform outwardly to the standards of this world," is strikingly relevant to the experience of aging persons in contemporary American life. The mature Christian is not the slave of the conventional judgments of society. Even if ageism is rampant in society it should not be so in churches and synagogues. In many congregations we who are over 65 are in the majority. We make the policy decisions. We have the freedom to "dream dreams and ask why not?"

COURAGE

A second key to creative aging is personal courage; for courage is the currency with which freedom is purchased. As Rollo May has pointed out, the opposite of courage is not cowardice. The opposite of courage is conformity.[11] Conformity is much easier than swimming against the currents of majority opinion.

Sometimes it takes a crisis in the church and community to challenge the theoretical stereotypes regarding aging and demand a paradigm shift.[12] Such a crisis appears to exist among most of the established churches. Mainline denominations are now recognizing that over half of their membership is over 60 years of age. The crisis for them has already arrived. Mainstream evangelical denominations are not far behind with a rapidly increasing population of "graying" congregations. The crisis is on the horizon.

Courage is often stifled by the fear of being isolated, or being laughed at, ridiculed or rejected, even in the face of a crisis. The person who is lacking in courage "goes along to get along," carefully avoiding the pain of disapproval by being compliant at all costs. But, when we speak of non-conformity as a virtue in the elderly, we must be careful to differentiate between courage and sheer cussedness. Persons who isolate themselves from others, who work at being rude, uncouth, and abrasive, just to prove that they can be different, are not necessarily acting out of courage. Because, as May points out, it takes courage not only to assert one's self but also to give one's self to others.[13]

Csikszentmihalyi again makes an astute observation that could be helpful to many older persons. Assuming that most people of any age want a joyful or happy life, he says that it "is an individual creation that cannot be copied from a recipe . . . Happiness, in fact, is a condition that must be prepared for, cultivated, and defended privately by each person."[14]

Perhaps the most important thing a person can do to prepare for, cultivate, and defend one's mental and spiritual health is to become involved with some meaningful activity outside one's own normal routine of living. A number of years ago Derrel was with a group of chaplains and other ministers who had gathered to hear the great psychiatrist Karl Menninger speak. During the question and answer time someone asked Dr. Menninger what advice he would give to older parishioners who were exhibiting signs of depression. Menninger said, "I would tell them to get outside themselves and become involved in the lives of other people whose conditions are worse." It takes courage to give up our own private "pity parties" and involve ourselves in someone else's life, but the personal and spiritual rewards are significant.

ADAPTABILITY

A third quality that lends itself to creative living in the later years is adaptability. Csikszentmihalyi, in his recently published book, *Creativity*, has written: "Creative individuals are remarkable for their ability to adapt to almost any situation and to make do with whatever is at hand to reach their goals."[15] He suggests this form of adaptation will include at least one of the following: (1) a task where there is a possibility of completion; (2) ability to concentrate on the task; (3) clear goals and immediate feedback; (4) involvement that is deep but effortless; (5) a sense of control; (6) concern for self disappears during the task but reappears with a stronger sense of self after the experience; and/or (7) an altered sense of the passage of time.[16]

One tool for creative thinking has been developed by Edward de Bono, called "lateral thinking." Logical or vertical thinking is most effective when paired with lateral thinking. De Bono says,

> Vertical thinking develops the ideas generated by lateral thinking. You cannot dig a hole in a different place by digging the same hole deeper. Vertical thinking is used to dig the same hole deeper. Lateral thinking is used to dig a hole in a different place.[17]

Kuhn, May, Csikszentmihalyi, and de Bono all emphasize the fact that traditional thinking and education have conditioned us to think in one dimensional or vertical terms. Creativity calls for new paradigms, attitudes, convictions, and thinking about our physical, mental, emotional, social, and spiritual conditions as we encounter our own aging. We can be confined by our own senescence or we can be challenged by it to achieve something more.

Not long ago, Lucien and his wife became quite concerned about a lovely red cardinal that insisted on flying against their bedroom window, repeatedly hurling himself at the glass with a loud thump. They tried to dissuade him in various ways, but nothing would deter the bird's suicidal plunges against the window. Some older adults resemble that cardinal in one respect. They beat themselves to death against the limitations that inevitably come with the passing years, rather than accepting and adapting to them.

The tragic story of Ernest Hemingway's demise is a case in point. Weakened by cancer, in his early sixties, he was no longer able to continue the physical exploits for which he was so wellknown–bullfighting, big game hunting, carousing, the pursuit of women–and he eventually ended his own life with a shotgun. Shortly before his suicide, he said to an acquaintance, "What does a man care about? Staying healthy. Working good. Eating and drinking with his friends. Enjoying himself in bed. I haven't any of them. Do you understand . . . None of them."[18] The very things that had defined his image of himself were the things he had lost; and he could find no substitutes for them.

Elders who dare to live creatively have the wisdom to come to grips with their limitations, but not in a mood of pathetic acquiescence. They not only adapt to their limitations, they even *use them* as an occasion for growth.

Shortly after Helen Parker had suffered a painful leg fracture, Lucien visited her in the hospital. Helen was propped up on pillows, busily writing with her Braille slate. He expressed surprise that she was able to concentrate on writing, under the circumstances. Helen retorted, "I broke my leg, not my head." (Helen, by the way, once insisted that a friend accompany her to a three-hour course in photography!)

Albert McClellan gives eloquent expression to his characteristic attitude toward the limitations imposed by age in a poem written in his retirement years. The poem explores the disappointments he experiences at each stage of life. With each stage and disappointment he vowed to keep on. Thus at the end of the poem he says: "Not for me, friend Waldo, not I! . . . The world is my firmament. No aging lament for me."

Paradoxically, the very tension imposed by limitations often proves to be essential to creativity. Just as a river can't exist without banks to restrain its flowing water, creative effort can be aimless and futile without restraints to channel thought and energy.

Rollo May tells of an occasion when Duke Ellington was explaining how he composed his music. It seems his trumpet player, and his trombonist, could reach certain notes beautifully but not other notes. So, Ellington explained, he had to write his music within those limits. Then he remarked, "It's good to have limits."[20]

Eric Rust stated the idea quite succinctly, on one occasion, when he said, "A violin string under pressure can make beautiful music; but turn it loose, and it can only wiggle."

EXPANSIVENESS

Yet another common component in the personalities of creative individuals is what might be called "expansiveness." They are broad-gauged in their interests, always pushing out the horizons, always open to new experiences. Csikszentmihalyi says of the 91 highly creative persons he and his students studied: "Every one of them is still deeply involved in tasks that are exciting and rewarding, even if they are ultimately unattainable. Like the climber who reaches the top of the mountain and, after looking around in wonder at the magnificent view, rejoices at the sight of an even taller neighboring peak, these people never run out of exciting goals."[21]

The actor Edward Asner (best remembered as the gruff Lou Grant on the Mary Tyler Moore show) is a case in point. Asner, born in 1929, told an interviewer that what was absorbing his attention now was demonstrating that his acting ability is better than it's ever been: "Doing it however and whichever way I can," he said. "In as many ways as I can. Radio, commercials, voice-overs, narrations for documentaries, on-stage, TV, films. It doesn't matter. I . . . burst at the seams, eager for the chase."[22]

A 77-year-old retired educator conveyed the same thirst for new experiences when he said:

> I had long planned to write three books, and I immediately set to work. Two have now been published, and the third is ready for the publishers. I had long wanted time to read far more than my teaching and administrative work permitted. Since retirement I have read scores of books and have kept up with journals in various fields.

Before retirement Lucien and his wife had made two European trips and traveled in Canada. They have since been traveling more in our own country and contemplate further travels as time permits. They have also kept busy with church work and correspondence and with various social activities. Time has, thus far, not been a problem.

The expansiveness, the hunger for experience exhibited by these and numerous other members of the older generation can very appropriately be described as a continual "renewing of the mind," to borrow a famous phrase from the Apostle Paul. Derrel, for example, retired from his position in the Department of Social Work at Southwestern Baptist Theological Seminary, and then accepted the Oubri A. Poppele endowed chair in Health and Welfare Ministries (gerontology) at Saint Paul School of Theology where he was able to engage in more research regarding the ministries of churches of all denominations with older persons. After retiring from Saint Paul School of Theology, he has found new challenges at Baylor University where he teaches courses in The Institute for Gerontological Studies. Many of those courses have called for him to engage in a thorough study of a discipline he has never taught before. He feels that he is involved in some of the most exciting experiences of his life.

OPENNESS TO GOD'S TRANSFORMING POWER

One final point comes, not from the behavioral sciences, but from the textbook of our faith. Call it "openness to God's transforming power."

When David O. Moberg, a distinguished sociologist from Marquette University, inaugurated the Kellogg lecture series at Southwestern Baptist Theological Seminary in 1987, he was one of the few academicians in the field of gerontology who dared to recognize that spirituality was a legitimate issue in the study of aging. In fact, Moberg has been called the "godfather of the religion and aging research field."[23]

At that time, most of the literature on aging was coming from the fields of behavioral, social and medical science and, to some degree, economics. The spiritual dimensions of older adult life were largely ignored, presumably because they were hard to define, measure and quantify.

But that has changed. Over the past decade, we have seen an increasing awareness of the importance of religion as a significant component in the study of aging. The Christian gerontology emphasis at Southwestern Seminary, in which the Kellogg Lectures and the Gulledge endowment fund have played substantial roles, has been a part of that trend. As a community of faith, our guiding conviction is that biblical revelation is an indispensable resource in addressing the experience of aging.

In keeping with that tradition, we want to re-emphasize a profoundly important biblical truth, a truth that hangs on a passive verb in Romans 12:2–"Be ye transformed." The passive construction implies that the believer is not the actor in this miracle of transformation; it is the action of the Holy Spirit. The *Today's English Version* translates Paul's words, "*let God transform you* inwardly by a complete change of your mind. Then you will be able to know the will of God–what is good, and is pleasing to him, and is perfect" (Rom. 12:2b TEV).

Persons of faith recognize that they cannot speak of creative living without acknowledging that God is the fountainhead of continuous renewal at the very core of one's being. This theme appears repeatedly in the Bible, in both the Old and the New Testaments. It is reflected, for instance, in Psalm 92, which assures us that "the righteous flourish like the palm tree" and that "they still bring forth fruit in old age . . . to show that the Lord is upright" (Ps. 92:12,14).

But particularly relevant to the experience of elderly Christians are the words of assurance in Isaiah 40:

> Even youths grow tired and weary,
> and young men stumble and fall;
> but those who hope in the Lord
> will renew their strength,
> they will soar on wings like eagles,
> they will run and not grow weary,
> they will walk and not be faint.[24]

Notice that fainting weariness, and exhaustion are not age-referenced. The renewal of strength is not reserved exclusively for those who can fly like eagles, or for those who run like gazelles. To those who are frail, to those who are weak, to those who can only walk, God's promise of renewed strength is unfailing. In the book of Joshua this theme is emphatically illustrated by Caleb when he says,

> So here I am today, eighty-five years old! I am still as strong today as the day Moses sent me out; I'm just as vigorous to go out to battle now as I was then. . . . but, the Lord helping me, I will drive them out just as he said.[25]

Do these passages suggest that God is going to magically remove all frailty and take away all limitations associated with growing older? While we believe that God could magically remove limitations we do not believe God chooses to do so in most cases. What God does is enable us to make creative use of our limitations and provide us with the means whereby we can accomplish realistic goals in light of our understanding of God's purpose in our lives. For example, Ms. Sadler worked in a greeting card shop all of her adult life. After retiring at age 65 she was involved in an automobile accident that caused her to need twenty-four/seven, medical supervision. She entered a convalescent hospital and then a nursing home where she has lived for the past seven years. One day when her pastor was visiting she asked him to bring her the names and addresses of all of the visitors to the worship services. She also wanted the names and addresses of members who were having birthdays and anniversaries each week. She began mailing cards to each of these persons each week. From her room in the nursing home she has now mailed over 6,000 cards. She feels that in some ways, being in the nursing homes has been a blessing to her. She said, "If I had simply retired and stayed at my home I probably would have just dried up, spiritually. Now, I receive visits and letters from people each week thanking me for my cards. God has been so good to me."

A majority of retired persons are not in nursing homes. They live in their own homes alone or with their own families or friends. Most older men are married, but most older women are not. Many widowed, divorced, and never married women find useful and creative ways of utilizing the time they might have spent caring for families or working outside the home. Numerous older men and women provide invaluable volunteer service to their churches and communities.

Younger persons seem to think that these able-bodied older persons have a great deal of time on their hands. If you listen closely to their conversations you will hear many retired persons say, "I am so busy these days. I don't know how I ever had time to go to work when I was younger." Unfortunately, this is not true for all of them. Some spend much of their time and energy bemoaning the fact that they are no longer useful. Our challenge to all senior adults is to reject the old paradigms and engage in creative approaches to everyday living. Engaging in activities that lead to new knowledge, new skills, and making new friends will make the latter years of life more profitable and more livable. God invites everyone to experience even greater spiritual blessings in their autumn years.[26]

NOTES

1. The terms "Future Shock," "Third Wave," and "Power Shift" are titles of three very influential books written by futurist, Alvin Toffler. Bantam Books published them.

2. From a personal conversation.

3. Antidotes in this paper are either stories garnered from personal observation, experience, or from personal conversations unless they are otherwise noted.

4. Quoted in Gordon Dryden and Jeanette Vos, *The Learning Revolution,* (Rolling Hills Estates, CA: Jalmar Press, 1994), 16.

5. Acts 2:17; Joel 2:28. New International Version. Bible scholars believe that the term "dream," as it is used here, does not refer to "day dreaming," but it is a parallel to the term "vision." It implies that God is calling persons of all ages and genders into Christian service during the eschatological age.

6. Mihaly Csikszentmihalyi, *(http://www.dailyobjectivist.com/Heroes/Mihaly Csikszentmihalyi.asp)*.

7. Thomas Kuhn, *The Structure of Scientific Revolutions*, (Chicago: The University of Chicago Press, 1962).

8. For a thorough study of a variety of theories of aging, read Vern L. Bengston and K. Warner Schaie, eds. *Handbook of Theories of Aging,* (New York: Springer Publishing Company, 1999).

9. Thomas S. Kuhn, "The Structure of Scientific Revolutions," as presented in a synopsis by Frank Pajares in the *Philosopher's Web Magazine. (http://www.emory. edu/EDUCATION/mfp/kuhnsyn.html)*.

10. Ibid.

11. Rollo May, *Man's Search for Himself* (Delacorte Press, 1992), 192.

12. Kuhn, 7.

13. Ibid., 194.

14. Csikszentmihalyi, (*http://www.dailyobjectivist.com/Heroes/MihalyCsikszent mihalyi.asp*).

15. Mihaly Csikszentmihalyi, *Creativity,* (New York: HarperPerennial, 1996), 51.

16. Ibid.

17. Edward de Bono, *Lateral Thinking: Creativity Step by Step,* (New York: Harper & Row Publishers, 1970), 12-13.

18. Betty Friedan, *The Fountain of Age,* (New York: Simon & Schuster, 1993), 225.

19. The poem was given to Lucien by Albert McClellan; it has not been published.

20. May, *The Courage to Create,* (New York: W.W. Norton & Company, 1994), 138.

21. Csikszentmihalyi, (*http://www.dailyobjectivist.com/Heroes/MihalyCsikszent mihalyi.asp*).

22. Csikszentmihalyi, 1996, 220.

23. James Seeber, *Journal of Religious Gerontology*, Vol. 7, Nos. 1/2, 1990, 2.

24. Isaiah 40:31, New International Version.

25. Joshua 14:10-12, New International Version.

26. Jane M. Thibault makes this point very pointedly in her book, *A Deepening Love Affair: The Gift of God in Later Life.* (Nashville: Upper Room Books, 1993).

Chapter 14

The Caleb Affect:
The Oldest-Old in Church and Society

Ben Dickerson, PhD
Derrel R. Watkins, PhD

SUMMARY. Persons in North America who are over 80 years of age are generally overlooked by religious leaders. They are, however, the fastest growing cohort in society. This *age crescendo* promises to be a significant factor in the future ministry of the rapidly increasing number of graying churches and synagogues. *[Article copies available for a fee from The Haworth Document Delivery Service: 1-800-HAWORTH. E-mail address: <docdelivery@haworthpress.com> Website: <http://www.HaworthPress.com> © 2003 by The Haworth Press, Inc. All rights reserved.]*

KEYWORDS. Age crescendo, overlooked, mainstream, ageism, Third Agers, centenarians, vitality, global aging, life-course, natural mecha-

Ben Dickerson is Director of the Gerontology Program, University of Indianapolis, IN, and former Director of the Institute for Gerontological Studies, Baylor University. Derrel R. Watkins is Adjunct Faculty, The Institute for Gerontological Studies, School of Social Work, Baylor University, Waco, TX; Professor of Social Work Emeritus, Southwestern Baptist Theological Seminary, Fort Worth, TX; and Oubri A. Poppele Chair (Gerontology) in Health and Welfare Ministries (retired), Saint Paul School of Theology, Kansas City, MO.

[Haworth co-indexing entry note]: "The Caleb Affect: The Oldest-Old in Church and Society." Dickerson, Ben, and Derrel R. Watkins. Co-published simultaneously in *Journal of Religious Gerontology* (The Haworth Pastoral Press, an imprint of The Haworth Press, Inc.) Vol. 15, No. 1/2, 2003, pp. 201-213; and: *Practical Theology for Aging* (ed: Derrel R. Watkins) The Haworth Pastoral Press, an imprint of The Haworth Press, Inc., 2003, pp. 201-213. Single or multiple copies of this article are available for a fee from The Haworth Document Delivery Service [1-800-HAWORTH, 9:00 a.m. - 5:00 p.m. (EST). E-mail address: docdelivery@haworthpress.com].

http://www.haworthpress.com/store/product.asp?sku=J078
Digital Object Identifier: 10.1300/J078v15n01_15

nisms, church, lifeline, future, age segregation, life-long learning, spiritual development, Christopraxis, Judeopraxis

For age is opportunity no less
Than youth, though in another dress
As the evening twilight fades away
The sky is filled with stars invisible by day.
–Longfellow

'For I know the plans that I have for you,' declares the Lord, 'plans for welfare and not for calamity to give you a future and a hope.' (Jeremiah 29:11 NASB)

A group gathered in the hallway outside the sixth-grade girls' classroom. Some were grandmothers, some were mothers and some were older sisters. They had come to honor Miss Bessie who had been their teacher. She had taught the sixth-grade girls for as long as anyone could remember. Not only did they want to honor her that day, they wanted to talk her into continuing to teach the girls' class for at least another couple of years. Some of the mothers wanted to be sure their daughters had an opportunity to be in Miss Bessie's class.[1]

Art stood at the same door of the church's worship center he had "manned" since it was dedicated in 1956. For over fifty years he had been a faithful usher and greeter. Today he would be honored for his faithfulness and asked to assume the role of chair of the usher committee for at least one more three-year rotation.

Chet and Millie were honored by their church on Easter Sunday. They had been members of the church since only a few months after its beginning. Now they are moving into a retirement home in another state. They are not retreating from work in the church, just moving to a place where they can be near their grandchildren and help build another church in an area where they will feel needed.

What do these persons have in common other than their loyalty and faithfulness to their churches? They are all over 80 years of age and they embody the attitude of Caleb, the Jewish leader who, at age 85, asked Joshua to give him the most difficult part of the territory to conquer. He knew the magnitude of the challenge and yet his faith in God motivated him to accept the task. "So here I am today, eighty-five years old! . . . Now give me this hill country that the Lord promised me that day. You yourself heard then that the Anakites were there and their cities were large and fortified, but, the Lord helping me, I will drive them out just as he said" (Joshua 14:10-12 NIV).

Even though the persons above have age and spirituality in common, it is important to realize that their lives elude categorization. These individuals are the unsung and often overlooked heroes of our churches and communities. They are often overlooked due to our limited understanding of persons in their 80 plus years.

We want to introduce you to a population of people characterized by an unprecedented history, and considerable potential. They generally possess a strong desire to continue to be a part of the mainstream of church and community life. We hope to: (1) awaken the churches and communities to the new challenges and opportunities of an aging society; (2) provide a realistic profile of the potentials and needs of these persons; (3) encourage church and community leaders to integrate these generations with younger generations; and (4) develop a proactive plan leading to more effective linkages between the church and community in utilizing persons 80 plus in more innovative and productive ways.

OLD IS NOT WHAT IT USED TO BE

This overlooked 80 plus crowd has a wealthy reserve of compassion and wisdom. They desire and need to utilize these qualities in the service of their God, church, and community. Yet, this potential is often unrecognized due to an overemphasis on this age group's frailty and sympathetic stereotypes. That is, more emphasis is given to cultivating sympathy and public support than recognizing the significant contributions this age group can make. This oversight is a form of "ageism," i.e., the focus is on the older persons that are least capable, least healthy, and least alert. A restricted view of the 80 plus age group in the church and community can mislead the best efforts in ministering to people of all ages. Additionally, this group is characterized as self centered, dependent, and lacking understanding of contemporary society and its technology. An older individual is thought of as either a Medicare or Medicaid recipient, and/or a resident in a long term care facility. Consequently, they are seen as contributing little to themselves, neighbors, churches or communities. As a result, many church and community leaders limit their perception of the 80 plus population to persons who are consumers of ministries and services, rather than contributors.

Research indicates that few resources for church or community leadership exist that are dedicated to gaining a better understanding of the importance of enlisting and educating this age group for service. To date, educational materials about senior adults are limited to the youngest old, their families, the church and the community. These limitations lead to generalizations about the aging population, but lack specifics about the heterogeneity of the advanced years. To meet the challenge of this growing population, a clearer understanding must be secured.

The way old age is experienced today is quite different from yesteryear. The differences lie in the increased life and health expectancy, and in their higher educational achievement level. This has contributed a new segment of the life course–the third age. This new segment challenges church and community leaders to recognize the presence of the 80 plus population along with their needs and gifts.

The 80 plus population is often referred to by demographers as the fastest growing population segment among the aged. This population is entering a time of life that is essentially uncharted or incorrectly mapped. In looking at the "Third Agers" we find that the majority of them are women. To be more specific, the sex ratio for persons 80 years and over approaches a high of 250 females for every 100 males. As a result a majority of women in this age group are widowed, single-never married, or single-divorced while a majority of men are married.

The majority of this age group lives in a community setting with a significant number living alone. As age increases within this group, women tend to live more outside a family setting. Living alone correlates with advanced age. Relatively small proportions of persons 80 plus, fifteen-twenty percent, live in nursing homes. Two percent of this group has no living siblings or children. Two-thirds of the population age 80 and over are high school graduates. Approximately fifty percent consider their economic resources to be adequate.

Narrowing our unit of analysis a little more precisely, it is increasingly important that we consider those persons who have lived 100 years or more as a separate category of the oldest old. The U.S. Census bureau issued a news release on June 16, 1999, with the following headline: "New Census Report Shows Exponential Growth in Number of Centenarians." The estimated number of centenarians nearly doubled during the decade between 1989 and 1999. A conservative estimate is that there were 37,000 in 1989 and at the end of the decade there were over 70,000.[2] Other studies have reported that the number is closer to 80,000. Richard M. Suzman, Associate Director of the NIA for Behavioral and Social Research, says, "The growing numbers of extremely old people give us the opportunity to examine their lives in more detail. By doing so, we will be able to discover the genetic, medical, social, and behavioral factors contributing to longevity and robustness in very advanced age."[3]

Not surprisingly, the report highlights that centenarians share most of the profiles that have commonly been noted regarding the 85+ group. Four out of five centenarians are women. Gains for men have been smaller and men still lag behind women in attaining 100. No change is expected in this phenomenon. Seventy-eight percent of today's centenarians are non-Hispanic white. That proportion is expected to decrease to about fifty-five percent by 2050.[4]

Prospects for the very oldest members of society may be more encouraging than anticipated. A number of research reports suggest that women who are 85 years of age can expect that two-thirds of their remaining years will be free of serious disability; for men that figure is closer to 80%. There appears to be a strong correlation with ". . . higher levels of education and increases in both the total life expectancy and the years of active life expectancy. In the future, the very elderly will be a much more heterogeneous group with a greater racial, ethnic, and economic diversity. The very elderly may therefore resist dependency and become more assertive as a group in demanding that communities meet their interrelated social and medical needs. The most successful outcome would be for the very elderly to take control of the last stage of life and make it livable and worth attaining."[5]

A significant number of news articles about the vitality of individual centenarians is appearing in newspapers and magazines. One hundred year old Howard Sturkie, for example, who has taught his "boys" (the youngest of whom is 74) Bible class for over 60 years. His son reports that Howard is never bored. "He studies his lesson and works jigsaw puzzles to keep his mind sharp and alert."[6] Or Vera Hogan, 103, says "I walked to work every day–about two miles each way. Now that I can't walk so much anymore, I stay busy by participating in every activity that's going on in the rest home . . . I can't slow down anytime soon; I'm in the middle of a thousand things." She took up landscape painting at 89.[7]

THE CRESCENDO OF THE THIRD AGE

Even though the graying of America is now a common phrase, anticipation of the potential of the rapidly emerging group of persons known as the oldest old is lacking. Consequently such questions as "Who are those people and what are we going to do with them?" are going to be posed more often. This group, both unexpected and often overlooked, represents a new social force we like to think of as an *age crescendo*. That is, the 80 plus population is steadily increasing in volume as well as in force and intensity throughout most of the societies of the world. Therefore, this population cannot be ignored by the church or other institutions in society. The 80 plus crowd can either be utilized to strengthen the necessary work of the church and institutions as they move forward, or this age group can become an incredible weight causing many resources to be expended without positive results. To a large extent we are un-prepared to incorporate such a large number into existing and newly created social roles.

It is important to note this age group's number has exceeded 8 million in the United States alone. Projections indicate that this same age group will increase to more than 26 million by 2040. Some demographers estimate that centenari-ans alone may increase to as many as 2.4 million by 2050.[8] Furthermore, the church in its mission zeal needs to note that the demographic shift being dis-cussed is altering age structure throughout the world. In Peter Peterson's book, *Gray Dawn*, the reader is alerted to the fact that "there is an iceberg dead ahead. It's called *global aging* . . . we will face unprecedented political, eco-nomic and moral challenges."[9] With the iceberg effect, only one-third of the iceberg, in this case the 80+ crowd, is visible and two-thirds remains hidden from view. Our population is to taking on the appearance of an upside-down pyramid where the older members of our population will equal or exceed the number of our younger members. This radical change in our age pyramid is challenging institutions in ways that were never anticipated. For example, fur-ther thought must be given to compensating for the labor shortage in the work force: (1) equal distribution of economic resources among the young as well as the old; (2) extending the work-life and shortening the retirement years; (3) greater emphasis on life-long learning; (4) improving technological liter-acy; (5) extension of caregiving responsibilities; (6) environmental modifi-cations; (7) establishing new specialties in elder-law and elder-health; and (8) developing new staff positions in both secular and sacred institutions.

TRANSITIONING TO A NEW LIFE-COURSE PATTERN

Furthermore the longevity revolution and the anticipated increase in health expectancy leads social scientists to view the life course more as a postmodern paradigm: as a cyclical pattern rather than a linear one. The linear pattern oper-ated on a rigid chronological age paradigm and offered little chance for innova-tion. The cyclical pattern provides increased opportunities as well as flexibility in organizing one's life course increasing the years of productivity. This pattern eliminates definitive boundaries defining participation in work, play, family re-sponsibility, church, and community. Each person has a new freedom to begin again, to experience the abundance of life throughout the entire course of living.

With the linear pattern, an individual's failure or disappointments often ne-gated any possibility of continuing the pursuit of his/her dreams and expecta-tions. Practically speaking, this new life pattern affords individuals new options in having more than one career experience, more than one educational experience, more than one family experience and more than one ministry experience. The cyclical pattern enforces what many gerontologists emphasize in understanding aging and its influence on the individual, the fact that old age is more of a sociological construct than a biological one. This fact enables us to recognize society's influence on defining how old is old. In other words, age is not an absolute. Rather it is relative to the definitions given to it by culture. The importance of this fact to church leadership is recognizing that the church, even as other facets of society, can redefine what certain ages mean, and insure that they are never major obstacles to utilizing individuals in the work of the Lord. Such redefinition acknowledges what Paul said regarding the church being comprised of many parts.[10] Accepting the relativity of age facilitates Paul's instructions regarding the composition of the church.

Fischer states that "though our stereotyping of the elderly has led us to view them as basically similar, there is probably no other point in life when personal diversity is so apparent. A lifetime of accumulated differences in experience, education, and social opportunities has sharpened individuality."[11] Two persons age 85 may be the same chronologically; however, they may be uniquely different in where they are located in the life course. One may be still be on the upward bound slope of involvement and achievement while the other is content to sit down and wait for the inevitable to happen. Recently published books and magazine articles help us to understand the difference in chronological years and real years and how these two concepts can be measured. The difference, according to Michael F. Roizen, is based on individual choices in everyday living. In his book, *Real Age: Are You As Young As You Can Be?*, he gives the reader the opportunity to identify "real age" by assigning values to life style choices. These choices include such things as exercise, blood pressure, physical activity, smoking, strength building, disruptive life events, and the presence or absence of pets. Based on your choices you either add or subtract years thus better defining how old you are. Thus, transitioning can be a matter of choice rather than chance. In other words, our aging experiences can be influenced by our choices and the environment in which we reside.[12] Based upon wise choices, the 80 plus crowd is able to transition to the third age with ease if given the proper encouragement from the faith community.

INTEGRATING THE FAITH DIMENSION

Fischer contends that a Christian perspective can help us to develop a more positive attitude toward the aging process. She believes that the Christian's relationship with Jesus can give them a renewed image of the future where they have assumed that hope was dead.[13] Anderson supports Fischer's conclusion by his summary of Paul's Philippian letter. The scriptural teaching reflects that no matter how old we are there is considerable life remaining and God can use it for his glory. Anderson derives from Paul's teaching ten goals for Christians at all stages of life: (1) loving with the love of Jesus; (2) living for the glory of God; (3) confronting life one day at a time; (4) remaining stable in a storm of suffering; (5) being a servant; (6) knowing Christ intimately; (7) keeping the joy; (8) maintaining an effective prayer life; (9) planning financially for a Christ-like finish; (10) depending on the adequacy of Christ all the way home.[14]

Research conducted by Koenig supports the conclusions drawn by Fischer and Anderson. He identifies three natural mechanisms by which religious belief and practice may promote mental health in later life: (1) "Religious beliefs provide hope and a sense of control over one's destiny. (2) Active participation in the religious community brings people into contact with others thus promoting positive social attitudes and self-sacrifice. (3) Religious doctrines promote a healthy balanced love of God, self, and others."[15] In addition to Koenig's remarks on the effects of religious beliefs on well-being in later life, Frankl, in his book *Man's Search For Meaning*, shares how one's faith made the difference between life and death: "The prisoner who had lost faith in the future–his future–was doomed. With his loss of belief in the future, he also lost his spiritual hold; he let himself decline and became subject to mental and physical decay . . . he simply gave up."[16]

The above-mentioned authors underscore the importance of building a faith foundation to adequately move into the third age and experience the abundant life that Jesus promises (John 10:10b). By accepting the faith element, the Scriptures assure us that "He shall direct our paths" even into the third age.

THE CHURCH–THE LIFELINE

Historically, the church is considered to be a lifeline to people of all ages. It is important that we extend this lifeline to include this new group of individuals entering a life period that few others have experienced in the past. This 80 plus crowd needs the church. The church is able to enhance this period of life by encouraging continued spiritual growth, accepting God's ministry, providing opportunity to pass on their wisdom to younger generations, providing opportunities for celebration of one's salvation, utilizing their material goods to further God's work, understand the presence of God in their daily lives, and being thankful for life's blessings. Furthermore this age group needs to acknowledge and claim God's promises of unconditional love and acceptance into eternal life with Him.

Likewise, this age group can serve the church. These individuals by their previous service to the church have proven that they can make valuable contributions to the church's ministry. This point is aptly illustrated by an experience that one of the authors had when taking his seminary students to visit a senior adult club in a local church. While visiting this senior adult group, one student asked an 82-year-old woman, "How does the church serve you?" With a somewhat puzzled look, the older woman looked directly at the student and replied, "The church gives me the privilege to serve."

STEPPING TOWARD THE FUTURE

It is our belief that the present 80 plus crowd can follow in the footsteps of Moses, Joshua, and Caleb and experience a good old age, full of years (Genesis 25:8). Noteworthy is the description of Abraham's advanced age. The scriptures describe it as a *good* old age. The fullness of years is directly correlated with faith. In Hebrews 11, the primary word is faith. The same is true of Moses, Joshua, Caleb and others. They believed as Paul did when he said, " Be anxious for nothing, but in everything by prayer and supplication, with thanksgiving let your request be made known unto God and the peace of God which passes all understanding shall keep your hearts and minds through Christ Jesus" (Phil. 4:6-7, KJV).

To capture the appropriate vision, church leadership must seriously consider the following steps to insuring the full utilization and integration of the 80 plus crowd:

1. *Redefine the life course where productivity is possible for any age group.* For example, the Rev. Herb Hawthorne, 84 years of age, had served as a lay leader in his church for over 50 years. When he told his pastor that he felt that God was calling him to be a pastor, instead of treating him like a senile old person who was out of touch with reality, the church leadership was sensitive to his request and at age 82 he was ordained. Soon he became the pastor of a small rural church just five miles from his home.

2. *Eliminate age segregation.* During the "industrial age" persons over fifty were considered to be on their "last legs." Younger persons with more physical strength were sought to work in the factories and fields. Industry leaders considered these younger persons to be more productive. Tragically, churches and community organizations adopted the same mindset although physical stamina was not usually a criterion for a majority of their tasks. Even many older persons themselves may be heard saying, "It is time for me to step down. Let the younger persons have their opportunity."

A beautiful example of age integration occurred when the Reformed Church in America held a family gathering at Estes Park, Colorado. In almost all of their group discussions, persons of all ages were intentionally included. This seemed to reflect their idea of what a family might look like. There were preschool children, elementary school age children, adolescents, young adults, median adults and senior adults in every group. Some visionary church and community leaders are promoting intergenerational education and recreational activities. Although the norm continues to be age-graded programs, some churches are moving beyond age-graded programs and are focusing more on intergenerational worship and Christian education.[17]

3. *Promote life-long learning.* "You can't teach an old dog new tricks" is probably not a totally accurate description of dogs and it certainly doesn't define older human beings. George Dawson is a prime example. At age 98 George wanted to be able to read his Bible for himself. He had never learned to read or write. An African American male and grandson of slaves, he had not had the privilege of formal education when he was young. He went back to school soon after his 98th birthday and he did learn to read and to write. At age 102 he was able to assist in writing a book about his life.[18] He spent a great deal of his time going to schools where he could speak with youth about making the most of life at the youngest age possible. Just before he died in 2001, a middle school in Southlake, a mostly European-American suburb of Dallas, Texas, was named for George Dawson because of his example and message. The movement to name to school for him was led by students at the school. They felt that no one was more deserving than George to have a school named for them.[19]

4. *Facilitate spiritual development.* Research indicates that a majority of the oldest generation acknowledges spiritual issues to be very important in their lives. A significant number of them do not perceive themselves to be growing in their faith. Many feel that there is little help available for them through their churches and other religious organizations. Spiritual development for the oldest old has not been a high priority in the development of church programs.

5. *Create new roles based on intellectual rather than physical capabilities.* Mr. Chester, 86, is a retired industrial engineer. He knows how to organize buildings and equipment for maximum benefit to the organization. The church trustees call upon him to advise them regarding any issues involving buildings and equipment. He doesn't have veto power over the trustees, but they do not make a decision without "running it by Mr. Chester." He was known in his manufacturing company for quickly spotting design flaws in products before they were put on the market. He feels that sharing his expertise and experience with the trustees is one way he can continue to make a difference in his church. From time to time the local school board calls upon him to advise them about the need and usage of school buildings and equipment.

Margaret Oliver, age 91, worked for 46 years as a copy editor for a national magazine. After retiring she volunteered to help the denominational office staff of her church to develop and produce literature for "capital needs" campaigns. She continues to help design and produce fund raising campaign literature. Her work has been copied by judicatories throughout her denomination and it has been used by other church denominations as well.

Carl Harrington, age 86, retired as a manager of a church supported children's home. After several years of searching for ways to use his experience with children, he started volunteering, at age 80, as the "Sunday School Granddaddy" in the two-year-old Sunday School department of his church. He has now enlisted seven other retired men who serve in a similar capacity in other Sunday School departments.

6. *Enable the discovery and utilization of spiritual gifts, talents and abilities, in the church's mission and ministry.* In community development classes we instruct students to ask three questions: One, "What do you have in your head?" (What do you know?) Two, "What do you have in your hands?" (What can you do?) Three, "What do you have in your heart?"(What do you care about?). These become the building blocks for empowering communities to help themselves to overcome whatever obstacles they face. The same process works with churches and a variety of community groups. In 1990, Derrel asked the same questions of a group of church members (most over 80 years of age) in a declining church. They discovered that when they quit waiting for a group of younger persons to come and take over they were able to reestablish a significant number of ministries. Their church became viable in the community once again. It attracted some younger persons from the community and they once again have an intergenerational church.

CONCLUSION

In order to appropriate "The Caleb Affect" the attitudes of at least two groups must be adapted to the current and future realities of the oldest old in our society: (1) There must be a change in the way we perceive old age. Stereotypes must be dismissed and individual valuations of persons over 80 must replace them. (2) Older persons themselves must cease to think of themselves as ineffectual and ineffective persons who are just waiting to die. They must learn that, like Caleb, Joshua, Moses, and Eli, of the Bible, they too are free to chose the difficult tasks and enjoy a great deal of success in whatever venture they decide to pursue. All of society, old and young alike, can truly learn that aging is not what it used to be.

The "crescendo" of the population cohort that we call the oldest old will get the attention of manufacturers, marketers, community leaders, political, and church and synagogue leaders in the very near future. Advertisements are already appearing in the media that recognizes the presence and buying power of an exploding old age population.

Faith development and spiritual formation is still possible and indeed desirable for persons in the oldest old category of church and synagogue members. In the past pastoral care of this age group has largely focused on the frail or infirm. Now, however, an overwhelming number of them are not frail or infirm. They, in great and growing numbers, continue to pursue personal growth activities outside their religious groups. Churches and synagogues, in the mean time, have generally ignored the special spiritual needs of the 80 plus cohort. The very presence of this age crescendo calls for some significant pastoral adaptations that may lead to a revitalization of faith on the one hand and the acquisition of new levels of faith on the other.

Practical theology has much to offer the oldest old. This is especially true in the ChristoPraxis or JudeoPraxis where doctrine and everyday lived lives intersect to form a vital connection with the unique features of older persons' lives and their spiritual growth potential.

NOTES

1. The case vignettes used in this article, unless otherwise stated, are not of actual persons, they are composites of cases the authors have known. The names and specific details have been changed but the type of activity described represents actual events.

2. Vicky Cahan and Claudia Feldman, *Embargoed* by the U.S. Census Bureau, June 16, 1999. Data from the report, *Centenarians in the United States,* P23-199, is available at http://www.census.gov/prod/99pubs/p60199/pdf.

3. Ibid.

4. Ibid.

5. Edward W. Campion, *New England Journal of Medicine*, Vol. 330, Number 25, 1819-1829.

6. Baptist Press, 1995, "100-year-old has taught his 'boys' for 60 years."

7. Randi Glatzer, "Living to 100" in *American Health,* July/August, 1997, 57.

8. Cahan and Feldman.

9. Peter G. Peterson, *Gray Dawn,* (New York: Three Rivers Press, 1999, 2000), 3.

10. 1 Corinthians 12; Romans 12: 3-9.

11. Kathleen Fisher, *Winter Grace,* (Nashville: Upper Room Books, 1998), 14.

12. Michael F. Roizen, *Real Age: Are You As Young As You Can Be?* (New York: HarperCollins, Cliff Street Books, 1999), 12-42.

13. Fischer, *Winter Grace,* 16.

14. Don Anderson, *Keep the Fire,* (Sisters, OR: Multnomah Books, 1994), 65.

15. Harold Koenig, *Is Religion Good For Your Health,* (Binghamton, NY: The Haworth Press Inc., 1997), 68-70.

16. Victor Frankl, *Man's Search for Meaning,* (New York: HarperCollins, 1968), 213-214.

17. James W. White, *Intergenerational Religious Education* (Birmingham, AL: Religious Education Press, 1988).

18. George Dawson with Richard Glaubman, *Life Is So Good: An Autobiography.* (New York: Rando m House, 1998).

19. Dave Lieber, "Dawson's life reflects century of progress," Fort Worth Star-Telegram, July 13, 2001; and Eva-Marie Ayala, "Man, 103 is remembered as inspiration," Fort Worth Star-Telegram, July 14, 2001.

Index

DATE DUE